DISINTEGRATING DEMOCRACY AT WORK

DISINTEGRATING DEMOCRACY AT WORK

Labor Unions and the Future of Good Jobs in the Service Economy

VIRGINIA DOELLGAST

ILR PRESS

AN IMPRINT OF
CORNELL UNIVERSITY PRESS
ITHACA AND LONDON

First published 2012 by Cornell University Press
Printed in the United States of America

Library of Congress Cataloging-in-Publication Data

Doellgast, Virginia Lee, 1976–
    Disintegrating democracy at work : labor unions and the future of good
jobs in the service economy / Virginia Doellgast.
        p. cm.
    Includes bibliographical references and index.
    ISBN: 978-0-8014-7799-7
    1. Call centers—United States.   2. Call centers—Germany.
    3. Telecommunication—Employees—Labor unions—United
States.   4. Telecommunication—Employees—Labor unions—
Germany.   5. Service industries workers—Labor unions—United
States.   6. Service industries workers—Labor unions—Germany.
    7. Industrial management—Employee participation—United
States.   8. Industrial management—Employee participation—
Germany.   I. Title.
    HE8789.U6D64   2012
    331.88'11000943—dc23   2011031367

Cornell University Press strives to use environmentally responsible
suppliers and materials to the fullest extent possible in the publishing
of its books. Such materials include vegetable-based, low-VOC inks
and acid-free papers that are recycled, totally chlorine-free, or partly
composed of nonwood fibers. For further information, visit our website
at www.cornellpress.cornell.edu.

Cloth printing   10 9 8 7 6 5 4 3 2 1

Contents

PREFACE

Labor unions across the global North are struggling to improve pay and working conditions in expanding service sector industries. This is by no means an easy task. The workplaces of the new economy remain poorly organized. Even in European countries known for their corporatist political traditions, politicians are designing new legislation intended to break the grip of strong labor laws and employment protections on a stagnant economy. Worker representatives find their role in national policymaking and in corporate decision making weakened at a time when more insecure, lower-paid jobs are expanding.

This book is about the role that labor unions can and should play in modern service workplaces. Its central motivating question is whether strong and cooperative industrial relations institutions characteristic of social Europe have the potential to give service workers similar benefits to those achieved in the golden age of postwar manufacturing: productive and stable employment characterized by high job quality and low wage inequality. Past academic and policy debates on the relationship between national institutions, management strategies, and worker outcomes have focused overwhelmingly on large export-oriented sectors such as the global auto industry. Institutions in most service industries look a lot less coherent than those described in these accounts. Union membership and works council presence are much lower in services than in manufacturing. Service workers are also less likely to be covered by a union contract or to have traditional occupational training, and their jobs tend to be lower paid and less secure.

As these poorly regulated service jobs become more typical of where Americans and Europeans work, the questions comparative researchers asked in auto assembly plants and steel mills need to be revisited. Is there an inevitable convergence on one "best practice" employment model, as managers adjust to competition unfettered by laws or unions? Or does context matter, even in more peripheral workplaces: Do different laws and collective bargaining arrangements make a difference for management strategies and employee outcomes? What influence do these strategies have, in turn, on the strength and coverage of collective bargaining? These questions are at the heart of debates over the future of work and worker welfare in increasingly interconnected, postindustrial economies.

I attempt to answer these questions here through the lens of a comparative study carried out in U.S. and German call centers. The analysis looks at how unions and works councils have shaped employer strategies to restructure these easily rationalized service jobs, and how these strategies have in turn refashioned industrial relations institutions. My focus is on industrial relations rather than other institutions, such as vocational training or corporate governance. While collective bargaining is only one part of broader systems of rules and incentives at the national level, it is unique in regulating the balance of power in the workplace and in laying out the conditions under which employees can participate in management decision making. Empirical findings are drawn largely from two industry sectors: telecommunications, which continues to have strong unions in many countries, and the third-party call center industry, which is a newer sector made up of firms with weaker or no unions that often perform subcontracted call center work for telecommunications firms. In both sectors, I examine the changes that occurred in the organization of call center jobs during the 1990s and 2000s, following the liberalization of U.S. and German telecommunications markets.

Call centers are in many ways the ideal setting for examining how institutions affect management strategy and worker outcomes in postindustrial economies. They are among the most highly mobile of service workplaces, with jobs that are increasingly easy to outsource and that are often viewed as peripheral to firms' "core competencies." In many countries, government-driven liberalization of service markets has increased pressure on managers to cut labor costs for these jobs. For all of these reasons, call centers are workplaces where we might most expect to see convergence on weak collective bargaining institutions and a management model based on reducing costs rather than investing in job quality. For these same reasons, they are a good place to look for the causes of past and continued divergence in management strategy and worker outcomes.

The dynamics of growing competition, organizational restructuring, and erosion of industry-level bargaining are hardly unique to call centers. In this sense, they are typical of a range of easily rationalized jobs in growing, poorly regulated industries. If unions can make a difference for management strategy in these workplaces, there is strong evidence for the continued relevance of national industrial relations institutions in the regulation of employment. Evidence of their failure to improve or maintain working conditions likewise suggests the need for more careful study of the causes of these failures and their labor market consequences.

During my field research in the United States and Germany, I observed a number of differences in how call centers were managed. German call center agents generally were paid higher salaries and had more control over their work than those in the United States. They were more likely to be treated like professionals, with flexible schedules and rules that protected them from the kind of invasive electronic monitoring that was common in U.S. centers. However, the most striking differences concerned the process of management decision making, and the effects that this had on employment practices. In Germany, independent works councils participated in democratic consultation and negotiation over these decisions. Worker representatives used their strong participation rights to help managers find compromise solutions that reduced costs and improved productivity and service quality, while ensuring that the privacy, dignity, and economic interests of the workforce were respected. Meanwhile, U.S. unions struggled to enforce the limited terms of the collective agreements that they were able to negotiate, against an often hostile management.

Where unions were not present, pressures to cut costs and the easy fix of new technologies seemed to leave managers with little choice but to intensify monitoring and discipline on a low-wage, high-turnover workforce.

The different practices and outcomes in these workplaces could thus be more or less directly traced to institutions that gave worker representatives widely diverging participation rights and bargaining power. German co-determination rights, exercised by strong and independent works councils, proved to be a crucial support for alternative, high-involvement employment systems—even in easily rationalized service jobs. Put another way, strong institutional supports for workplace democracy pushed call center managers to take the high road in workplaces where there were many incentives to reduce pay and rationalize work.

At the same time, I also found that worker representatives were facing formidable challenges to maintaining these institutions. In both the United States and Germany, the number of call center jobs in workplaces with strong unions was shrinking. Market liberalization and technological change meant that telecommunications employers faced growing price competition in increasingly volatile markets. They responded by developing similar organizational strategies that downgraded pay and working conditions through moving work to subcontractors and subsidiaries. Employers then renegotiated pay at lower levels or simply shifted calls wholesale to companies with weaker collective agreements. These trends were weakening coordinated collective bargaining and undermining unions' and works councils' bargaining power.

Based on these findings, I argue that institutional supports for workplace democracy and for the maintenance or extension of encompassing collective bargaining are essential for encouraging high-road practices where there are strong countervailing pressures to cut costs. Managers have a range of different incentives to invest in skills and employee discretion in workplaces servicing value-added market segments. In the service workplaces studied here, variation in the ability of workers to participate substantively in management decisions was a critical factor explaining why some call centers adopted high-involvement employment systems and others did not. This ability to participate in democratic arrangements depended, in turn, on legal participation rights and bargaining structures, which influenced worker representatives' countervailing power in negotiations with management.

One objective in this book is to bring this political dimension of management strategy and practice back to the center of debates over contemporary change in national models. Comparative theorists often treat strategy and institutions as coherent bundles or systems. Taylorism, diversified quality production, and high performance work systems are by now well-known ideal type production models. They have most often been studied for their promise to improve firm performance, albeit through more or less worker-friendly practices. Analyses of hybridization of these models describe the mechanisms through which institutional change occurs based on increasingly complex categories of complementary institutions and their relationship with firms' strategic choices.

This focus on firm strategies in much of the comparative literature neglects the negotiations and conflicts that accompany changes in work organization, as well as their concrete effects—in the short term, on pay and working conditions; and in the longer term on bargaining power and institutions. While worker participation undeniably can produce benefits for firms, it has also traditionally been resisted by managers seeking to reduce costs or expand their own scope to implement new strategies unilaterally. An important question is under what conditions worker representatives are able to encourage qualitatively different employment models that produce some possibility of "mutual gains," in settings where their own power or scope for maneuver is changing. To answer this question, it is necessary to take a closer look at how negotiations over restructuring play out in those firms and workplaces that face the most intense pressures to rationalize jobs and lower wages. By unbundling strategy, institutions also begin to look more like heterogeneous resources that unions can draw on to effect meaningful changes in pay and working conditions.

A further objective is to more closely examine the social costs of market liberalization, or what is lost as collective bargaining becomes increasingly disorganized and as unions lose power and influence. In the past, the social market countries of continental Europe were held up as representing an alternative model to free market or liberal capitalism, with political and economic institutions that ensured the benefits of economic growth were more broadly distributed. Strong labor market regulations and powerful labor unions encouraged employers to invest in high wages and worker skills, while supporting competitive advantage in more value-added segments of global markets. Labor unions in Europe played a leading role in promoting quality of working life as a central principle in work design, encouraging managers to invest in expanded job discretion and worker participation at a time when similar U.S. companies were cutting costs and downsizing.

Today, inequality is also on the rise in social Europe. Governments are deregulating their labor markets to encourage job growth and unions are declining in power and influence. Germany was long the best-practice case of a national economy that managed to compete in global markets on the basis of well-engineered, quality products, while distributing the benefits of value-added production more broadly across the workforce. In contemporary Germany, wages are stagnating and low-wage and precarious forms of employment have increased, while firms are reorienting their strategies to better pursue shareholder value.

This book draws on the experiences of the individuals and organizations who are both driving institutional change and experiencing the costs of more flexible labor markets, changing organizational boundaries, and weakened unions. The accounts of the workers, managers, works councilors, and union representatives interviewed in the course of this study give insights into the social and strategic advantages of the kind of workplace democracy that was (and to some degree still is) characteristic of the textbook "German Model." Strong codetermination institutions support deliberation over the goals and practices that firms adopt when faced with similar market challenges. In the cases presented here, these institutions gave works councils the tools to propose and enforce alternatives to rationalization and intensified monitoring. The loss of this power has had devastating consequences for employees and has created new kinds of management problems for their employers. A closer examination of the politics of restructuring helps us better understand these consequences and their causes.

ACKNOWLEDGMENTS

This book is the product of many years of research, starting with my Ph.D. studies at Cornell University and continuing through rounds of follow-up interviews, data analysis, and successive redrafting in the five odd years since. In this time, I have accumulated an extensive debt to many colleagues and institutions who provided support along the way.

The union representatives, works councilors, managers, and employees who explained their work and organizations to me are too numerous to list here (and because of promises of anonymity many cannot be listed). In the United States, Debbie Goldman, Beverly Hicks, Annie Hill, Robert Patrician, Teri Pluta, and Pat Telesco at the CWA answered numerous follow-up questions, and gave valuable feedback on written drafts. In Germany, Siegfried Balduin at IG Metall and Otmar Dürotin, Christoph Heil, Sylva Hieckman, Frank Sauerland, Hans-Juergen Klempau, and Ado Wilhelm at ver.di explained evolving developments in the industry (some of them over many follow-up interviews) and provided contacts at case study companies. Wittich Rossman from IG Metall helped me to develop a more intuitive understanding of "Rheinland style" social partnership. Agnes Schreieder provided much patient tutelage on ver.di's internal politics and the difficulties of organizing low-wage workplaces in Germany. In addition, librarians at the Hans Böckler Stiftung and ver.di assisted with archival research over the course of several research trips.

My colleagues in the Global Call Center Project have been an important source of contacts and ideas. Ursula Holtgrewe and Karen Shire helped me to figure out what was particularly interesting about call centers in Germany, and then integrated me into their research team and generously shared their survey data. Frank Kleeman and Ingo Matuschek encouraged my developing research plan (and German language skills) during my stay in Chemnitz. Ingo invited me along for several week-long research trips at Deutsche Telekom, which provided data and insights that became the core of this study. I owe Ingo and Ursula special thanks for sharing copious interview notes from their past research projects in German call centers. Members of the other country teams gave valuable feedback during several working conferences and contributed insights from their own research. My more recent work with Hiroatsu Nohara and Robert Tchobanian on a comparison of the French and German telecommunications industries helped me to better understand the distinctiveness of the German case and is the basis for the French case study in chapter 5 of this book. My work with Ole Sørensen editing a special journal issue on call centers in Europe was also useful in developing the ideas and analysis in that chapter, particularly concerning the interpretation of developments in Danish call centers.

Many institutions provided financial and logistical support. My Ph.D. field research in Germany was funded by a Fulbright Fellowship, small grants from the Einaudi Center and the Benjamin Miller Scholarship Fund at Cornell, and a grant from the Council of European Studies. My field research in the United States was conducted while I was working as a research assistant on the Cornell-Rutgers Telecommunications Project, supported by the Alfred P. Sloan Foundation; and the Global Call Center Project, supported by the Russell Sage Foundation. Both foundations funded the U.S. call center survey. The German call center survey was supported by a grant from the Hans Böckler Stiftung. Other surveys in the Global Call Center Project were supported by a range of funding bodies (see www.ilr.cornell.edu/globalcallcenter/sponsors/). Günter Voss hosted me at the Technische Universität Chemnitz during the first month of my research year in Germany, providing a useful introduction to East Germany. Wolfgang Streeck at the Max Planck Institut für Gesellschaftsforschung in Cologne gave me the opportunity to enjoy the institute's excellent office and research facilities during the remainder of my stay, as well as to participate in seminars and lectures with a thoughtful community of scholars. Discussions with Martin Höpner, Till Müller-Schoell, Myung-Joon Park, Britta Rehder, Christine Trampusch, and Josh Whitford helped with thinking through the research design and interpretation of findings. At Cornell, Marco Hauptmeier, Rob Hickey, Hyunji Kwon, Julie Sadler, and Danielle van Jaarsveld gave feedback and support during many doctoral seminars and discussions.

In the years since completing my Ph.D., I was able to conduct follow-up research in Germany with the help of funding from King's College London and the London School of Economics. I worked on parts of this book manuscript while a visiting scholar at the Wissenschaftszentrum Berlin (WZB), the University of New South Wales, and the Laboratoire d'Economie et de Sociologie du Travail (LEST). Arndt Sorge, Steve Frenkel, and Ariel Mendez were gracious hosts during these visits, and seminars at each institute were useful in figuring out what was particularly interesting in my research findings for an international audience of scholars.

My advisors and colleagues have provided valued mentoring and support throughout. Katherine Stone, Lowell Turner, and Sarosh Kuruvilla gave feedback on early proposals and drafts. My committee members John Bunge, Susan Christopherson, and Harry Katz helped with data analysis and interpretation of findings. Rose Batt deserves a special heartfelt thanks for her support during my Ph.D. studies and in the years since. This book benefited enormously from her detailed feedback on research design, interpretation, and through several stages of writing. Lowell, Harry, Rose, Chris Tilly, and Pat McGovern all read and commented on recent drafts of the book manuscript, providing useful suggestions for revisions. My colleagues at King's College London and London School of Economics helped to sharpen my analysis through feedback on a series of articles based on this research, including Olivier Butzbach, Tony Edwards, Howard Gospel, David Guest, Richard Hyman, Gregory Jackson, David Marsden, Riccardo Peccei, and Matt Vidal.

Several chapters in this book draw on previously published material. Chapter 2: Virginia Doellgast, "Still a Coordinated Model? Market Liberalization and the Transformation of Employment Relations in the German Telecommunications Industry," *Industrial and Labor Relations Review* 63(1) (2009): 3–23. Chapter 3: Virginia Doellgast, "Collective Voice under Decentralized Bargaining: A Comparative Study of Work Reorganization in US and German Call Centres," *British Journal of Industrial Relations* 48(2) (2010): 375–99. Chapter 4: Virginia Doellgast, "National Industrial Relations and Local Bargaining Power in the US and German Telecommunications Industries," *European Journal of Industrial Relations* 14(3) (2008): 265–87. Chapter 5: Virginia Doellgast, Hiroatsu Nohara, and Robert Tchobanian, "Institutional Change and the Restructuring of Service Work in the French and German Telecommunications Industries," *European Journal of Industrial Relations 15(4) (2009): 373–94.*

A conversation with Fran Benson at Cornell University Press five years ago planted the idea that my Ph.D. research could be turned into a book. She gave much valued support to this project during the past year, as I set out to write that book. The copyediting of Jack Rummel and production work of Karen Laun significantly improved the clarity of the text.

Finally, I owe a big debt to my family. My husband, Ian, has been a true partner during the research and writing of this book, first encouraging me to take an interest in German industrial relations; and then serving as my best sounding board and critic for numerous ideas and drafts. My mother, Janet, enthusiastically supported my studies and work, even when they took me far from home; while my father, George, shared his wisdom accumulated from years as an academic. He was particularly pleased when I decided to study in Germany, to which he felt a close connection through his German parents and the immigrant community in New York where he grew up. His death two years ago was a great loss. This book is dedicated to him.

Abbreviations

BDA   Bundesvereinigung der Deutschen Arbeitgeberverbände (Confederation of German Employers)

CFDT   Confédération française démocratique du travail (French Democratic Confederation of Labour)

CGPT   Christliche Gewerkschaft Post und Telekommunikation (Christian Postal and Telecommunications Union)

CGT   Confédération générale du travail (General Confederation of Labor

CLEC   Competitive local exchange carrier

CTI   Computer Telephony Integratio CWA Communications Workers of America

DBP   Deutsche Bundespost

DGB   Deutscher Gewerkschaftsbund (Confederation of German Trade Unions)

DPG   Deutsche Postgewerkschaft (German Postal Union)

DPV Kom   Kommunikationsgewerkschaft DPV (Communications union DPV)

DT   Deutsche Telekom
FMLA   Family Medical Leave Act
HBV   Gewerkschaft Handel, Banken und Versicherung (Retail, Banking, and Insurance Union)
IBEW   International Brotherhood of Electrical Workers
IG BCE   Industriegewerkschaft Bergbau, Chemie und Energie (Mining, Chemicals, and Energy Union)
IG Metall   Industriegewerkschaft Metall (Metalworkers Union)
ILEC   Incumbent local exchange carrier
ISDN   Integrated Services Digital Network
ISP   Internet Service Provider
MCO   Mannesmann Customer Operations
NDA/CA   National Directory and Customer Assistance
NL   Niederlassung (Region)
NLRB   National Labor Relations Board
ÖGB   Österreichische Gewerkschaftsbund (Confederation of Austrian Unions)
ÖTV   Gewerkschaft öffentliche Dienste, Transport und Verkehr (Public Service, Transport, and Traffic Union)
PSA   Personal Service Agentur
PUC   Public Utilities Commission
RBOC   Regional Bell Operating Company
SEC   Securities and Exchange Commission
SUD   Solidaires, Unitaires, Démocratiques (Solidaristic, United, Democratic)
TIM   Telekommunikation, Informationstechnologie, Medien (Telecommunications, Information Technology, Media)
TKG   Telekommunikationsgesetz (Telecommunications Act)
UNETEL   Union Nationale des Entreprises de Télécommunications (National Association of Telecommunications Employers)
UNI   Union Network International
VCS   Vivento Customer Services
VDSL   Very High Speed Digital Subscriber Line
ver.di   Vereinte Dienstleistungsgewerkschaft (United Service Sector Union)
VoIP   Voice over IP
WPOF   Workplace of the Future Agreement

DISINTEGRATING DEMOCRACY AT WORK

1

Introduction

Ronald Dore begins his book *British Factory, Japanese Factory* with the statement, "Factories look very much alike anywhere..." One could easily make the same observation about call centers, often described as the assembly lines of the information age.[1] Call center agents use the same tools regardless of what country they are in or task they are performing: a headset, a computer, perhaps reference files and a list of phone numbers. Most call centers are located in large rooms divided into many small cubicles, with slightly larger desks or offices for team leaders and managers. Signs of varying degrees of sophistication, perhaps centrally located, perhaps on the bottom of each agent's computer screen, flash the number of customers on hold. The technology behind these white collar factories is becoming close to identical, as consultants and suppliers sell common platforms for predicting call volumes, routing calls to different agents and centers, and developing scheduling plans.

However, seemingly identical call center workplaces can be entirely different kinds of places to work. Managers use a range of approaches to organize these jobs and to motivate employees to sell an ever-expanding number of products while still providing efficient (yet high-quality) customer service. The service companies that operate call centers experiment with performance incentives, different ways of splitting up tasks, and team-based or individualized models of work organization. Some call centers rely heavily on electronic monitoring systems that record every key stroke and conversation, while others use more personalized side-by-side coaching. In the course of my research for this book, I interviewed highly skilled call center agents who had been in their jobs for twenty years, were making solid middle-class salaries, and took a great deal of pride in their work. I also met a good share of low-paid and overworked employees who felt they were trapped in dead-end jobs with little control over their day-to-day work.

The present study attempts to make sense of these differences through asking how national and workplace institutions influence management choices in what seem at first glance to be uniformly lower-skilled and easily rationalized service jobs. Under what conditions will employers adopt high-road, or "high-involvement," employment models in workplaces where there are strong pressures to cut labor costs? Is there evidence of cross-national divergence in these models—and if so, what explains these differences?

Matched case studies of call center workplaces in the United States and Germany provide a first look at the experiences of worker representatives in both countries as they have sought to shape management strategies at the workplace and organizational levels. The first pair illustrates contrasting outcomes from negotiations over work reorganization in two large telecommunication firms. The second shows the increasingly similar challenges unions experience in both countries as a result of the outsourcing strategies adopted by those same firms.

The Diverging Politics of Work Reorganization

A manager steered me through his service and sales call center at a brisk pace, apologizing for the chaos. I was visiting a former regional Bell company, which had been part of the U.S. monopoly AT&T/Bell system before divestiture and deregulation in the 1980s. The company was in the midst of restructuring its call center jobs, in response to recent regulatory changes that had opened up their regional market to competition—putting pressure on management to cut costs.

That day the company was sponsoring an "international party" to promote international long-distance plans. The large open-plan rooms were decked with streamers and balloons, and supervisors milled around in Hawaiian leis, grass skirts, and African headdresses. Each team had made food and decorated its set of cubicles to represent a different country, giving an eerily festive sheen to an otherwise cavernous white room. The center managers were in the process of judging the teams based on their costumes and level of participation, which seemed to roughly translate into the number of team members who had shown the proper amount of enthusiasm in preparing for the competition. They could expect a material payoff for demonstrating that extra team spirit: the members of the winning team would gain points toward their monthly sales bonus, with the tie breaker going to the team that sold the most international long-distance plans.

A perky team leader told me about the many exciting changes they had put in place in the last few years: "We're really much more about sales now. And that means I have to always come up with new ways to motivate my team." She held up some plastic hands, and showed me how you could shake them together to make a clapping sound "to show employees we appreciate them, that they're doing a great job." As we were talking, one of the center leaders came around to take a team photo. The agents reluctantly got up from their desks and grimaced at the camera as the team leader tried to egg them on: "Come on, smile! Don't look so gloomy, this is a party!" "Honestly," she confided later, "the employees we get today just aren't what they used to be. In my day, we were motivated by doing the job well. Now these kids just come in to make some money, and are out the door next week."

Along with building team spirit and rewarding sales, managers were trying to enforce stricter rules on this more difficult-to-motivate workforce. The company had just adopted a new monitoring policy to catch fraud as employees racked up huge bonuses selling products that customers never ordered. Those who did not make their sales targets were put on progressive discipline, and dismissals for poor performance had skyrocketed. The company had also started hiring private investigators to catch employees who were taking unfair advantage of paid sick leave. "When employees see a supervisor come out to a desk with a buggy and empty out that desk, they might think twice next time."

Union representatives complained that these policies combining tough discipline and individual sales incentives were undermining their work. They were processing a constant stream of grievances against unfair dismissals and several attempts at partnership had fallen flat. Moreover, this new high turnover, sales-focused workforce was proving to be difficult to convince to get active in the union. Union representatives felt their ability to influence management decisions or protect workers was restricted to filing grievances, along with regular fights during formal bargaining to keep in place some negotiated rules about how and when managers could monitor performance or change schedules.

"Team spirit" was also the buzzword among managers and team leaders at Deutsche Telekom's service and sales centers. Deutsche Telekom was seeking to adjust to growing competition in Germany's fixed-line markets, where they had only recently lost their monopoly. As at the regional Bell, these changes were accompanied by new pressures to cut costs and compete for customers. "Sales offensives" and competitions had become just as much a part of their new culture. Large posters announced how many DSL and long-distance packages teams had sold each day, and how far they had to go to meet their goal for the week. "Employees can add a mark when they sell something—that helps build team solidarity, gives them the feeling they're moving toward something." The company sponsored special win-back offensives, with prizes or bonuses for the winning team. Team leaders admitted they had gotten the competitive bug as well: "I look and see, ah, this week I'm number three, and last week I was number ten in the rankings, good job!"

Also similar to their counterparts at the former regional Bell, Deutsche Telekom's managers were seeking to transform the culture in their call centers, trying to encourage workers to move from their traditional focus on customer service to more of a sales orientation. They had introduced performance-based pay, were teaching selling techniques, and had set up competitions and prizes. Still, call centers belonging to the two companies looked completely different. There were no clappers, balloons, or streamers at Deutsche Telekom. Employees dressed more professionally and tended to be older, making it difficult to tell the team leaders from the agents. Team leaders discussed their employees respectfully, instead of like a parent explaining the challenges of disciplining unruly children. "It is impossible to do this job without the trust of your team. They have a certain expectation of us as well: that we will help them to develop, that we will give them some room to use their skills and not look over their shoulder every minute."

Scratch beneath the surface and these differences widen. While the former regional Bell made heavy use of individual bonuses, all sales incentives at Deutsche Telekom were group based. While the U.S. managers constantly monitored their employees, Deutsche Telekom managers had to rely on "mystery calls" to evaluate service quality and could only report results at the team level. Most striking was how much more control employees had over their work and working time. Disciplining agents for poor performance was extremely difficult, break times were flexible, and "working time accounts" meant employees could take time off when they needed it within certain negotiated boundaries. A joint labor-management committee decided on sales goals, and employees could formally challenge these goals if they believed they were unfair. There was also practically no turnover and minimal fraud.

The Company Principles hung on every wall announcing Deutsche Telekom's goal to match customer orientation and professional service: (1) Quality of life in an open information community; (2) We impress customers through innovative solutions and individual service. In one room, a team leader had put up a Goethe quote: "Es hört doch jeder nur, was er versteht" (Each hears only what he understands). In addition to regular training on selling techniques and product updates, employees and supervisors attended special seminars at the company's training centers to develop "professional competence."

At one point during a site visit, I was standing in the hall with a group of call center agents on a smoke break. I listened to their complaints about the new competitions and incentives, growing pressure to make sales goals, constant reorganization in the company, and downsizing. As in many of my visits to German call centers, the employees were curious about whether I observed any differences in the United States. "What is it like there? Aren't all call centers the same?" I told them that supervisors could listen to agents without their knowledge and fire them for poor performance. Several mouths dropped open. "How can they work under those conditions? Aren't they afraid all the time? Does the works council just let that happen?" And then I explained that there are no works councils in the United States and that unions do not have the legal right to block remote monitoring or decide on the appropriate criteria for evaluating performance. This was a revelation for them: workers in the United States did not have codetermination rights even where they had a union. They conceded that while they may have troubles, conditions were probably worse for their American colleagues.

The Converging Politics of Organizational Restructuring

Upstate New York experienced deindustrialization in the 1970s but is still dealing with the problems associated with job loss and social dislocation. Abandoned factories line the roads and waterfronts in many cities and unemployment is persistently high. Buffalo has gone through changes typical of the region. As employment shifted to services, union density and per capita earnings declined. Call centers moved in to take advantage of attractive government subsidies and a large potential pool of workers.

One of Buffalo's large call center subcontractors, Telespectrum, won a contract in the late 1990s to handle DSL sales and customer service for Verizon. Verizon is a "legacy" telecommunications firm coming out of the former AT&T and regional Bell monopoly, with a long history of collective agreements with the Communication Workers of America (CWA) and the International Brotherhood of Electrical Workers (IBEW). The unions had been trying to halt or reverse outsourcing at Verizon for years with some limited success but had no wins from organizing campaigns in its subcontractors. The conventional wisdom held that these companies were impossible to organize, as it was too easy to intimidate the workforce with threats of moving call center jobs to another center or region. Union representatives and workers with any experience trying to organize call centers repeated one phrase like a mantra: "It's just a matter of flipping a switch, then those jobs are gone."

However, it seemed like they might have a chance at Telespectrum. The IBEW had a number of unemployed members in Buffalo who were willing to take jobs and organize the workforce at the subcontractor, and the union thought it could use its leverage at Verizon to put pressure on management. These union activists organized an election and won union recognition in 2000—the first successful organizing campaign at a U.S.-based call center subcontractor. After fourteen months of difficult negotiations, management agreed to a contract that raised pay 14 percent, from $8.75 to $10. Although this was still less than half of the average salary in the company's unionized call centers, it was substantially higher than the typical wage for subcontracted jobs. However, three months later, Verizon withdrew its contract with the company and moved the work to several nonunion subcontractors in southern "right to work" states. The call center closed, and three hundred employees lost their jobs.

A similar chain of events unfolded in Siegen, a small city in the German state of Nordrhein-Westfalen, which is the historic center of West German manufacturing. Like many cities in the region, Siegen has shed population over the past decade due to the decline of the steel industry, and has been steadily losing its remaining manufacturing jobs. Abandoned factories line the main highway through town, and unemployment fluctuates around 10 percent. Similar to Buffalo, the local government sought to attract call centers as part of more service sector–focused economic development strategies. In 1999 T-Online, a subsidiary of Deutsche Telekom, set up a technical support call center in Siegen. The company was attracted to the region by generous training subsidies and relocation assistance, and management easily recruited a skilled workforce for the new, high-paying jobs. The company's central works council helped to coordinate elections for a local works council, which established a good working relationship with management. In line with the policies across T-Online, the works council negotiated team-based incentives, strict limits on management's ability to remotely monitor calls, and regular pay increases.

After several years, T-Online sold this center to the U.S.-based subcontractor Sykes as part of a plan to outsource the majority of its call center work. The new company retained the existing workforce, who kept the terms of their former contracts for eighteen months. However, toward the end of that period, management gradually introduced individual performance-based pay and flexible scheduling. New employees were hired on short-term contracts, at two-thirds the pay of tenured agents. While agents continued to handle the same kinds of calls, they were expected to answer a greater number of calls each hour and to take shorter breaks. Cooperative negotiations with management turned into daily fights, and the works council began to go to court regularly to protest labor law violations. Some employees struggled to hold on to the protections they had won in the past, supporting the works council and consulting with local union representatives on their rights. Others felt they should accept the new employment terms, and accused the works council of putting their jobs at risk. Managers fed this fear with threats that they would close the center. After three years of hostile relations, Sykes decided to reroute the calls to a call center in another region with a more "employer-friendly" works council and 25 percent lower pay. As a result, close to two hundred employees lost their jobs.

These two stories look quite similar, despite having taken place in two very different institutional settings. Large telecommunications firms with strong unions outsourced their call center jobs to nonunion subcontractors with lower pay and poor working conditions. Worker representatives then tried to organize resistance to changes or negotiate new collective agreements, relying on what they believed to be a stable base of bargaining power or member support from the unionized company. However, in the end these efforts were unsuccessful. In the U.S. case, the telecommunications firm withdrew the contract and sent the work to other subcontractors that did not have union agreements. In the German case, the subcontractor moved the work to another region where the workforce was more willing to accept management's terms.

I spent an afternoon in Siegen with several former T-Online works councilors talking with them about their experiences leading up to the closure of the Sykes call center. They described the growing stress and animosity between formerly close colleagues, the daily arguments, and the constant fear of job loss. They continued to engage with management despite all of this based on the persistent belief that it was worth the personal sacrifice to try to maintain high pay and good working conditions for these jobs. The former head of the works council put off meeting with me for several months after the center had closed because she felt she could not talk to anyone about it yet. "I was just so mad, you know, I was depressed and demoralized and felt like it would be too much to go back over everything that happened." These former call center agents had held the same high-road, professional jobs as their colleagues at Deutsche Telekom's in-house centers, but the protections they had enjoyed were easily undermined by a simple change in ownership.

Divergence and Convergence

These case studies illustrate two closely related dimensions of service work restructuring, and the different tools worker representatives have at their disposal to influence these decisions. On the one hand, management practices are often significantly shaped by industrial relations and labor market institutions—and these institutions do vary in a systematic way between countries. In core firms like the regional Bells and Deutsche Telekom that have strong unions and, in Germany, independent works councils, worker representatives have access to different resources in negotiations over work reorganization. Simply put, German workers have more potential bargaining power at an individual and collective level compared to U.S. workers. Participation rights in Germany's national *Betriebsverfassungsgesetz,* or Works Constitution Act, give elected works councils the right to be consulted over decisions ranging from the design of variable pay to how electronic monitoring is used. Board level rights mean that workers can elect representatives to company advisory committees, which gives unions and works councils access to privileged information about company finances and consultation rights over the effects of restructuring on the workforce. The United States has very different labor laws and collective bargaining institutions. Unions' statutory bargaining rights are restricted primarily to pay and layoffs; and power often comes either at the bargaining table or in enforcing the contract through grievances.

These differences are real and persistent. However, the second of the two matched cases above shows that these formal rights and structures are increasingly easy to undermine or bypass by employers seeking labor cost savings. Organizational restructuring strategies like outsourcing allow firms to move work out of core workplaces and avoid many of the institutions that in the past encouraged alternative approaches to work organization.

Outsourcing has more often been associated with union avoidance and the downgrading of working conditions in liberal countries like the United States. Low bargaining coverage and a high union wage premium meant that unionized firms could gain large cost savings by moving jobs to typically nonunion subcontractors or subsidiaries. Today, outsourcing strategies are increasingly used in Germany to reduce pay and avoid negotiated constraints on management. Despite strong unions, extensive participation rights, and high bargaining coverage, it has proved surprisingly easy for companies to move work (and workers) to new companies that lack strong and independent collective bargaining institutions.

This book investigates the causes and consequences of these dual trends: divergence in employment systems and growing convergence in organizational restructuring strategies. Case studies show that institutional supports for collective worker participation in decision making can lead to substantively different management strategies in easily rationalized service jobs, where technology is standardized and there are intense pressures to cut labor costs. In settings like call centers where managers have obvious incentives to downgrade pay and working conditions, the decision to invest in worker skills and participation (rather than monitoring and discipline) requires some form of negotiated or collective constraints on unilateral management prerogative. Strong participation rights have traditionally provided worker representatives in Germany with the resources necessary to exercise this kind of countervailing power at the workplace level. The lack of equivalent resources in the United States mean that management is not obliged to compromise with its workforce in the same way, and thus more likely to seek productivity increases through intensified monitoring and discipline.

At the same time, sustaining equity in access to good jobs also requires institutions that close off possibilities to escape collective agreements through moving work outside of traditional workplace boundaries. The lack of encompassing bargaining has long been a challenge for U.S. unions. It has recently become a more serious and growing challenge for German unions due to expanding gaps in bargaining coverage in traditional industries and the growth of new, poorly regulated sectors or employment categories. The unraveling of traditional sources of countervailing power has encouraged intensified labor market segmentation and created downward pressure on pay and working conditions. These employer strategies threaten to further erode collective power based on encompassing and coordinated bargaining.

These findings contribute to ongoing debates in the comparative political economy and industrial relations literature on the changing relationship between national institutions, management strategy, and worker outcomes. In the following sections, I review the history of these debates and lay out my argument based on the current study.

National Models of Capitalism

The French businessman Michel Albert popularized the notion of national models in *Capitalism vs. Capitalism* (1993), in which he described Germany's "Rhineland Capitalist" system as a successful alternative to the Anglo-Saxon model. This book expressed an idea with a long tradition, that distinct institutions shape approaches to organizing production, investing in skills, and competing in international markets. However, scholars have long debated exactly how stable these alternatives are, given pressures from best practice institutional systems and the management strategies they support.

In traditional Marxist theory, the dual forces of technological change and market competition were believed to determine the path of industrial development, as countries moved at different paces toward greater concentration of capital and rationalization of production (Marx and Engels 1986: 78). Industrial sociologists of the 1960s and 1970s agreed that similar innovations would spread and have a leveling effect across countries. However, they argued that the force driving these changes forward was industrialism rather than capitalism (Form 1979). According to Kerr, Dunlop, Harbison, and Meyers (1964), the spread of industrial production methods would lead to similar social structures, which included dominance by large enterprises, a hierarchically differentiated workforce, and growing government involvement in industrial relations. The Keynesian welfare state and industrial unions provided the political coordinating muscle, and countries would gradually adopt similar institutions as they industrialized. Behind these convergence theories was the idea that there was one best way or most efficient set of exchange relations. Progress marched forward in an orderly manner as firms adopted production methods based on new technological advances and governments put in place institutions that supported the successful adaptation of these methods.

These insights were extended to explain the diffusion of similar employment systems across industries and workplaces. In the postwar period,

Fordist mass production came to dominate both manufacturing best practice and academic discussions about the future of work. Firms produced standardized goods for mass markets using semiskilled labor and tight managerial control. This production model was in turn supported by strong industrial unions and redistributive policies through the Keynesian welfare state. Taylorist principles of scientific management governed shop floor work organization, which sought productivity improvements through a more narrow division of labor that separated "conception from execution." At the same time, efficiency gains often had negative effects on workers in the mass market factory (Braverman 1974) and its white collar equivalent of large, hierarchical bureaucracies (Kanter 1978; Whyte 1956), as jobs were divided into fragmented and repetitive tasks.

Developments in the late 1970s and 1980s posed new challenges for convergence theories. The oil shocks of the 1970s, growing instability in international financial markets, and the breakdown of the Breton Woods system meant that employers faced more volatile competitive conditions. Marxist interpretations of technological convergence lost credibility with the decline of state socialism in the 1980s. Markets and production technologies were also changing rapidly, as innovations in microelectronics increased opportunities for flexible production methods and niche market strategies, while contributing to fragmented customer demand (Piore and Sabel 1984).

At the same time, the superior economic competitiveness of Germany and Japan in the 1980s inspired research on the institutional underpinnings of alternative national models. Neocorporatist theories, associated with the work of Schmitter and Lehmbruch (1979), held that social arrangements characterized by strong and hierarchically organized labor unions encouraged tripartite bargaining between unions, organized private sector or business interests, and the government. These in turn produced both social and economic benefits, as they divided productivity gains among the social partners and promoted wage restraint. Katzenstein (1985) argued along these lines that Europe's small, open economies, such as Austria, Sweden, and the Netherlands (and to a lesser extent Germany), relied on a distinct "democratic corporatist" model to manage their relationship with more competitive global markets, as an alternative to the liberal U.S. model or statist French and Japanese model. Approaches to economic restructuring could thus be broadly categorized along national lines, based on the extent to which labor and the state were included in negotiations over industrial adjustment (Zysman 1983).

Comparative researchers also began to describe alternative production models in these countries. Dore (1973) showed that industrial relations and employment systems looked quite different in superficially similar British and Japanese electronics factories. Diverging preindustrial histories, the degree and nature of state control, and systematic variation in the path to industrialization had produced contrasting management approaches that were stubbornly resistant to convergence. Maurice, Sellier, and Silvestre (1986) took up similar themes in their study of matched pairs of German and French manufacturing firms. Despite having similar tasks and technology, French firms adopted a more centralized, bureaucratic, and individualized management style compared to those in Germany, where blue collar workers enjoyed higher qualifications and professional status. Each system led to different levels of skill across employee groups, which were in turn rewarded differently. These processes of skill formation were embedded in unique social arrangements that developed over time, constituting "societal effects" on work systems.

The conclusions researchers drew from these comparisons carried with them an assumption—to varying degrees implicit or clearly articulated—that certain institutions produced better outcomes than others. These "better" outcomes ranged from improved productivity and efficiency to benefits for workers, such as the ability to share in productivity gains and exercise autonomy and discretion in their work. However, the ideal best practice model would produce some mutually beneficial combination of these outcomes, overcoming the equity-efficiency tradeoffs assumed in most neoclassical economic models. Management practices that relied on a high degree of workplace democracy were a viable and perhaps even a more competitive alternative to the managerial control models associated with Fordist mass production. Moreover, these practices seemed to be more common in countries like Germany and Japan, where unions were involved in extensive workplace-level participation structures and committees.

In the 1980s and 1990s, scholars also began giving more attention to the dynamics that sustained these kinds of best practice models, as well as discussing the conditions necessary for the diffusion of these models across countries or regions. "Flexible specialization" typical of Italian industrial districts (Piore and Sabel 1984) and Japanese-style lean production (Womack, Jones, and Roos 1990) came to be viewed as technically superior alternatives to Fordist-style mass production. In Germany, Kern and Schumann (1984) argued that the "New Production Concepts" taking hold in industrial production required general skills and subjective participation, as workers were called on to be more creative and autonomous in their work. Popular books, such as Best's (1990) *The New Competition* and Porter's (1990) *The Competitive Advantage of Nations,* added further fuel to arguments that organizational change along the lines of Japanese lean production or flexible specialization were needed to break the grip of command and control production organizations prevalent in American big business.

At the same time, national differences proved remarkably persistent. As the workplace innovations associated with lean production became increasingly popular, comparative research showed that firms implemented innovations like teams and quality control in different ways across workplaces and countries. Scholars attributed these differences to a range of factors, such as industrial relations institutions, systems of skill development, and management cultures. Streeck's (1984, 1991) work on German diversified quality production, Jaikumar's (1986) research on flexible manufacturing in Japan and the United States, Turner's (1991) and Thelen's (1991) studies of auto manufacturers in the United States and Germany, and Berggren's (1992) study of sociotechnical systems at Volvo in Sweden all became important references in a growing literature on the institutional foundations of national production models and their resistance to convergence (Marsden 1999; Locke, Kochan, and Piore 1995; Berger and Dore 1996).

These researchers continued to be far from neutral about their preferred model. Their studies did much to promote the view that the more organized, corporatist, or "Rhineland Capitalist" economies produced superior outcomes to those relying more heavily on unfettered markets: strong unions secured mutual gains at the workplace level, and—through a combination of wage moderation and redistribution of productivity gains—produced equity with efficiency at the national level. Researchers took this as evidence that regulated labor markets and centralized or coordinated collective bargaining institutions could be a source of competitive advantage for firms rather than an obstacle to the smooth functioning of the market. Dore (1986) described lifetime employment, seniority-based payment systems, and long-term relationships between manufacturers and suppliers in Japan as a source of "flexible rigidities"; while Streeck (1991) argued that Germany's apprenticeship-based training system, occupational labor market structure, and dual system of collective bargaining served as "productive constraints" on firms. These institutions forced employers to focus on their long-term interests rather than respond to short-term market shocks, and thus provided them with unique competitive advantages in world markets. Instead of convergence, foreign best practice was transformed into a "social-institutional hybrid" (Streeck 1996: 168).

Meanwhile, research in the United States found that new "high performance work systems" that gave frontline employees the opportunity and incentives to participate in decision making were catching on in a minority of U.S. firms as they tried to compete in more quality-conscious markets (Appelbaum and Batt 1994). There was a great deal of early optimism that these models would transform U.S. companies and provide a vehicle for stronger labor-management partnerships based on mutual gains. However, survey research showed that only a minority of companies adopted these practices in a systematic way (Gittleman, Horrigan, and Joyce 1998; Osterman 2000). Those partnerships that did succeed for a time at unionized firms, such as Saturn or AT&T, eventually folded as firms pursued more unilateral downsizing or restructuring strategies that undermined trust and cooperation. This seemed to bear out earlier predictions by Katz and Sabel (1985) and Turner (1991) that the United States' weak industrial relations institutions—with fragmented and decentralized bargaining, weak bargaining rights, and little institutional security for unions—would undermine the long-term success of joint efforts to implement new flexible or high-involvement employment systems.

The New Convergence Debates

The researchers involved in these studies agreed that different national models could be identified based on coherent systems of institutions; national production models were embedded in unique histories of industrial and institutional development; and many of these institutions persisted despite changing markets and technologies. However, the contours of these debates changed again in the mid-1990s as the United States and United Kingdom became dynamic settings for the expansion of new economy industries and as unemployment began to climb in countries with more strongly regulated labor markets. Manufacturing firms in continental Europe lost market share to new lower-cost competitors, while Japan entered a prolonged economic slump.

Convergence theorists turned attention back to the U.S. economy, but this time its competitiveness was popularly attributed to its more liberal, market-based institutions that combined weak unions, low regulation, cheap capital, and shareholder value-oriented financial markets. Radical innovation or speed of reaction became the new best practice and a key resource for competitive advantage in more volatile markets. The rise of international finance rapidly increased the pace of capital investment and disinvestment, encouraging employers to step up pressure on governments to replace protective regulations with more flexible labor market rules.

The new advocates of convergence theory argued that the increasing speed and magnitude of flows of goods, services, and capital investment diminished the importance of boundaries and regulation as transnational corporations took center stage (Ohmae 1994). Optimists see these trends as improving employment opportunities and job quality in the long run, as advanced countries increasingly specialize in capital intensive activities requiring a well-educated workforce (Friedman 2007). According to more pessimistic accounts, however, globalization is driving low-road convergence, as firms face intensifying pressure to reduce labor costs. Multinational corporations use "coercive comparisons" between unionized plants to secure concessions on pay or working time arrangements, threatening to withdraw investment if terms are not met (Edwards, Rees, and Coller 1999; Greer and Hauptmeier 2008; Royle 2004). "Global Japanization," in the form of the widespread adoption of lean production techniques in manufacturing, has intensified union avoidance and work speedups (Elger and Smith 1994; Stewart et al. 2009). These changes are not only driven by firms: across social Europe, the EU and national governments have encouraged the liberalization of labor markets through measures aimed at increasing employment flexibility, reducing welfare expenditures, and increasing competition in formerly protected markets (Brandt et al. 2008; Keune, Leschke, and Watt 2008).

Meanwhile, recent theory and research in comparative political economy continues to emphasize continuity in coherent national systems of complementary rules and resources, and to articulate the underlying logic behind those systems (Deeg and Jackson 2007). According to the varieties of capitalism approach developed by Hall and Soskice (2001), distinct national models have persisted with coherent systems of rules and incentives. The United States is an example of a "liberal market economy" where firms rely on market relations to resolve coordination problems, giving firms a competitive advantage in market segments requiring rapid innovation. In contrast, Germany is a "coordinated market economy" where firms rely more heavily on nonmarket or relational forms of coordination and perform best in value-added and niche product segments.

This framework has encouraged a flowering of alternative typologies, in which scholars debate the appropriate number of ideal-type national models and exactly which dimensions of those models matter most for constructing these groupings (e.g. Whitley 1999; Schmidt 2002; Amable 2003). A central argument in this literature is that complementary sets of institutions help to solve different coordination problems, and thus support distinct competitive strategies in international markets. Using the language of management strategy theorists, firms develop and exploit "core competencies" based on their unique resources—however, these resources are not only internal to the firm but also derive from the institutions that developed over time in different national economies. Globalization has thus made institutionally based differences *more* important for firms, and competitive success in each best practice model depends on the continued presence of strongly complementary institutions (Hancke, Rhodes, and Thatcher 2008). This, in turn, should give employers in coordinated economies an incentive not to defect from expensive training obligations and collective bargaining arrangements, and encourage governments to maintain the regulations that support these arrangements (Thelen 2001).

Convergence or Divergence?

These two groups of scholars stake out different positions on whether national institutions will continue to shape the strategies employers adopt to compete in increasingly globalized markets. Proponents of convergence theories argue that globalization has opened up location options, leading to the "death of distance" (Cairncross 1997) and diminished differences in pay and working conditions for similar jobs across countries. Proponents of varieties of capitalism theories agree that intensified global competition is transforming corporate strategies but argue that this instead creates incentives for companies to exploit their unique competitive advantages, intensifying the divide between distinct national models.

At the same time, the two positions are based on similar assumptions about the relationship between institutions and employer strategies. First, both treat firms as central actors. Second, both focus on whether and how institutions matter for competitive strategies writ large, and tend to read employment practices off of these strategies. Low-road convergence arguments predict that as firms face intensifying pressure in global markets, they will be more likely to seek out institutional settings that facilitate low-cost strategies, leading to wage concessions and work intensification. Varieties of capitalism theorists argue that as firms pursue competitive advantage in market segments that require "comparative institutional advantages," they will adopt complementary organizational and human resource strategies—which in coordinated economies should rely on high skill levels, cooperative labor relations, and commitment-oriented employment practices.

Both perspectives conflate strategies to compete in different market segments, reorganize production, and redesign work, assuming that these make up a coherent system. According to convergence arguments, the growing *similarity* of competitive conditions in a globalized economy drives firms to mount a neoliberal offensive against constraining institutions (such as unions) and to adopt a common set of employment practices. The conventional wisdom in the comparative political economy literature is that *divergent* strategies to compete in distinct product niches in globalized markets explain both the stability of different national institutional arrangements and their effects on employment systems.

The Argument

The analysis in this book seeks to explain why firms compete in *similar* market segments using *divergent* management approaches. Instead of treating strategy as functional and coherent, I look at how political processes of negotiation shape (or fail to shape) employment systems and the organizational restructuring decisions that influence patterns of inequality. Contemporary debates on convergence and divergence focus overwhelmingly on employer strategies. This study, in contrast, focuses on unions and works councils as important strategic actors that combine different institutionally and organizationally embedded resources to influence management decisions through negotiations and political action.

The central argument in this book is that strong forms of workplace democracy backed by encompassing collective bargaining are necessary to encourage investment in high-involvement employment systems and to prevent the degradation of job quality in employment settings where managers face strong pressures to reduce labor costs. Workplace democracy is defined here as representative structures within establishments and firms that give employees an independent voice in, and direct influence over, a range of management policies and practices. Similar terms used for these kinds of structures include "collective voice" mechanisms, "representative participation," or "codetermination." The important common denominator is the presence of formal negotiations over management goals and practices that involve a high degree of power-sharing between employers and worker representatives. The main outcomes I focus on are employment systems within workplaces and patterns of inequality in pay and working conditions across networked workplaces. I categorize the employment system as falling along a continuum between high-involvement models that rely on investments in skills and worker discretion; or managerial control models, in which jobs are narrowly designed and decision making is centralized.

My argument rests on two propositions. First, market liberalization puts common pressures on firms to reduce labor costs for easily rationalized jobs. Employers adopt different strategies to externalize or segment these jobs within institutional systems that provide them with distinct resources and constraints. However, growing inequality in pay and working conditions is a common and converging trend that is accomplished through rather than against existing institutional arrangements.

Second, differences in labor power, and how that power is exercised and supported, are central to explaining differences in the employment systems adopted across networked workplaces that perform these secondary jobs. Two dimensions of national institutions are crucial in this regard: strong participation rights and encompassing collective bargaining institutions.

Participation rights are particularly important because they ensure that employee interests are represented where employers have a clear interest in reducing labor costs. Management researchers have shown that employers are more likely to use high-involvement practices for groups of workers who are viewed as core or of high strategic value (Lepak and Snell 1999; Batt 2000). The varieties of capitalism literature argues along similar lines that national institutions serve as a resource for investing in these core competencies, allowing German firms, for example, to pursue competitive advantage in high-value-added segments of global markets (Hall and Soskice 2001). Employers have stronger incentives to rationalize work or reduce investments in human capital in secondary or peripheral workplaces. In these settings, countervailing power exercised by worker representatives is necessary to challenge a focus on cost-cutting and to help management implement alternatives. Employers often gain benefits from these alternatives, including worker acceptance of productivity-enhancing changes to work design and more flexible scheduling arrangements. However, managers are unlikely to make sustainable investments in high-involvement models without the constraint of mandatory worker participation in decision-making.

At the same time, encompassing institutions are necessary to protect worker access to participation rights and structures across increasingly fluid organizational boundaries. The erosion of bargaining coverage, changes in employment protection legislation, and the rise of a poorly regulated sector of subcontractors mean that managers in both liberal and coordinated countries have growing opportunities to escape negotiated constraints on unilateral decision making through organizational restructuring. The degradation of job quality often follows from organizational strategies that take advantage of these growing gaps in a broader regulatory framework to externalize once core jobs. Expanding opportunities for employers to exit formal bargaining arrangements not only reduce the size of the core workforce but also weaken the countervailing power and institutional security that support high-trust labor relations in this core. As unions lose power and influence, remaining participation structures often become a resource for firms to gain worker acceptance of and cooperation with desired changes, rather than a means for developing negotiated alternatives. Maintaining and strengthening workplace democracy requires building encompassing institutions that constrict these exit options, thus providing employers with clear incentives to cooperate with worker representatives in secondary as well as in core workplaces.

Strategic Choice and Institutional Change

This argument—and the findings it is based on—contribute to recent debates in the comparative literature on the changing relationship between management strategy and national institutions. Industrial relations theory has explained variation in employment systems as the outcome of different strategic choices that actors make within a set of institutional resources and constraints (Dunlop 1958; Kochan, Katz, and McKersie 1986). Comparative studies in the 1980s and 1990s mapped out the relationship between strategy and structure in different political economies, arguing that industrial relations institutions played an important role in enabling or constricting strategic choices (Katz and Sabel 1985; Turner 1991; Wever 1995).

Recent research in this vein has had more difficulty describing exactly how national institutions are related to management strategy as collective bargaining arrangements become less coherent. Studies have shown that the growth of nonunion sectors, new production models, and the decentralization of bargaining have contributed to growing diversity in human resource practices and increased wage spread within coordinated countries (Jacoby 2005; Katz and Darbishire 2000; Marginson, Sisson, and Arrowsmith 2003; Gautié and Schmitt 2009). These scholars argue that strategic choices are becoming more important and national institutions less robust as a causal factor explaining employment systems. However, there is no consensus on how institutions influence these choices, and at what level of decision making.

A second group of researchers from the historical institutionalist tradition has begun to analyze the dynamics of institutional change within coordinated economies (Yamamura and Streeck 2003; Kitschelt and Streeck 2004; Streeck and Thelen 2005; Crouch and Voelzkow 2009; Crouch 2005; Gospel and Pendleton 2005; Djelic and Quack 2003; Morgan, Whitley, and Moen 2005). These scholars argue against the functionalism of varieties of capitalism and examine the political processes through which laws, collective bargaining structures, and corporate governance systems are being renegotiated under pressure from economic liberalization.

One argument holds that these institutional changes represent managed change. Old laws and bargaining arrangements are adapted through hybrid models that "accommodate more marketized capital within regimes of industrial citizenship for employees" (Jackson 2003: 263). Vertical disintegration, declining bargaining coverage, and expansion of nonstandard employment arrangements may encourage growing "segmentalism" (Thelen 2009) but do not threaten the core logic of employer coordination that serves as a source of competitive advantage for firms (Herrigel 2008; Höpner 2007). Others view these trends as part of a gradual shift in coordinated economies toward the adoption of a more liberal political and economic model. Lehndorff et al. (2009) point to stagnating wages and an increase in low-wage and precarious employment as evidence of a breakdown of the German model, particularly in new and growing areas of the economy (see also Bosch and Weinkopf 2008). Streeck (2009: 87) argues that the general trend in Germany is toward "dissolution of the broad political camps and economic risk pools that were at the center of postwar German corporatism."

These researchers give a more up-to-date analysis of neocorporatist institutions, describing the mix of path dependency and negotiated change occurring in coordinated countries. However, the focus of their research is often on the changes occurring in the institutions themselves, rather than on how residual and emerging institutions influence or interact with management strategies. Studies that do look at outcomes like pay and work design tend to look at one country (usually Germany or Japan) and aggregate findings across large employers. They lack a more focused empirical lens that examines how the dynamics of institutional change they describe play out within organizations, on countries with different political and economic institutions.

Findings from the present study contribute to debates in these two literatures. First, instead of simply describing the growth of poorly regulated employment segments, I analyze the restructuring processes that have contributed to the growth of these segments. The dynamics of internal labor markets in manufacturing were at the heart of research on the development of employment systems under Fordist capitalism (Jacoby 1985; Osterman

1984). The varieties of capitalism literature has concentrated overwhelmingly on export-oriented manufacturing or high-end services, as these are viewed as central to sustaining competitive advantage in international markets. Strategic choice and historical institutionalist arguments improve on the functionalism of the varieties of capitalism literature, but they are similarly biased toward the experience of core employees.

In contrast, the call centers studied here are labor-intensive service workplaces that tend to serve a (mostly) domestic market, are characterized by the breakdown of internal labor markets, and are typically not treated as a "core competency" by employers. As such, they are representative of a growing segment of secondary employment that has expanded in the global North over the past several decades. The influence of institutions on working conditions in these kinds of jobs has become the recent focus of both policy debate and comparative research (Gautié and Schmitt 2009; Bosch and Lehndorff 2005; Batt, Holman, and Holtgrewe 2009). This study takes a closer look at negotiations involved in work restructuring in secondary workplaces, their strategic context, and their outcomes. This provides new insights on how firm strategies are changing, and what their effects are on working conditions for different groups of service workers.

Second, this study examines the relationship between management strategies at the workplace and inter-organizational levels. The industrial relations literature has traditionally focused on employment practices at the workplace level. Both varieties of capitalism theorists and historical institutionalists have turned their attention to product market strategies and institutions aggregated at the national level, and say little about how these relate to the micropolitics of work reorganization. Organizational restructuring has figured in both traditions as an explanation for more decentralized bargaining, but there has been little comparative analysis of collective negotiations over these decisions.

The present study analyzes the negotiations that have accompanied change in employment systems, based on detailed findings from workplaces linked through subcontracting and subsidiary arrangements. Looking at the workplace and organizational dimensions of restructuring in parallel gives a useful window on exactly how institutions matter for employers' strategic choices across the "networked firm," as well as the effects of these choices on pay and working conditions for different employee groups.

Findings contribute concretely to the above debates through showing how and why national differences in industrial relations institutions shape job quality in peripheral service workplaces. They demonstrate that participation rights and bargaining structures can have a large influence on work organization and patterns of inequality in these more challenging settings, even where firms compete in similar markets. While globalization and market liberalization create universal pressures for more differentiated management strategies, these strategies do not necessarily lead to low-road convergence on "bad jobs." However, unions' growing difficulty in closing off escape routes from existing institutional protections is contributing to the degradation of work in formerly protected service industries. Unions thus not only face the challenge of rebuilding past sources of collective power but also of finding new ways to narrow these gaps in regulation.

Outline of the Book

The research presented in this book is based on a multilevel and mixed-method study. To analyze industry developments and organizational restructuring strategies, I draw on interviews with managers and union officials as well as archival sources. Findings on work reorganization and employment systems are based on a structured case comparison, focusing on four matched pair firms in the telecommunications and call center subcontractor industries. In total, I conducted close to three hundred interviews with key informants, managers, team leaders, union representatives, works councilors, and workers in the case study firms (see appendix A). Most of this work was carried out over three years (2002–4) with follow-up interviews between 2007 and 2010 to track more recent developments at the case studies and in the industry. In addition, I examine the broader generalizability of the qualitative findings using survey and case study research from the Global Call Center Project, an international study involving teams in twenty countries (Batt, Holman, and Holtgrewe 2009). Most of the research from this collaborative project was carried out between 2003 and 2005.

The following three chapters compare the politics of restructuring in U.S. and German telecommunications firms at three levels—the industry, the workplace, and the firm or corporate group. In chapter 2, I compare changes in markets and industrial relations in the U.S. and German telecommunications industries. Government-led market liberalization (and, in Germany, privatization) has meant that market conditions and ownership structures are increasingly similar between the two countries. The former monopolists face growing price competition from new firms with lower fixed costs and weaker or no unions. As a result, bargaining coverage has declined and bargaining has become increasingly decentralized in unions' traditional strongholds. At the same time, German unions have held on to past sources of power at the workplace level in core firms, primarily through their relationships with strong and independent works councils.

Chapter 3 compares the strategies that U.S. and German telecommunications firms and their subcontractors adopted to reorganize call center jobs, as they sought to improve the productivity and quality of customer service and sales. Matched case studies in these two industries show that despite similar strategies and objectives, managers in each country put in place very different employment systems. Unions in the United States were unable to prevent managers from intensifying monitoring and discipline to increase productivity. In contrast, German unions and works councils used their strong codetermination rights to promote a more professional, or high-involvement, model of work design that safeguarded employee autonomy and discretion.

The case studies also show variation within each country. In the United States, unions had some success in forming partnerships with management over work reorganization, but the strength of these partnerships varied over time and across firms and locations. Managers in the German cases were under growing pressure to adopt remote electronic monitoring and individual incentives, and these initiatives proved more successful where coordination between worker representatives at different establishments or companies was weakest. In both countries, subcontractors paid lower wages and monitored workers more intensively, while their works councils (where they were present) faced large challenges in negotiating strong collective agreements.

Chapter 4 focuses on organizational restructuring in major telecommunications firms or corporate groups, and the implications of these restructuring measures for employees working across their networked call centers. Telecommunications employers have used restructuring measures such as outsourcing, subsidiary creation, and consolidation of jobs in both the United States and Germany to reduce costs, often with the effect of weakening or avoiding collective agreements. Managers either moved work or sold locations to call center subcontractors with substantially lower union density, few collective agreements, and in Germany, weaker works councils. At the same time, many firms established new subsidiaries or job classifications for service and sales work, and negotiated contracts for these groups at lower pay rates. Together, these trends contributed to growing diversity in pay and working conditions and increased worker-to-worker competition for highly mobile jobs. Unions in both countries faced the new challenge of redefining their roles in less clearly bounded industry sectors and developing new strategies to regulate work across their major employers' production chains. Thus, although formal participation rights in Germany remained stable, new organizational strategies were driving radical institutional change and contributing to increased differentiation in pay and working conditions on a scale very similar to that in the United States.

In chapter 5, I ask how representative these case studies are of broader trends in the U.S. and German call center industries, as well as of international developments. Survey data support the case study findings: German call centers were more likely to adopt high-involvement practices, but take-up of some of these practices was strongest where both unions and works councils were present. At the same time, patterns of inequality were similar. Average pay and working conditions differed between centers, with subcontractors having low pay and low bargaining coverage in both countries.

A comparison of survey results from other countries in North America and Europe also show within-country variation in pay and working conditions, with the most obvious gap between in-house call centers and subcontractors. However, countries varied quite a bit in the structure of union and works council representation as well as in patterns of outcomes. France stands out for having low levels of wage inequality and so is examined in greater depth. A case study of the French telecommunications industry shows that state support for extending collective agreements to all firms in a sector and different union structures and strategies together ensured that collective bargaining institutions remained relatively encompassing.

However, French call centers had quite low levels of discretion compared to similar centers in Germany, which may be traced to weak participation rights and union presence at the workplace level. Denmark represents a contrasting case where participation rights, strong local unions, and encompassing bargaining appear to have supported positive outcomes in both areas: Danish call centers were both high adopters of high-involvement employment systems and had among the lowest levels of wage inequality. This further supports the argument that persistent national differences in bargaining coverage and rights are critical for explaining different patterns of outcomes.

In chapter 6, I summarize the findings from the book and discuss their implications for policymakers and labor unions.

2

CHANGES IN MARKETS AND COLLECTIVE BARGAINING

In the 1990s, telecommunications markets were transformed by a range of new technologies and by legislation aimed at easing the entry of new competitors.[1] The industry's history as a regulated monopoly left a legacy of strong unions and public sector involvement. However, former monopolists initially pursued different strategies as they adjusted to more competitive markets. In the United States, AT&T and the regional Bells aggressively cut costs and downsized. Meanwhile, unions and works councils at Deutsche Telekom in Germany successfully slowed deregulation, promoted up-skilling, and eased worker displacement.

The U.S. and German telecommunications markets looked more similar by the 2000s. Deutsche Telekom was privatized and local telephone markets in both countries were opened to competition. A once-stable industry made up of vertically integrated firms was locked in perpetual restructuring, while customers faced rapidly expanding choices among competing technologies and providers. This chapter compares these recent developments and asks what their implications have been for industrial relations and union strategies. Findings show that market liberalization was followed by a transformation in industrial relations in both the United States and Germany, marked by bargaining decentralization and the growth of nonunion competition. As unions found that they could no longer rely on established forms of bargaining power, they began to seek new forms of leverage, though with mixed success.

Liberalization and Industry Restructuring

United States

AT&T dominated the U.S. telecommunications industry until a federal court judge ordered the separation of its competitive and regulated business areas in 1984 following a lengthy Department of Justice suit. The twenty-two operating companies that provided local telephone service were split off from AT&T's long-distance arm, becoming seven separate Regional Bell Operating Companies (RBOCs): Ameritech, Bell Atlantic, BellSouth, Nynex, Pacific Telesis, Southwestern Bell, and US West. The court order that dismantled the Bell System also opened up full competition in the long-distance market but protected the monopoly status of the RBOCs within their regions. The so-called "Baby-Bells" were in turn prohibited from competing in the long-distance, cable TV, or information services markets.

The initiative for these reforms came from a well-organized group of large businesses in the airlines, computer, and financial services industries that were paying top dollar for long-distance services, which AT&T used to subsidize more costly local telephone service. A federal court ruling in 1978 had granted MCI entry to the long-distance market. However, the 1984 decision went further, eliminating cross-subsidies while setting up "asymmetric regulation" to overcome AT&T's market advantage. These court rulings, which created the framework for market liberalization, occurred with little political support or input from stakeholder groups. Although AT&T led a coalition opposing divestiture that included unions, state PUCs, independent telephone companies, and consumers, its efforts ultimately held little sway over the divestiture decision or new industry regulations (Batt and Darbishire 1997).

In the decade following divestiture, different product market segments were typically serviced by separate companies, including long-distance, cable, within-state toll calls, local telephone service, cable TV, and wireless. Of these segments, local service remained the most highly regulated, enjoying protection from the often cutthroat competition in markets like long distance. Beginning in the early 1990s, a number of small nonunion firms, such as Teleport, began to either construct their own competing fiber-optic networks or lease phone lines—often targeting corporate customers with larger profit margins. However, the impact on the residential market was marginal. In 1995, the seven RBOCs and GTE still provided 95 percent of local telephone service (Keefe 2005: 40).

Since the mid-1990s, formerly rigid boundaries between industry segments and the firms operating in these segments have broken down. Three developments had the greatest impact on firm strategies.

First, regulatory changes cleared the way for telecommunications firms to compete in new markets and ended the monopoly of the RBOCs over local telephone service. The 1996 Telecommunications Act allowed local telephone companies to offer long-distance services, provided they gave competitors access to their local markets. However, the RBOCs could still protect their local networks with access charges, which were initially set high with phased reductions over five years. This meant that they only experienced the full brunt of competition beginning in the early 2000s. By 2004, Competitive Local Exchange Carriers (CLECs) had grown to 18 percent of total end-user access lines bringing them into direct competition with the RBOCs or Incumbent Local Exchange Carriers (ILECs) (FCC 2005a).

Second, new technologies encouraged the expansion of competing market segments. Internet service providers (ISPs) like America Online, Earthlink, and Net Zero took advantage of new access to local phone lines in the late 1990s to compete for share in the emerging market for Internet services. Between 1998 and 2003, wireless subscriptions more than doubled, and in 2005 the number of wireless subscribers was actually higher than the number of switched access lines (Keefe 2005: 4). Wireless providers also expanded into multimedia services and high-speed broadband. Independent Voice over Internet Protocol (VoIP) providers like Vonage offered cheap local and long-distance phone service over the internet. Cable companies began to compete across segments with video-on-demand, high-speed Internet, and VoIP.

Meanwhile, traditional fixed-line providers replaced copper wires in large markets with high-speed or fiber optic cables, which increased data transmission speeds and allowed them to sell their own packages of high-speed DSL Internet, television, video on demand, and wireless services. The businesses and large institutions that traditionally were the most lucrative customer groups moved to high-speed private data access lines. By the 2000s, a variety of mobile, cable, and fixed network service providers were competing directly with one another across market segments to sell customers "bundles" of information services, packaged on one bill for a flat fee.

Third, major telecommunications firms reorganized their operations vertically and horizontally. Throughout the 1990s, companies established new subsidiaries and adopted divisional structures as they entered new segments, in part because these markets were regulated differently. Incumbent firms also decentralized decision making to these divisions and subsidiaries to improve operational flexibility, diversify employment contracts, and avoid unions. Subsidiaries of major telecommunications firms, such as AT&T, Sprint, and BellSouth, came to dominate the mobile industry, but had considerable autonomy from their parent companies and typically remained nonunion. In many cases, business units were spun off, bought out, or operated as joint ventures with domestic or multinational firms.

By the late 1990s, the pendulum had begun to swing back to growing industry concentration and centralization. The RBOCs went through a series of high-profile mergers, which resulted in a smaller number of national players that were better able to realize economies of scale and to compete in a diversified information services market. In August 1997, NYNEX and Bell Atlantic merged, and in July 1998 they joined with GTE to form Verizon. SBC bought Pacific Telesis in 1997, Southern New England Telecommunications in 1998, and Ameritech in 1999. In 2005, SBC bought AT&T, shortly after AT&T exited the long-distance consumer market. The new company then merged with BellSouth in 2006. This meant that after two decades, Ma Bell was brought back together with two of its largest Baby Bells. The newly branded AT&T moved into the position of market leader, controlling 45 percent of "telephone loops" and 34 percent of the fixed-line market (FCC 2008). Meanwhile, its mobile subsidiary, AT&T Mobility, controlled the largest share of the wireless market with more than 70 million customers in the United States.

These developments suggest dual trends. At the same time that competitive local exchange carriers grew in number and traditional carriers began to compete with each other in formerly segmented markets, former regional providers became national players. Most major U.S. companies also expanded internationally. Sprint, MCI, and AT&T formed strategic partnerships with overseas telecommunications providers like British Telecom and France Telecom to compete in the global business network market. Verizon Wireless was formed as a joint venture of Verizon Communications and the British mobile company Vodafone. All of the former RBOCs established fixed-line and wireless communications operations and investments throughout the Americas and Europe, increasingly orienting themselves to international markets.

Corporate restructuring was given a push by a financial crisis at the end of the 1990s. The U.S. telecommunications industry had enjoyed a sustained boom, with expanding employment and profits. That boom turned to bust due to overbuilding of capacity, the bursting of the Internet bubble, and the exposure of financial fraud at several major firms (including WorldCom and Qwest). Financial instability increased across segments and firms tightened their belts, laying off employees and outsourcing jobs.

These regulatory changes, technological innovations, and corporate restructuring strategies refashioned the U.S. telecommunications industry as it moved from a stable monopoly focused on fixed-line telephone services to a highly competitive information services industry. At the same time, the Bell system left an important legacy. In 2005, the traditional fixed telephony or fixed-line network still provided basic telephone service to 90 percent of U.S. households and employed around half of the workforce in telecommunications (Keefe 2005). The former RBOCs continued to dominate this market, with around 70 percent market share in fixed-line markets and majority interests in the major wireless companies. Growing competition was coupled with growing concentration, as firms that were once restricted to distinct regional and product markets became national and global players.

Germany

The liberalization of Germany's telecommunications market occurred more slowly and involved more union and worker participation than in the United States. A federal court set out the framework for the breakup of AT&T in 1984 and the first phase of deregulation—a process that involved little input from telecommunications firms or their consumers and unions. In contrast, a series of legislative reforms and stakeholder negotiations guided an incremental process of liberalization and privatization in Germany. These differences in the timing and substance of deregulation shaped the structure of the emerging telecommunications markets in each country. At a time when a variety of private sector companies in the United States were competing for market share in a fragmented industry, Deutsche Telekom remained a publicly owned company that dominated not only long-distance and local phone services but also the growing mobile, Internet, and until recently, cable markets. However, over the past decade regulatory changes, technological advances, and corporate restructuring have also refashioned the German telecommunications industry.

Telecommunications services in Germany were traditionally bundled together with postal services under the Deutsche Bundespost (DBP), which was an administrative part of the Ministry of Posts and Telecommunications. This structure allowed the DBP to operate as a "parapublic institution" (Markovits 1986) steered by informal tripartite negotiations between the ministry, the major union (Deutsche Post Gewerkschaft, or DPG), and equipment suppliers. When deregulation and privatization finally did occur, they were guided by a drawn-out series of legislative reforms. Post Reform I (*Poststrukturgesetz*) went into effect in 1989 and separated the postal service, the post bank, and telecommunications services. At this time, mobile and satellite communications were opened to limited competition, but network telecommunications services continued to be protected as monopolies.

In 1993, the European Council passed a directive requiring all EU member states to end monopolies on telecommunications network infrastructure and voice telephony services by January 1, 1998. Germany responded with Post Reform II (*Postneuordnungsgesetz*) in 1995, which further deregulated the market and laid the groundwork for privatization. The DBP-controlled postal service, post bank, and telecommunications services were converted to private corporations, and the Deutsche Telekom AG (DT) was established as a joint-stock company with 100 percent state ownership. In 1996 the *Telekommunikationsgesetz* (TKG) set a deadline for opening up competition to DT's network in 1996 and fixed network voice telephony in 1998.

Throughout this period, deregulation and industry restructuring in Germany looked quite different from the United States. While AT&T was split up into multiple companies that specialized in different regional and product markets, DT retained much of its monopoly power and was able to diversify into new industry segments. By the mid-1990s, DT still controlled around 90 percent of the data services market and 90 to 95 percent of the cable TV network (Darbishire 1997: 195). DT also benefited from "asymmetrical" regulation that gave the company a number of advantages, including low-incentive price regulation and few limitations on cross-subsidization or market entry (Darbishire 1997: 195–96). This was comparable to the protections enjoyed by RBOCs at the time in their regional fixed-line markets, but very different from the competitive market conditions that AT&T faced in national and international long-distance markets.

The two major parties negotiating over regulatory reform had an ongoing interest in protecting DT's monopoly position. The German government wanted to promote the international competitiveness of the country's major telecommunications firm and protect the public revenues it provided, while the DPG stood to lose members and influence from market liberalization. The DPG also had considerable influence over strategic decision making within the Bundespost through its close work with the union-dominated personnel councils (*Personalräte*) and representation on the company's supervisory board.

Starting in the late 1990s, however, conditions in the German telecommunications market began to converge on those in the United States. First, regulatory changes led to growing competition across market segments and placed further restrictions on DT that curbed its market power. In 1998, only two years after the 1996 Telecommunications Act opened up competition in local telephone service in the United States, legislation came into effect that ended DT's monopolies for network infrastructure and fixed network voice telephony. Almost overnight, the German telecommunications market shifted from one of the most protected to one of the most liberalized in the world, with no restrictions on the entrance of foreign companies. New competitors quickly established themselves in several emerging segments. A small number of large national network operators like Mannesmann and o.tel.o and a variety of smaller utilities and city carriers like Net Cologne built their own competing network infrastructure, often targeting lucrative urban and large business markets. At the same time, service providers or resellers benefited from new rules that allowed them to resell network capacity from Deutsche Telekom at lower rates.

This led to intensified price competition in fixed-line communications, particularly in the long-distance segment, where prices declined by 50 percent in some markets within the first several years. Call charges in Germany fell more than 60 percent between 1998 and 2000, representing "the steepest cuts in any European market for years" (Althaus 2000). These falling prices cut dramatically into DT's bottom line, as the fixed-line market has continued to represent around 50 percent of the corporate group's revenue.

Private ownership of DT stock gradually increased over this same period. In 1996, DT made an initial public offering (IPO) and 1 million private investors purchased 26 percent of its stock. State ownership was further eroded following second and third public offerings in 1999 and 2000, and in 2001 DT used stock sales to raise additional capital to acquire the U.S.-based VoiceStream and Powertel. By 2004, the federal government directly held 26 percent of shares, with 17 percent held by the federal Loan Bank for Reconstruction; while by the end of 2007 their joint ownership had dropped further to 32 percent. Meanwhile, the price of DT shares fell by more than 90 percent from their peak by 2002 (Economist 2002), prompting a class-action lawsuit by investors who claimed the company had been overvalued when new shares were issued in 2000 (Economist 2008). Large institutional investors, such as the private equity firm Blackstone, began playing a more active role in advising management (Schröder 2007).[2] This put additional pressure on the firm to turn steady losses into profits and reorient itself to increasing shareholder value.

Second, as in the United States, innovations in the diversified information services market gave rise to a variety of competing technologies and blurred boundaries between market segments. Deutsche Telekom was better positioned than most German or U.S. firms to develop an integrated competitive strategy in these segments, as the dominant market player in mobile, Internet, and cable services. However, it lost market share in all of its businesses. Mannesmann Mobilfunk (now Vodafone) vied with T-Mobile for the position of market leader since the mid-1990s. By 2009, DT continued to control around 46 percent of the broadband and fixed network market, but local providers and DT's major competitor Arcor were gaining. As in the United States, companies were in a race to develop attractive bundles of services, and the major wireless providers had become direct competitors to broadband with their own internet products.

Third, corporate structures changed rapidly following market liberalization, both within Deutsche Telekom and among its competitors. In the 1990s, firms targeted different markets by decentralizing strategic decision making to new divisions and subsidiaries. An eclectic mix of metalworking, chemical, and public-sector organizations established wireless and fixed network subsidiaries throughout the 1990s. Mannesmann, a large metalworking conglomerate, was given the first license for a competing mobile network in 1989, and by the mid-1990s its subsidiary Mannesmann D2 was competing on equal footing with T-Mobile. A spate of mergers and buyouts then increased consolidation and the presence of multinationals in the industry. DT's two major fixed network competitors, Arcor and Mobilcom/Freenet both formed through a series of mergers among smaller companies that were spun-off subsidiaries of large conglomerate firms. The energy firms RWE and VEBA jointly owned o.tel.o, the third largest fixed-line competitor, until it was acquired by Mannesmann in 1999. A major reshuffling occurred when the British firm Vodafone took over Mannesmann in 2000, rebranded their lucrative D2 wireless network, and retained majority ownership of Arcor (Höpner and Jackson 2003). DT also expanded internationally, entering into a variety of joint ventures and extending the international reach of its wireless business through purchases and joint ventures.

These three trends—liberalization of fixed network services, growth of competing technologies, and acceleration of corporate restructuring—contributed to growing convergence on U.S.-style liberal markets and increasingly differentiated and cost-focused competitive strategies. Some differences have proven to be more persistent. DT long enjoyed the advantages of its diversified structure and monopoly power, which allowed it to remain the dominant competitor across a variety of segments. It was accused of using judicial review to delay or block unfavorable regulatory decisions and leveraging its market power to delay provision of leased lines and introduce artificially low "dumping prices" in certain markets, such as DSL (OECD 2004: 59–60).

More recently, DT lobbied Germany's coalition government to exempt new investments in its high-speed fiber-optic network, VDSL, from regulation. In 2006, the Federal Network Agency (Bundesnetzagentur), backed by the EU, required DT to offer local loop unbundling on the network. However, in February 2007 a new clause in the German Tele-communications Act came into effect that exempted new markets from regulation, allowing DT to prevent competitors from gaining full access to the majority of its fiber-optic network for a fixed period. The EU Commission instituted breach-of-contract proceedings, arguing that these provisions conflicted with the EU's legal framework. In the United States, the incumbent telecommunications providers have sought to regain the market power they lost at divestiture through merging with other regional fixed-line network carriers and buying out smaller wireless companies.

DT also had more influence over how the telecommunications infrastructure developed in Germany, which continued to give it a competitive advantage in some markets. For example, the company did not invest in its cable network infrastructure, and instead promoted its DSL services and expansion of its high-speed integrated services digital network (ISDN). DT was forced to sell majority stakes in its 9 regional cable companies in 2000, following the Cable Directive (*Kabelrichtlinie*). However, DT initially retained 25 percent plus one vote share in each of these companies, which gave it strong veto rights and potentially allowed DT to block mergers. In addition, the direct customer connections continued to be owned and operated by a large number of small private companies, which made it both complex and expensive for the large cable operators to invest in upgrading their infrastructure. As a result, the cable network has been slow to materialize as a serious competitor to fixed voice telephony and fiber.[3] In contrast, nonunion U.S. cable companies have engaged in major price wars with incumbent RBOCs.

A final important difference was the absence of a major telecommunications "bust" in Germany. DT suffered from plummeting share price and consistent losses until 2003 when it finally managed to turn a profit. Heady growth in the industry after liberalization gave way to consolidation and tighter margins. However, Germany did not experience the accounting scandals, overbuilding of capacity, and plummeting share price that U.S. telecommunications firms went through at the end of the 1990s. Despite a shift to a "shareholder value" orientation, the German market remained more stable—which some observers attributed to the continued strong presence of banks and institutional investors, as well as corporate governance arrangements giving employee representatives oversight over company finances (Boersch 2007).

At the same time, liberalization, technological innovation, and globalization unleashed fierce competition in a long-protected market. While DT continued to dominate the industry, particularly in the local calls segment, it rapidly lost market share and was constrained by new regulations that sought to curb its monopoly power. DT's share of the telecommunications market fell from 70 percent in 1998 to 61 percent in 1999, and then further declined to 46 percent by 2008. Competition was introduced in the local telephone market at around the same time as in the United States and has become similarly fierce. Deutsche Telekom's market share in local telephone services (measured in connection minutes per day) fell more than 30 percent between 1998 and 2008, compared to a drop of around 12 percent among incumbent local exchange carriers in the United States since the 1996 Telecommunications Act. DT faced a rapid hemorrhaging of customers in the mid-2000s, which declined by 1.5 million in 2006, and shrinking net profits.

Changing Industrial Relations and Union Strategies

The changes in markets described above dramatically reshaped industrial relations. To understand their effects and union responses in each country, it is useful first to review the major differences between the U.S. and German industrial relations systems.

First, the structure of bargaining is quite different. In the United States, bargaining takes place between one union and one employer. While there used to be a mix of multiemployer and firm-level agreements, this began to break down in the early 1980s, and today most bargaining has shifted to the firm level or regional level within large firms. While unions typically have an industry focus, they represent workplaces across industries, sometimes competing head to head in organizing drives. Another important feature of collective bargaining in the United States is the limited range of "mandatory" subjects of bargaining, basically restricted to pay and working conditions (including benefits, promotions, layoffs, and dismissal procedures) while excluding such things as investment decisions and implementation of technology. Finally, a key means of enforcing collective contracts is through the grievance procedure, and a central role of local union officials is often filing grievances on behalf of employees.

In Germany, bargaining is organized at two distinct levels, often described as a "dual system" (Markovits 1986; Thelen 1991). Traditionally, one union is responsible for negotiating a sectoral agreement (*Flächentarifvertrag*) with the employers association for a particular industry over key issues like wages, benefits, and working time. However, there is a growing trend of company-level agreements negotiated between one union and one employer (*Haustarifvertrag*), which today make up close to half of all agreements in Germany. Separate works councils then consult with management on a much broader range of issues, including scheduling, performance measurement, performance-based pay, and employee health and safety. Local works councils (*Betriebsräte*) are elected by the employees in a workplace and negotiate over working conditions in that workplace. Company-level, or general works councils (*Gesamtbetriebsräte*), are made up of delegates from local works councils and have broader rights to consult with top management and receive information about business decisions. In some cases, a corporate group-level works council (*Konzernbetriebsrat*) is formed to consult on decisions that affect the corporate group.

National unions typically help to coordinate negotiation of works agreements at these different levels, and works councils are in turn responsible for recruiting new union members. Finally, representatives of unions and works councils are elected to serve on a supervisory board, or *Aufsichtsrat,* of companies with five hundred or more employees, which has some oversight over strategic decisions (though the actual influence of this body varies considerably). When the relationship between unions and works councils works well, it gives labor formidable bargaining power, as both organizations can participate in or block decisions at multiple levels of the company. However, there is also a great deal of potential for conflicts between these different bodies, particularly as the strength of unions erodes at the sectoral level.

Second, the process of setting up collective bargaining is different in each country. In the United States, organizing drives are more "all or nothing" than in Germany. A union typically initiates a campaign with an organizing committee of employees, which then try to convince a majority of the workforce to vote for the union in elections overseen by the National Labor Relations Board (NLRB). If they win, the employer is obligated to bargain with the union; but if they lose, organizers have to start over or give up. An alternative route is through "card check recognition," whereby the employer agrees to recognize the union if a majority of employees sign cards supporting the union (thus bypassing elections). All employees in that bargaining unit are obligated to join the union and pay dues, unless the location is in a "right to work" state with laws that prevent these kinds of union shop arrangements (most of which are in the southern United States).

In contrast, German unions typically rely on works councils to get a foot in the door at an unorganized workplace. They often first help to organize works council elections and run a slate of prounion candidates who then compete against a separate slate of candidates chosen by management. Unlike the U.S. requirement of majority employee support, German employers are required to negotiate with elected works councils if there is any employee support, and there are strict legal limits on employer efforts to discourage works council elections. Then, if the union's candidates win, local union representatives advise the works councilors and provide them with legal support, often under the condition that they join the union. Ideally, the works council would then convince employees to also become union members and would use its leverage in bargaining to convince managers to negotiate a collective agreement with the union. Of course, this depends on a lot of things—most important, getting candidates elected who are sympathetic to the union and convincing employees and works councilors that the union can offer some value added over the elected works council, both of which can be a challenge. Employees are not required to pay dues, even if they are covered by a union-negotiated agreement, so unions rely on voluntary membership. In other words, "union shops" are illegal. In addition, multiple unions can be represented at a workplace and run their own candidates in works council (and supervisory board) elections.

This brief overview illustrates that both systems have strengths and weaknesses from the perspective of unions. While German unions and works councils clearly have more potential means of influencing management strategy, gaining this leverage requires a great deal of coordination between separate groups of worker representatives at different levels of the firm and industry. Unions in the United States have to overcome substantial obstacles to organize a workplace or firm, but once they do, they typically can rely on dues from employees and face a clear procedure for setting up bargaining. The following comparison looks at how these differences play out more concretely in the telecommunications industry.

United States

Collective bargaining in the U.S. telecommunications industry became increasingly decentralized in the period following AT&T's divestiture. The CWA and the IBEW primarily represented workers at AT&T and the RBOCs, where they continued to have a well-organized membership base and institutionalized bargaining relationships. The CWA has been the most important union in U.S. telecommunications, representing around 90 percent of the industry's unionized workforce. Throughout the 1980s and 1990s, the CWA merged with a number of smaller unions that represented employees in the telephone, broadcast, and cable industries, and today negotiates contracts in the public sector, health care, and airlines. While there have been past conflicts between the CWA and IBEW, for the most part they work closely on a number of campaigns, bargain joint contracts, and typically respect each others' organizing jurisdiction based on the regions or companies where they have historically represented workers.

By 1974, the CWA had succeeded in setting up a national bargaining structure that covered AT&T as well as all of the regional operating companies. The union gained a national contract for wages, benefits, and employment security, while AT&T gained union support for its efforts to protect the Bell System (Boroff and Keefe 1994). However, the different parties were unable to reach agreement on a new postdivestiture structure in 1983 negotiations, and in 1986, national bargaining was replaced by a two-tiered system, with each regional union negotiating pay and benefits at the company level, and below that scheduling, work practices, and overtime at forty-eight separate tables. The union relied on informal pattern bargaining for more than a decade to maintain similar wage increases, with AT&T as the pattern leader. This also broke down in 1998 after SBC settled early in negotiations and other companies negotiated contracts with varying expiration dates, from thirty-two months to five years.

Firm strategy, profitability, and union bargaining power came to differ radically across incumbent firms and in some cases across business units within these firms. This in turn drove variation in agreements. The combination of a growing profit center focus and the growth in mergers and joint ventures meant that the CWA has faced constant changes in negotiating partners. Firms decentralized and recentralized decision making as they sought to balance control and coordination with autonomy for different business units. This, in turn, affected the ability of union representatives to influence strategy at these different levels. The CWA continued to bargain over issues like wages, benefits, and employment security at the company level in many firms. However, it was not able to push for harmonization of agreements. The union's strategy by the 2000s was to negotiate a "lead" contract that then became the benchmark for negotiations with other companies. Different groups within the CWA also disagreed on the right balance between centralization and decentralization, as some locals feared that national bargaining in large companies could result in the erosion of working conditions in regions with stronger contracts.

The result was a system in which firms negotiated multiple collective agreements, often with large variation in pay and working conditions. Verizon, which was formed in 1998 through the merger of three regional telecommunications firms, had more than eighty agreements in the mid-2000s. SBC had four separate regional contracts for network operations and a number of smaller ones for its subsidiaries. By 2010, AT&T had six regional contracts, along with a number of special contracts for newer areas such as "internet services." Within most companies, contracts expired around the same date and bargaining was coordinated, with some national or regional language around things like health care plans.

Mergers between large employers created opportunities and challenges for the CWA. For example, Cingular was one of the union's few success stories, where it was able to set up bargaining across the company under a card check neutrality agreement with the wireless company's parents SBC and BellSouth. After its merger with the fiercely antiunion AT&T Wireless in 2004, Cingular went from close to 100 percent organized to 45 percent organized. At the same time, the CWA secured an extension of the neutrality agreement and made substantial progress in helping the technicians, customer service and sales reps, and store employees on the AT&T side to organize. The union had gained more than five thousand new members by the end of 2005 and incorporated all nineteen thousand employees under three collective agreements by the late 2000s.

Despite these successes, the nonunion sector has been steadily growing. New entrants are nearly impossible to organize. AT&T's two major competitors in the long-distance market, MCI and Sprint, were from the beginning virulently antiunion. Cable TV companies resisted organizing efforts through aggressive antiunion campaigns and decertification elections. The wireless industry has also remained unorganized outside of AT&T Mobility. These trends contributed to a growing wage gap between segments. By 2001, median annual pay for call center workers at wireless companies was 85 percent and at cable companies 73 percent of pay in the fixed-line segment (Keefe 2009).

The CWA adopted new strategies as they adjusted to these changes in markets and bargaining structure. One of its early campaigns focused on improving union influence over management decisions at major employers like AT&T, US West, and BellSouth through labor-management partnerships. The CWA got involved in designing and implementing new models of work organization such as team-based systems and put in place partnership committees that gave its representatives input in decisions such as the deployment of new technologies (Boroff and Keefe 1994). However, the union largely abandoned or scaled back these efforts in the late 1990s as management continued to resist partnership and pursue disruptive restructuring measures—including workforce reductions, labor-saving automation, reclassification of nonmanagement jobs as managerial, and outsourcing—which were typically implemented through central fiat rather than negotiated compromise.

At the same time, the CWA initiated a series of new campaigns targeted at gaining influence over organizational restructuring. Organized firms set up nonunion subsidiaries to compete in growing markets, such as wireless, telemarketing, and data communications. From the beginning, these companies adopted a "union containment strategy" that prevented unions from entering the new units (Bahr 1998: 111). In 1989, CWA won an election to represent NYNEX Mobile employees in New York following a long strike but were unsuccessful in other regions and companies, where they faced hostile antiunion campaigns. In 1991, the CWA made organizing these new business units a key goal and launched a "wall-to-wall" organizing campaign.

By the end of the 1990s, the CWA had negotiated a variety of security clauses such as neutrality pledges, card check recognition, and standards of behavior at almost all major unionized companies.[4] Often these were the quid pro quo for the union's support in key regulatory battles and company mergers, such as the mergers between NYNEX, BellAtlantic, and then later GTE that formed Verizon. These agreements helped the CWA to organize new units in the fixed-line business of their core firms and gave them some advantages in the new business units they viewed as strategically important. SBC held up its pledge in a 1997 agreement not to interfere in union organizing and card check recognition for all business units, which proved a valuable foot in the door in the difficult-to-organize wireless industry. The CWA organized a number of workplaces in SBC's subsidiary Pacific Bell Wireless in 1998 and extended neutrality to the new company Cingular Wireless as SBC expanded its market share through mergers and acquisitions. However, the union experienced more disappointments than successes. In two familiar cases, AT&T and Verizon signed neutrality agreements in exchange for concessions but then later aggressively opposed organizing drives: at Verizon, this encompassed their Wireless, MCI, and yellow pages subsidiaries.

These initiatives focused on the CWA's core firms and their subsidiaries, where the union already had members and bargaining leverage. The union also supported organizing drives in nonunion companies, though these have for the most part been a disappointment. Over the years, the union organized some bargaining units in companies like Sprint (now part of Century Tel) and GTE (now part of Frontier), but contracts were much weaker than at the RBOCs. It has had no long-term success in organizing the call center subcontractors that handle outsourced telecommunications work.

Germany

Decentralization of industrial relations in the German telecommunications industry occurred only over the past decade but has dramatically reshaped collective bargaining and union power. The Deutsche Postgewerkschaft (DPG) long operated as a single-company enterprise union in the postal services, banking, and telecommunications branches of the Deutsche Bundespost, and continued to negotiate with the three firms after they were separated. By the late 1980s, around 75 percent of the Bundespost's 500,000 employees were DPG members, making it the fourth largest union in West Germany (Turner 1991: 184). Personnel councils (*Personalräte*)—the public sector version of works councils—were dominated by DPG members, and the union was closely involved in coordinating works council activities. The DPG also enjoyed a great deal of influence over strategic decision making through its members on the supervisory board, or *Postverwaltungsrat*.

In the 1990s, as DT moved toward majority private ownership and liberalization pushed ahead, the DPG continued to enjoy strong influence over firm and industry restructuring. Member density in core areas of the business remained high, at around 70 percent. Almost half of the former Bundespost's employees were civil servants (*Beamten*), which meant that a substantial portion of the workforce enjoyed lifetime job security along with a slew of other special employment rights. Personnel councils were transitioned to the private sector works councils,[5] entailing some loss of members, but membership on the councils was largely stable. The DPG leveraged its strong position in the firm to negotiate collective agreements that preserved high social standards for the workforce, with good pay and strong job security protections.

In 2001, the DPG merged with four other service unions to form the new union ver.di.[6] The old leadership was given considerable autonomy within the new telecommunications and IT division of ver.di (Fachbereich 9), which then became responsible for carrying out negotiations with DT. Ver.di continued to have close, institutionalized ties with DT's works councils. Union membership remained high in traditional areas of the business, and union and works council representation on the company's supervisory board gave them considerable oversight in strategic decision making. Two minority unions, Kommunikationsgewerkschaft DPV (DPV Kom) and the Christliche Gewerkschaft Post und Telekommunikation (CGPT), shared about 10 percent of works council votes, but their influence in bargaining remained minor (Sako and Jackson 2006: 12).

However, the DPG, and now ver.di, have had less success in organizing new areas of the industry. Because DT was a monopoly, collective bargaining in telecommunications was organized exclusively at the enterprise level—a structure that was unusual in Germany, where industry-level collective agreements are the norm. Furthermore, no employers' association formed to negotiate a sectoral agreement after market liberalization. Several peculiar characteristics of the emerging telecommunications industry made it particularly difficult to set up coordinated bargaining. First, new companies entering the market saw their interests as often sharply opposed to those of DT, particularly in the regulatory arena. Local exchange carriers and competing network operators were unwilling to cooperate with the former monopolist or its union, which continued to place a priority on slowing market liberalization. The employees and works councilors of these firms were likewise wary of joining a union that represented the interests of a competitor. Even after the DPG became part of ver.di, it carried the stigma of its history as the union of the old Bundespost.

Second, other unions began to compete with the DPG in new telecommunications firms. U.S. unions often organize across sectors, but as mentioned above, there has been surprisingly little competition across unions in telecommunications. In contrast, typically in Germany one union negotiates a collective agreement for an industry and is then responsible for the employees and companies in that industry. However, this structure assumes that each company falls neatly within the boundaries of one industry. As firms in the public, metalworking, chemical, and energy sectors expanded into telecommunications and IT, their unions sought to represent employees in new business units. By the late 1990s, Transnet, ötv, IG Metall, and IG BCE all either had negotiated collective agreements or were in the process of negotiating agreements with DT's new competitors in telecommunications services. This added to jurisdictional battles that were already raging among seven different unions in the related IT industry.

The constant reorganization of telecommunications and IT firms exacerbated competition among unions, particularly the metalworking and manufacturing union IG Metall and the new service union ver.di. The unions negotiated a formal agreement in 2000 through the Deutsche Gewerkschaftbund (DGB) that divided up responsibility for new telecommunications and IT companies, but this has not prevented conflict at a time of shrinking membership and changing firm boundaries. For example, ver.di had agreed that the mobile phone subsidiary D2 Mannesmann Mobilfunk fell under IG Metall's jurisdiction, as Mannesmann had a long-standing relationship with IG Metall. However, after the British company Vodafone took over Mannesmann, ver.di representatives initially argued that they should be responsible for the new company, sparking renewed conflict. This added to tensions in the DT subsidiary T-Systems, which had an agreement with both unions since DT's telecommunications and IT service division DeTeSystem merged with debis Systemhaus, a service division of the automaker DaimlerChrysler. Deutsche Telekom's major fixed-line competitor, Arcor, was formed through the mergers of subsidiaries that had separate agreements with IG Metall and Transnet, and continues to bargain with both unions. This fragmentation in collective representation made it difficult for unions to develop a coordinated strategy at the industry level, while dividing works councils and weakening support for union-negotiated collective agreements at the firm level.

A third reason for the lack of a coherent bargaining structure was the overall weak union presence in new, growing industry segments. Many firms managed to avoid negotiating with unions altogether—particularly the large number of small service resellers and internet service providers. New entrants to the telecommunications market in the mid- to late-1990s either came from outside Germany or grew out of diversified multinationals that were reluctant to negotiate new agreements for their new, dynamic (and often poorly organized) telecommunications subsidiaries. D2 Mannesman Mobilfunk began negotiations with IG Metall in the mid-1990s but did not conclude a collective agreement until 2001, after the company was taken over by Vodafone. Membership remained low, at around 5 percent, and in some regions works councilors broke off all ties with the union. Vodafone's and T-Mobile's major wireless competitors E-plus and O2 had established works councils but, again, union membership was low, union affiliation of the works councilors was fragmented, and there had been no progress toward an agreement. Even within the Deutsche Telekom corporate group, the DPG was unable to negotiate a common framework agreement for subsidiaries, which had widely varying union density levels, from 70 percent in the parent company to around 5 percent in T-Online. T-Mobile and T-Systems negotiated their own contracts that differed substantially from the fixed-line agreement at T-Com, while T-Online remained without an agreement until a decision was made in 2006 to pull the subsidiary back into the parent company.

As a result of these developments, works councils became the central bargaining partners representing worker interests in many telecommunications workplaces. However, unions found it quite difficult to organize or work closely with works councils outside of DT. This lack of traditional "dual system" bargaining institutions has important implications for works councils' independence from management, as well as the extent of bargaining coordination within a company. The lack of strong union ties in much of the telecommunications industry means that works councils must set up their own coordinating mechanisms. Because companies are constantly restructuring, works councilors at individual locations often do not know each other. Membership in company-level councils changes frequently as divisions get spun off and former competitors merge. Moreover, in diversified firms like Mannesmann or DT, works councils in different subsidiaries and business units often view their interests as distinct or conflicting (Sako and Jackson 2006; Höpner and Jackson 2003). The result is considerable fragmentation in bargaining at the works council level as well.

These trends are similar to the growth of nonunion competition and decentralization of collective bargaining in the United States in the 1990s. However, changes have occurred more quickly and represent in many ways a more substantial challenge to traditional collective bargaining structures and union roles. In the United States, divestiture happened well before the mobile phone and internet boom, and meant the splintering of a former monopoly into multiple firms that retained embedded and relatively strong unions. The CWA remained the dominant union with a coherent bargaining strategy and maintained a generally cooperative relationship with the IBEW.

In Germany, unions accustomed to industry-level bargaining and social partnership faced the challenge of building new relationships with firms and organizing new members with no centralized bargaining partner. They lacked both "union shop" rules and a clear strategy for member recruitment or retention, which made it difficult to reverse the steady erosion of union density. The industry was already substantially globalized when the full force of market liberalization hit. Many of DT's competitors are partially or fully owned by companies located outside of Germany. This has made it more difficult to establish strong bargaining relationships or to influence corporate policy. The DPG faced the additional challenge of adjusting to the ver.di union merger in 2001, which took attention and staff time away from strategic planning. Both the DPG and IG Metall thus faced a variety of new stresses at a time when industrywide collective bargaining and strong coordination between works councils and unions were eroding.

Despite these new pressures, union strategies have been slow to change. The CWA began to focus on maintaining institutional security and organizing new workplaces in the 1980s, while German unions are only beginning to respond to similar threats. The CWA also went through an ideological transformation from a militant union embedded in a monopoly system to one committed to partnering with companies to improve competitiveness and secure union jobs in a diversified information services industry. Ver.di representatives are still struggling to develop new approaches to regulating working conditions in a more competitive sector, without the institutional moorings of a national bargaining system and in the context of declining employer commitment to partnership.

The DPG's and IG Metall's past strategies focused on regulating wages and working conditions at the industry level, keeping overall levels high while supporting enterprise-level codetermination through their membership on works councils and advisory boards. As an enterprise union, the DPG was more closely involved in workplace-level negotiations at DT, relying on close relationships with works councils to coordinate codetermination and bargaining. Following the merger, ver.di continued to use these traditional forms of leverage in DT. However, ver.di, IG Metall, and other competing unions have had more difficulty reorienting their strategies to organize new firms.

The DPG and then ver.di worked closely with large telecommunications employers to pass legislation favorable to the incumbent firm, similar to the CWA. Traditionally, the DPG sought to constrain competition and preserve competitive advantage for Deutsche Telekom. More recently, ver.di worked with the employers association of large telecommunications firms (Arbeitgeberverband BreCo) to lobby for provisions in the 2004 Telecommunications Act (Novilierung of the Telekommunikationsgesetz— TKG) that restricted full access to smaller service providers. The union also worked with DT to propose and lobby for reforms to EU regulations for the sector passed in 2009. However, unlike the CWA, ver.di has not placed conditions on this kind of joint work. The CWA became quite savvy about negotiating "memoranda of agreement" on things like card check recognition in exchange for its support of national and regional legislation or regulatory approval. Card check neutrality at SBC and Cingular began with joint work to get legislation passed in Texas favorable to the company. A local union leader convinced all the locals, "every time you meet with the company, the message you've got to give them is, if you want us to help you, you've got to help us" (Interview, CWA representative, May 2005). In contrast, a ver.di representative stated that the main benefit they saw coming out of their lobbying efforts was to show the firms, "look, the unions can be good for you as well," eventually bringing them around to a more cooperative relationship (Interview, April 2004). This is in keeping with the traditional German "social partnership" spirit but did little to strengthen membership or organize new workplaces.

These strategies sought to leverage relationships with core firms. German unions also initiated campaigns to recruit members and set up collective bargaining. They made very little progress in organizing or bargaining with new competitors in telecommunications in the 1990s, mirroring a trend across new industry sectors. Then in 1998, the DPG formed an organizing initiative called Telekommunikation, Informationstechnologie, Medien (TIM). TIM established and advised works councils in new firms, organized information exchanges, developed informal working groups (*Arbeitskreise*), and worked toward a branch-level collective bargaining agreement in both telecommunications and the third-party call center industry (DPG 2001). Union representatives succeeded in getting works councils elected at most large telecommunications firms and call center subcontractors, and provided them with advising and legal services.

The DPG focused its campaign efforts on enforcing labor laws in the new firms. For example, German employees who work at a computer are entitled to a *Bildschirmspause,* or a break from the computer screen every hour, but many employers were not providing this for their call center workforce. This was an easy target for improving working conditions, allowing the union to use its legal resources and knowledge to support new works councils. The TIM project also organized to win equal pay for full-time and part-time workers under the terms of a widely disregarded EU directive. These campaigns helped the DPG to establish a strong membership base among works councilors in some new firms. However, it did not contribute directly to new collective agreements and union membership remained low, and so the project was eventually discontinued under ver.di. IG Metall likewise started its own organizing initiative, putting resources into a new telecommunications and IT department and building up membership in some new telecommunications firms. But again, despite these efforts, the union was unable to extend bargaining beyond its traditional firms and their subsidiaries.

Unions also sought to organize call center subcontractors. They began taking notice of the sector in the late 1990s as services began to be privatized and deregulated and as call center employment exploded. Both ver.di and IG Metall (along with other smaller unions) tried to organize works council elections, recruit members, and bargain with employers. However, union rivalry in Germany also splintered efforts to organize this sector. The two unions advised works councils from different subcontractors, and ver.di has had internal conflicts over which department is responsible for these workers. Both unions also had difficulty allocating resources to organizing or advising works councils in new industries at a time of shrinking membership, and this contributed to a perception among works councilors that their concerns were a low priority in union politics. In 2004, ver.di had around three thousand members in call center subcontractors, which represented less than 7 percent of employment in the industry. By 2009, there was still only one union agreement in the industry, which ver.di first negotiated in 2003 with Walter Telemedien, one of the largest subcontractors in Germany and the largest German-owned firm in this industry.

Discussion

The introduction of competition contributed to the fragmentation of collective representation in both the U.S. and German telecommunications industries. Membership density is difficult to compare because there are no official statistics on union membership by industry in Germany, and managers are able to join unions in Germany but not in the United States. In 2006, ver.di representatives claimed to have 70 percent density in Deutsche Telekom's broadband/fixed network operations and headquarters (with around 115,000 employees), an average of 40 percent in DT's other subsidiaries (45,000 employees), and 5 percent in new industry entrants (56,000 employees). It thus appears that union density was at most around 47 percent (including managers—and probably based on overestimation). This had fallen from an estimated 57 percent in the mid-1990s (Funk 2004). Collective bargaining coverage remained higher, due to the continued dominance of DT. However, based on similarly rough calculations, it appeared to have fallen from close to 100 percent to around 80 percent in 2009.[7] In the United States, between 1986 and 2009, membership density fell from 51 percent to 20 percent in "wired telecommunications" and

6 percent in "other telecommunications"; while bargaining coverage fell from 56 percent to 22 percent in wired and 7 percent in other telecommunications (Hirsch and Macpherson 2009).

Union influence also depends on the structure of bargaining, which has become more similar over time. While the CWA and the DPG enjoyed industrywide bargaining prior to deregulation, both experienced a shift of bargaining to the firm level (or multiple contracts within one firm). The CWA moved from forty-eight separate bargaining tables with informal pattern bargaining in the late 1980s to more than one hundred agreements with no pattern. Again, change looks less dramatic in Germany's incumbent firm; however, Deutsche Telekom similarly shifted from one contract in the early 1990s to a number of separate agreements at each subsidiary. Multiple works agreements within each subsidiary further increased variation in work rules and working conditions. In addition, several different unions negotiated agreements with DT's major competitors and did not coordinate bargaining with ver.di. In contrast, the CWA remained by far the dominant telecommunications union in the United States: the IBEW represented 12 percent of the industry's workforce but generally worked closely with the CWA in contract negotiations.

Both countries thus had moved toward less coordinated bargaining and weaker unions by the late 2000s. It is particularly noteworthy that German unions lost members so quickly in such a short time. While bargaining coverage is certainly important for holding the line on pay and working conditions across the industry, there was no sectoral bargaining structure, and union agreements outside of Deutsche Telekom were weak. Low membership density in companies like Vodafone, Arcor, and even T-Mobile affected bargaining power and made it more difficult for unions to work closely with works councils.

These trends encouraged unions to adopt new strategies. In both the United States and Germany, telecommunications unions began to focus on extending collective representation to subsidiaries of their core firms, preventing work from being outsourced, and partnering with unionized employers to pass favorable legislation. Despite its institutionally weaker position, the CWA had more success in organizing new workplaces and using its support in regulatory battles strategically to build membership and influence. The DPG (and then ver.di) had been trying to make this shift since the deregulation of fixed-line in 1998 but had not enjoyed major successes outside of DT.

Taken together, this demonstrates the iterative relationship between convergence on more competitive markets, competitive strategies that are differentiated within (rather than across) firms, and more disorganized industrial relations institutions. In the next two chapters, I ask what these trends have meant for employer strategies at the workplace and organizational levels. As firms compete in more differentiated markets, and as unions find that certain key areas of strategic decision making are taken off the bargaining table, to what extent are worker representatives still able to influence approaches to work reorganization and organizational restructuring?

3

Using Power in the Workplace

This chapter compares strategies by U.S. and German telecommunications firms and their subcontractors to reorganize call center jobs, during a period when they were under considerable pressure from declining prices and increasingly competitive markets. To do this, I analyze changes in employment practices, and the reasons for these changes, in eight case study firms. These are organized in four matched pairs: (1) two fixed-line telecommunications companies with strong unions ("U.S. Telecom" [a former RBOC] and Deutsche Telecom); (2) two new mobile companies with recent union agreements ("U.S. Mobile" and "German Mobile"); (3) two large call center subcontractors that contract with telecommunications companies ("Client Help USA" and "Client Services Germany"); and (4) U.S. and German call centers belonging to one multinational subcontractor ("U.S. Vendotel" and "German Vendotel") (see table 3.1).

These case studies represent a range of industry segments and companies with stronger and weaker collective bargaining institutions within those segments. Client Help USA, and Vendotel's U.S. and German call

TABLE 3.1 Case studies

	Telecommunications firms		Call center subcontractors	
	Established fixed-line	**New wireless**	**Established**	**New (MNC)**
U.S.	U.S. Telecom (former RBOC)	U.S. Mobile	Client Help USA	U.S. Vendotel
Germany	Deutsche Telekom	German Mobile	Client Services Germany	German Vendotel

centers do not have union agreements, and so give some benchmark for comparing workplaces with no formal collective bargaining. In each case study, I visited customer service and sales centers that perform similar work for mass market or residential customers; and interviewed managers, team leaders, works councilors, and employees (see appendix A). In most cases, multiple locations were visited, and in the German cases, I visited centers in both West and East Germany (with the exception of "German Vendotel," which only had centers in the West).

In the following sections, I describe the employment practices adopted in each matched pair, focusing on work organization, such as scheduling practices and job design; and performance management, such as monitoring, coaching, and performance incentives. I then compare negotiations over changes in these practices where there was collective bargaining, or the considerations that drove changes where no unions or works councils were present. Taken together, this gives a window on not only to what extent but also why practices diverged between each pair of U.S. and German companies.

Negotiating Flexibility in the Core: U.S. Telecom and Deutsche Telekom

U.S. Telecom and Deutsche Telekom were both established telecommunications firms. The two companies received most of their revenues from fixed-line services and have faced fierce competition from new entrants since the 1990s. They also had similar bargaining structures, with a single, centralized bargaining unit, high membership density, and a history of cooperative labor relations. These are thus cases where unions and works councils should be strongest. Findings show that although both companies had similar goals, the U.S. case adopted an employment system that emphasized rules and discipline, pervasive monitoring, and unilateral management control over performance management; while the German case adopted practices that emphasized professionalism, protected job stability, and included democratic checks and balances on new initiatives to improve performance.

U.S. Telecom

The call centers I visited at U.S. Telecom fall under the broad umbrella of consumer or mass market call center operations. The company had recently gone through a major consolidation of call centers that brought together territories with distinct operating procedures and varied performance. Call center jobs in the consumer division were divided into three separate groups. Consumer services included acquisitions and sales and support call centers, while a separate division supervised the collections call centers. Strategies to improve performance were somewhat different across divisions due to separate management, but were guided by a similar goal "to drive, to direct, to be consistent, to drive uniformity [and] to take away a lot of creativity and ingenuity at the center leader level" (Interview, collections manager, July 2003). This was accomplished through a range of new policies.

First, managers tightened attendance and scheduling rules as they implemented a leaner staffing model. The centers were networked across the region for the first time, whereas before they had serviced several smaller regional markets. This made it easier to forecast call volume and measure "compliance" with staffing and scheduling plans. Before consolidation, each center had its own Force Team that was responsible for predicting call volume and adjusting scheduling, but afterward these responsibilities were centralized. The new central Force Team put in place a "commitment index," which measured in fifteen-minute increments whether each center had the appropriate number of employees online. This allowed U.S. Telecom to drive up its compliance numbers from 65 percent to 90 to 95 percent. It also meant that each center's Force Administrator was required to have much tighter control over scheduling. Each team and center had a certain amount of "closed key time" each month set aside for coaching and development, which had recently been negotiated in the union contract. When employees were absent or call volume peaked this time was cut, and managers used voluntary or forced overtime to make up gaps.

> Scheduling for us—you want to talk about being flexible, we're hard as hell about scheduling. For our representatives and our coaches, call center work is an extremely difficult job. We need 3,206 people at this quarter hour, each center's got its particular target, and one person needs to go to the bathroom or call their kids, we make them get in the chair and take the call. We are not very flexible. (Interview, consumer manager, February 2005)

Another manager described stricter rules on breaks: "Say I have a 10:00 to 10:15 break—if I take it 12:00 to 12:15, you just changed the way I look. You've changed the number of people that we have, and we don't really need the people then. It's basically, following your schedule to the letter of the law" (Interview, February 2005).

Managers were also attempting to create more consistency in scheduling through fixed shift plans. U.S. Telecom had put in place open-ended scheduling in the mid-1990s when the company moved to twenty-four-hour service, with shift tours that were adjusted every week based on changing call forecasts. The company then moved back to a more restricted number of opening hours, and in 2003 adopted basic scheduling, which allowed employees to choose their schedules up to thirteen weeks ahead of time based on seniority.

Attendance became a key focus. Absenteeism was creating major scheduling problems and was relatively easy to measure and enforce. One manager in collections noted, "They [the union] argue with us all the time that it's our responsibility to develop the employee, performance-wise. But when it comes to attendance, it's their [the employees'] responsibility, so we never lose a grievance" (Interview, collections manager, July 2003). The Family Medical Leave Act (FMLA), supplemented by provisions in the union contract, allowed employees to take up to 450 hours a year paid time off with a doctor's approval for their own illness or that of a family member. In some cases, employees used FMLA to excuse themselves for coming in late or leaving early. In addition, the contract allowed employees to take a vacation day and break it into fifteen-minute increments at their discretion. Employees were routinely using this on weekends or the day after a holiday, increasing absenteeism rates. The most recent contract placed more restrictions on when this flex time could be used. However, combined with FMLA time, absenteeism rates at times were still running up to 46 percent. This increased substantially with a younger, higher-turnover workforce: where the same policies resulted in rates of 2 or 3 percent five years before, it had become typical to have 10 to 20 percent absenteeism.

> The FMLA laws are killing us. Part of the problem for [U.S. Telecom] is that we pay for absence. There's no real incentive to come to work if you can't be penalized. If you get paid to stay at home, it's kind of a disincentive to come to work.... I don't think we've been smart enough yet to figure out what incentive we need to put out there to get people to come to work. (Interview, consumer manager, February 2005)

There was little managers could do about FMLA or flex time absences. However, they had begun to contract with company security to track down employees who they thought were fraudulently absent, which had resulted in some dismissals. Managers and supervisors were also cracking down on "unexcused" absences. "You might have an individual who has been out 450 hours, but they have no occurrences because they used FMLA. We have to be ready to pounce on them. We cannot let an opportunity pass us by" (Interview, collections manager, February 2005).

A second group of changes with consolidation affected performance management. Managers began to be held more accountable for their centers' ranking, and U.S. Telecom increased the proportion of supervisor and center leader pay that was "at risk," or contingent on meeting performance goals. The company also standardized measurements of customer satisfaction through a new system that matched customer survey scores with individual employees.

Agent pay also became more tightly linked to performance measures. In collections, performance evaluations placed a stronger emphasis on measures of talk times and percentage of follow-through with payment arrangements. In the service and sales centers, the union agreed to a new "sales associate" position. These employees had a higher salary, but their evaluation was tied to meeting a sales quota. Management would be able to set the quota levels, subject to (nonbinding) consultation with the union.

Before consolidation, if a certain percentage of employees did not get a satisfactory performance rating, management would often adjust the measures downward under union pressure. As the company centralized control over these policies and shifted to the new bonus system, the union lost influence and managers steadily increased targets. However, they ran into a number of new problems as they tried to design incentives that would promote the "right kind of selling behaviors." The first year after consolidation, U.S. Telecom provided a bonus if representatives sold six out of seven products at a certain target level. Very few employees made this target, and so the following year the targets were reduced, employees were asked to hit satisfactory attainment on all products, and they were paid a bonus for hitting more than 100 percent attainment. Employees started making money, but the company was not having a good retention rate on products sold to the customer. In 2005 they moved to targeting incentives to sales of certain strategic products, such as high-value bundles or DSL, but employees stopped selling other products that the company also wanted to promote. More recently, they tried to move to a "net sales" system, where any returned sales would be taken out of the bonus calculation. Managers continued to raise and change targets frequently, and admitted they had not yet figured out the right incentives for the behaviors and outcomes they wanted.

U.S. Telecom also adopted performance management initiatives that focused on improving the consistency of coaching and employee discipline. The company put in place a new administrative position in each center to handle paperwork and free up coaches to be "on the floor" listening to employees and answering questions. Managers required coaches to use more systematic metrics, expected them to spend 85 percent of their time coaching, and held them accountable for doing a standardized number of development sessions with "less than satisfactory" performers every week. The union worked with U.S. Telecom to create a new leadership position in sales and support, where an experienced representative in each team took over some responsibility for mentoring her peers and received a 10 percent wage premium during her coaching time. This helped to ease some of the performance problems associated with a less knowledgeable, newer workforce and provided a small career ladder. Both collections and consumer services adopted a new system to improve efficiency of the call flow that specified the different steps the agent should go through for each call and that added additional scripting.

One of the most significant changes in coaching methods was increased latitude to monitor employees, negotiated in a recent collective agreement with the union. Previously, supervisors were allowed to do only several observations per month and had to inform employees and give them the option of either remote or side-by-side monitoring. While they could listen to employees at any time, if they heard someone abusing a customer or not adhering to her script, they could not discipline her unless they had informed her that she was being evaluated. Under the new agreement, supervisors were allowed to do up to twenty-five observations per month and did not have to inform employees. However, they were required to use the additional monitoring for "coaching and development" and thus had to give employees a "free pass" if they observed a major mistake other than customer fraud. The company's main goal was to provide better oversight of fraud, such as employees putting products on customers' lines that they had not ordered, but employees experienced this as a new form of discipline:

> The company would like to listen to them twenty-four/seven. They would. And then come to them with every nit-picky little thing. There are many styles of management, and intimidation is not the one that they should go with. But unfortunately for many of them, that's the only form that they know. So if they keep monitor, monitor, and never come out with anything positive, like you did really great on this, I really like the way you sold that...package, you really did a wonderful job. They're going to come out and say, why didn't you offer [the package] to the next guy? They're not going to mention the good job they did. They're going to mention what they didn't do. And that's why we don't want them to monitor all the time. Because these people are already industrious. And just to hear negative feedback all the time, that's not going to help anybody, the employee or the company either. (Interview, Employee, July 2003)

These new staffing and performance management initiatives created more standardized metrics and increased the use of progressive discipline for "less than satisfactory performers." Dismissals based on performance had increased, under the general rubric of "holding reps more accountable." Managers viewed the new policies as successful—sales had increased, collection rates were up, personnel costs had declined, consistency in outcomes improved, and customer satisfaction scores remained among the highest in the industry.

However, the new structure and policies also had costs. The company lost experienced employees, larger centers presented new management challenges, and absenteeism rates began to climb. The company had eliminated some very high performing centers from smaller towns with an older, more motivated workforce, replacing them with a less committed, younger workforce.

> When we were in smaller towns, you got into [U.S. Telecom], that's it. You got a good paying job, great benefits, a job for life, a steady and reliable company you could be proud to work for. Very community-oriented, very service-oriented. That has changed. Now we are in big cities, people walk out our door and go somewhere else. (Interview, consumer manager, February 2005)

One of the biggest challenges this had created was a dramatic growth in employee turnover. In 2005, two and a half years after consolidation, turnover was running around 50 percent a year in consumer services call centers, up from less than 10 percent in the late 1990s; with most of it concentrated in the younger, low-tenure workforce. Only 60 percent of turnover was voluntary, meaning that a substantial portion was due to dismissals for behavior or failure to meet performance goals. Average seniority dropped from twenty-nine years in the late 1990s to around four years. This created additional training costs, requiring centers to hire their own trainers and invest in ongoing classes for new recruits that lasted from eight to twelve weeks. It also took resources away from ongoing training and skill upgrading. While managers complained bitterly about the problems these changes had caused, both in employee motivation and commitment, they had chosen a staffing strategy that relied on this younger workforce through their decisions to consolidate centers and step up discipline.

At the same time, high turnover rates provided some degree of external or numerical flexibility that had not existed before. The organization did not use temporary workers but described the high-churn portion of their workforce as serving a similar function: whereas previously management would be much more careful about hiring new employees during seasons when call volume peaked, they could now rely on some amount of attrition to decrease staffing levels during lower volume times of the year:

> If we know we are going to keep an average of a thousand people in the acquisitions channel, we may start the year, because January is busier than

December, we may start the year with twelve hundred knowing that attrition will eventually get us to the point where we need to be by the end of the
year with eight or nine hundred. We also use overtime to fill in the gaps. So
we have a staffing plan that goes up-and-down, and then we use overtime
to manage peaks within the week and within the month. (Interview, Force
manager, February 2005)

Management was still trying to figure out how to address turnover, dis-
agreeing about whether it was really a problem—or instead an acceptable
cost of moving to a more sales-focused, accountability-driven organization.
One center with particularly high attrition adopted a policy of "nothing
but positives" in coaching employees, and center managers were struggling with how to raise morale and enthusiasm at a time when discipline
was increasing. The most concrete steps toward improving job quality
were attempts to create a more "fun" environment, particularly in sales
and support, with balloons, parties, special rewards, team competitions,
and promotions—though managers admitted none of these had yet been
particularly effective in raising commitment.

Deutsche Telekom

Deutsche Telekom's call centers were still relatively new but had quickly
become a key strategic area of the business. In contrast to U.S. Telecom,
which had divided consumer call center jobs into three separate rep positions, Deutsche Telekom had created "universal representatives" in the
customer service and sales centers who handled all customer requests, including billing, sales, and customer service. These centers primarily serviced regional markets, with around twelve thousand employees at more
than one hundred locations nationwide.

Most call center employees at Deutsche Telekom had apprenticeship
training, either within or outside the company. The standard career path
was to go through two or three years training through the company to
become qualified as a *Kaufmann für Bureaukommunikation* (management
assistant in office communication). At one center I visited in West Germany, 40 percent of the employees were trained in this occupation, while
the rest had either technical training or university education. In the company's East German locations, employees came from a variety of different

backgrounds. Deutsche Telekom's call centers had expanded rapidly after unification and hired workers who had lost their jobs from other contracting industries. One human resource manager explained, "When personnel were no longer needed somewhere, call centers always needed them. Then regardless of what you can or can't do, now you go into call centers" (Interview, October 2003). At the same time, most of these workers had some form of related occupational training.

While Deutsche Telekom employees were more likely to have formal vocational qualifications than those at U.S. Telecom, in practice internal labor markets and training investments at the former RBOC had long served a similar function—allowing the company to develop and retain a highly skilled workforce. However, restructuring at U.S. Telecom had driven up turnover and led to the replacement of a large proportion of this stable workforce with a higher turnover, primarily high school–educated workforce. In contrast, Deutsche Telekom retained a majority of its highly qualified and experienced employees.

Like U.S. Telecom, Deutsche Telekom's call centers were a target of company efforts to cut costs and improve sales and service quality. There was also a trend toward tighter scheduling, stricter rules, and more pressure to raise sales and cut talk times. However, changes in work organization were accomplished through a negotiated process of restructuring that resulted in a more professional, or "high-involvement," employment system.

First, management was implementing more flexible scheduling policies to better match employee availability with more unpredictable call volumes. After 1996, the company adopted a system of fixed shifts in which each team was given its "tour plan" eleven weeks ahead of time. This was then replaced by a system based on variable tours and scheduling handled through a new electronic shift planning program. Employees gave their team leaders their requested schedules six weeks ahead of time, and the program tried to match these as closely as possible to staffing needs based on call volume predictions. Formally, employees were scheduled on six shift tours of "core" work time, and rotated across these shifts. Unlike at U.S. Telecom, seniority was not used as a factor in deciding shifts.

Working time accounts were also adopted in a works agreement as a compromise to help address seasonal fluctuations in call volume while giving employees more control over their working time. When call volume was high, team leaders encouraged employees to come in earlier or leave later, building up "plus" hours in their account. Then when volume dropped off, especially in the summer months, they could draw on this account to take additional time off. Employees had a great deal of formal control over whether they stayed late and when they used their "plus" hours—there was nothing like the regular forced overtime at U.S. Telecom.

Agents were expected to adhere to a more loosely defined schedule of break times, as well. Every employee was given twenty minutes for a computer screen break, in addition to regular break times. This was negotiated with the works council in 2002, as part of an initiative to improve employee health and workplace ergonomics. Employees were free to take breaks within some limits, and team leaders came up with different strategies to make sure these were staggered. In one center, there were several tennis balls on a table that employees picked up when they went on their breaks to make sure no more than four were up from their desk at any one time. Absenteeism was also a problem, running sometimes as high as 20 percent (though this is still much lower than the 46 percent reported at U.S. Telecom). As it was difficult to discipline employees, team leaders tried to use "softer" forms of pressure, such as spending more time coaching and talking with individuals about the effects of their behavior on the team.

A second set of changes affected performance measurement and management. The union renegotiated the structure of compensation in 2001, as Deutsche Telekom sought to move to a payment system based on job skill and experience. An important part of the new agreement was the introduction of performance-based pay. Deutsche Telekom put in place a bonus system with team-based sales goals that management negotiated with the union and works councils. They agreed on two systems for calculating variable pay. In the first system, 7 percent of what employees earned in sales was put into a pooled budget for performance pay at the center level, and management then distributed all of this money across the teams. Each team was evaluated on a twenty-point scale and received a portion of the total based on the number of these points. An oversight committee at each workplace, with an equal number of employee and employer representatives, was responsible for deciding how performance-based pay was distributed. Under the new system, 10 to 12 percent of employee pay and 20 percent of supervisor pay was performance-based.

In the second system, Deutsche Telekom managers made a recommendation for team-based goals, which were then discussed with the team leaders. If the employees disagreed with the goals, the joint committee made a final decision. These goals were then incorporated into a collective agreement that regulated what goals could be measured, based on whether they were "plausible." The goals were set between 70 and 150 percent, with a cap that prevented them from going up too quickly. If the goals were thought to be too high, employees could again bring the issue before the commission—for example, if too many employees had been laid off and there was more work to do than originally forecast, or the computer systems were not working that month.

A notable feature of this system, and a clear difference from U.S. Telecom, was its strong focus on coaching and performance evaluation at the work group level. This contributed to a more team-oriented form of work organization. Deutsche Telekom sponsored ongoing competitions among the teams, typically made up of twelve to fifteen employees, for sales of certain products or "customer win-backs." Supervisors, now called "team leaders," saw their role as developing team spirit and making sure that all employees were pulling their weight. Team leaders described a complicated system for coaching and motivating individuals while staying within the strict limits that works councils imposed on *Einzelplatzkontrolle* (or individual job control):

> We negotiate individual goals—we can't write them down like we do with performance-based pay because that is seen by the works council as *Einzelplatzkontrolle,* which isn't allowed and doesn't bring much benefit when I want to nurture team thinking. But it's clear that everyone has her personal goal—it is more an orientation: when I bring this part and everyone brings theirs, then we meet the team goal. But I can't say: you have only four, you should have five—that's not allowed. (Team Leader, October 2003)

The works agreement allowed individual coaching, but it could only be used for development and training. Deutsche Telekom put in place a new system in 2002, as part of an effort to improve the professionalism and "leadership competence" of the team leader while increasing the consistency of coaching. Team leaders did regular side-by-side listening with employees and gave them feedback on their selling techniques and how they dealt with customers, while identifying areas where they needed additional training. Once a year each employee met formally with her team leader to discuss what kind of training she needed to do her job better, and what resources could be provided to help her improve. The team leader and employee had broad discretion over how many side-by-sides were done and what kinds of training and development measures were adopted.

These policies created a very different work climate than that at U.S. Telecom: employees were treated as professionals and given considerably more discretion over how and when they worked. The limits on managerial control of individual performance extended to team leaders' ability to monitor adherence to schedule and talk times. While in the United States these metrics were easy to link to individual agents, the collective agreement prohibited tracking any performance outcomes that could influence discipline or compensation. Again, team leaders were creative in getting around these rules to maintain order in their teams, based largely on developing trust with employees:

> I see in the display how the availability is and how many people are logged in, but I don't know who is there. For example: here there are no names next to numbers. If I see seven are available and I have ten working, I ask where are the other three and look and see. The works council would not be able to say that this is *Einzelplatzkontrolle*. ... With my team, we tell each other everything. When someone's missing, I go through the rows and talk directly with the agents. They don't see it as control, but—oh, right, I've worked too long on the order. I don't need their names to do this. (Team leader, October 2003)

Employees felt that scheduling rules had become more strict over time, but experienced this pressure differently from their counterparts at U.S. Telecom. Team leaders motivated employees by developing strong relationships within the group rather than with progressive discipline and intensive monitoring.

At Deutsche Telekom the union and the works councils were able to negotiate compromises to employer demands for improving sales performance and adopting lean scheduling practices that maintained employee autonomy. This more professional model relied on an experienced, stable, and self-motivated workforce. There were growing stresses on employees from the new policies, which introduced pressures to sell that had not existed before—particularly within the new teams. There were also continued costs from variation in performance that managers were unhappy about. While many were positive about the team model, some felt that the system was less successful in motivating persistently weak performers. Nonetheless, outcomes represented negotiated compromises that moved toward a more sales-based model through incentives and commitment rather than discipline.

Comparison

The companies in the two case studies adopted distinct strategies to organize work and develop and motivate employees (see table 3.2). Basic tasks were similar, the market segment was identical, and both companies faced similar competitive pressures. However, U.S. Telecom had moved toward an employment system that relied on a young, high-turnover workforce, gave agents very little working time flexibility or control over scheduling, and designed jobs narrowly with few mechanisms for employee participation in decision making. In contrast, Deutsche Telekom continued to rely on an older, more stable workforce, created more broadly skilled universal rep positions, established extensive opportunities for employee participation, and gave agents broad discretion over their schedules and break times. While U.S. Telecom was moving to a performance management system that relied on individual appraisal and incentives, continuous monitoring, and a strong focus on discipline, Deutsche Telekom had put in place group-based incentives and strong limits on individual monitoring, and focused on coaching and development.

One explanation for these different approaches may be skill levels or training systems. Deutsche Telekom was able to draw on a more experienced, well-trained, and committed workforce, compared to the younger, high-turnover workforce at U.S. Telecom. However, differences in skill profiles were not necessarily inherent to the two companies, but rather created by management strategies. U.S. Telecom long enjoyed a high-tenure workforce, which had acquired broad skills through the company's internal labor markets. The unilateral decision by U.S. Telecom's management to consolidate centers, crack down on discipline, focus on sales incentives, and tighten scheduling led many of these experienced employees to leave

TABLE 3.2 Employment systems at U.S. Telecom and Deutsche Telekom

	U.S. Telecom	Deutsche Telekom
Staffing and skill		
Typical tenure	• < 5 years	• > 10 years
Typical ed. level	• High school	• Kaufmann/frau apprenticeship
Initial training	• 6 weeks	• Based on need
Scheduling		
% Part time	• < 5%	• 15–20%
Scheduling	• Set 13 weeks in advance	• Set 6 weeks in advance
	• Fixed schedules with some agent choice; FMLA paid leave and flex time; inflexible break times	• Broad agent choice, negotiated with team leaders
	• Seniority or forced overtime	• Working time accounts, with broad agent discretion
Work design		
Breadth of skills	• Separate customer service, sales, and collections positions	• Agents handle all calls; division between front and back office
Use of teams	• Limited use for competitions and 'building spirit'	• Strong use for incentives, competitions, and training
Compensation		
Av. base pay	• $30,000–$40,000	• $32,000–$40,000
Pay at risk	• 8% for sales reps	• None
Av. % variable pay	• 15–20%	• 10–12%
Level of variable pay	• Individual-based	• Group-based
Worker rep. influence	• Limited oversight	• Substantial oversight
Coaching		
Basis for coaching	• Individual performance	• Training needs
Discipline	• Steps leading to dismissal if targets not met	• Dismissals for poor performance rare
Monitoring		
Electronic	• Some limits, individual-based	• None
Other	• 25 remote observations allowed per month	• Mystery calls aggregated to the team level
Outcomes		
Absenteeism	• 20–46%	• 10–20%
Turnover	• 50%	• Close to 0%

and attracted a younger workforce. Indeed, the union viewed management's consolidation and relocation strategy as an explicit effort to eliminate the company's more skilled, higher-paid workforce, whom they assumed would not be willing to relocate to another city to follow their work.

While employee skills were no doubt an important resource for German managers, case study findings suggest that differences in institutional supports for worker participation in decision-making are a central explanation for diverging employment systems. Both companies had strong unions that tried to partner over work redesign. The management challenges were almost identical: how to implement sales incentives, how to monitor and measure performance, and how to design more lean staffing and scheduling practices. However, unions and works councils in Germany were able to push management to adopt a more high-involvement approach in responding to these challenges. A closer look shows how two bargaining systems—the one based on contract rules and grievances and the other on more substantive rights to negotiate over work design—led to distinct management strategies.

The union at U.S. Telecom was able to influence compensation, evaluation, and staffing policies mainly through contract negotiations and the grievance process. Labor-management partnership had given the union stronger influence in the past—however, this influence typically waxed when management decided to implement changes in the workplace that need the union's support and waned when the company shifted to a strategy of downsizing and consolidation. Changes in top management also played an important role in the quality of labor-management relations. For example, the president of consumer services who was responsible for the consolidation of U.S. Telecom's call centers came from outside the company and had a finance background. His unilateral approach to restructuring angered union representatives, leading to ongoing conflicts and expensive grievances. A new president came in a couple of years after consolidation who grew up in the company, and as a "Bell-head" knew how to work with the union and was able to immediately improve working relations.

Despite a sometimes rocky relationship, union representatives and managers agreed that over time both parties had become more willing to work together. Call center managers described cooperation with the local president and shop stewards on a range of issues, from improving sales and collections to reducing absenteeism. The union decided to allow sales quotas and increased monitoring for the first time in the late 1990s to help the company better compete for customers, even though these decisions were unpopular with employees. At the same time, after they changed the rules, union representatives lost some control. Once managers could use sales quotas, the union had no way of influencing how these were set. While the contract could restrict the allowed number of "silent observations," it had little sway over company policies to discipline employees based on those observations.

The most recent partnership agreement came out of bargaining in the late 1990s, and put in place a system to consult at the workplace level. These committees had two managers and two union representatives, typically shop stewards, who met at the local level once or twice a month to discuss performance issues and employee concerns. Issues that could not be resolved were sent to a quarterly meeting at the district level between union and management representatives. This allowed for more labor input and local "trouble-shooting." During consolidation, when relations with management broke down, the union suspended the boards for about a year. After they were reinstated, they continued to play only a marginal role. While meetings could be useful for resolving smaller issues like "putting a bigger clock on the wall" or improving coaching styles, most substantive decisions were handed down from central management. A shop steward gave one example of a new initiative the local partnership had come up with to reward good attendance with special gift certificates, but when word got out, the corporate human resources department told them it was not consistent with U.S. Telecom's compensation policies and so it had to be discontinued.

One manager described how partnership and consultation over changes in employment policies worked in practice:

> It's sort of a variable process. If it's something where the [union] has no jurisdiction, for example, but as a good business partner we do want to work with them productively, we go by to make sure they're aware of that. The communication is more a one-way informative communication—we want you to be aware that we're doing this, and this is the effect of it. We do have some things that we struggle for, what will be the best approach. Then, we do actually engage with the [union] saying, here is something we are working on, and we would like to get some ideas. If they have not been engaged, they will push back much harder than if they've been involved and come to a reasonable conclusion. Sometimes we think we are communicating a change, and we get some feedback that causes us to reevaluate and change what we do. (Interview, manager, February 2005)

The union could influence decisions in these kinds of discussions, but only if managers felt proposals were in the company's interest. Consultation was often more about communicating changes and getting buy-in. Real power came at the bargaining table, in more narrowly prescribed areas such as pay, transfer rights, overtime rules, and vacation time.

At Deutsche Telekom, partnership over work redesign was backed up by more extensive consultation and real countervailing power at multiple levels of the organization. Partnership was not a choice, but rather a clear obligation. Deutsche Telekom's strategic reorientation to become a more "sales oriented" organization was a unilateral decision, as management sought to respond to a rapid growth in low-cost competition and declining market share. However, the union and works councils were able to shape implementation of management strategies to reduce stress on employees and ensure the structure of new policies was jointly designed.

First, the presence of worker representatives on Deutsche Telekom's supervisory board meant that the union and works councils were much better informed than U.S. Telecom's union of strategic decisions and the effects these would have on employees. For example, when the company was facing changes in customer demand and trying to figure out how to adjust staffing to respond, worker representatives were able to look at call projection numbers and make their own recommendations based on how accurate these projections had been in the past (as it turned out, not very). The works councils eventually hired their own consultants to study staffing, and found that call volume was consistently above projections. This allowed them to successfully argue that the company should increase staffing levels in some regions, making the business case that customer satisfaction and service quality were at stake.

Second, strong codetermination rights meant that works councils were able to negotiate much broader agreements that covered the design of performance-based pay, how employees were evaluated, and detailed scheduling practices. Formal codetermination rights did not necessarily mean that the works council could block unpopular changes, but works councilors used these rights to receive information about proposed changes and as leverage to influence decisions:

> The works council can't stop us, when we have a good reason, from changing the work time or deciding how big the room will be where the employees work. But they can say, we need to measure how high the oxygen level is in the room, how loud it is, and then the process will last longer. When we have measured and have a bad result, then they have a basis to say, okay the size of the space is okay, but the loudness in the room is too high, which

means they can lengthen the process or stop it if they know the laws, and can use the laws to influence change. And this process works well, also, to make sure that we adhere to the laws. That means, they can't directly take part in the decision, yes or no, but they can influence the circumstances of the decision. (Interview, team leader, March 2004)

A comparison of negotiations over new, leaner staffing and scheduling policies shows how these differences in industrial relations institutions led to different outcomes. At U.S. Telecom, the union contract created numerous constraints that management had to work around when trying to staff its call centers. Rules laid out how far in advance schedules were set, how overtime was handled, and when employees would take their vacations. Management was required to adopt schedules three weeks in advance and notify employees several days in advance when overtime was needed. When there was a last-minute need for employees to work overtime to clear the phone queue or handle an unexpected spike in calls, supervisors had to ask employees one-on-one based on seniority, within the constraint that no one could work more than eleven hours overtime a week. The contract also specified that all centers must remain open on the same schedule, making it difficult to create a more staggered plan.

Negotiated FMLA rules that provided paid sick leave and flex time rules that allowed employees to take vacation days in fifteen minute increments also created unique staffing challenges. Managers accused employees of abusing policies that let them take time off and were frustrated that the union agreement made it so difficult to discipline agents. Managers had to work within these constraints that created a clear procedure and more predictability for employees, as well as some working time flexibility. However, they experienced this as a struggle for control over scheduling. Managers felt employees were taking advantage of flexible working time and described the various restrictions as rigid rules.

Rather than giving us flexibility within our working agreement to allow people to bid on their off days, they have to be rotated equally. So everybody works the same number of holidays, everybody works the same number of Saturdays, everybody gets the same number of Tuesdays, Wednesdays, Thursdays, and Fridays off. We have to maintain that day to day, and administer that in the fairness rules. That constrains the creativity you can do around scheduling. If you didn't have that kind of restriction, we could say, this group of folks always want to work Thursdays, Fridays, this other group is always a Fridays and Saturdays group. We can't do that. We are about to go to a new scheduling system that will allow us the flexibility to bid on your tours as well as your off days. If we are able to do that, it's going to require negotiating with [the union] to get a different set of work rules around these issues. Those are constraints. (Interview, manager, February 2005)

The union had an interest in maintaining these rules to provide some measure of predictability and fairness, and was mistrustful of management strategies that relied more on flexibility and individual negotiation.

At Deutsche Telekom, the problem of adjusting staffing was handled through working time accounts, which, as mentioned above, allow employees to build up "plus" hours in their account when there is a spike in call volume, and then draw on this account during quieter times. Employees formally had control over when they would take this time, requiring team leaders to negotiate somewhat over schedules:

We have flexible work time here in the firm. But I can't have employees regularly taking flexible time when I have to make sure availability stays at a certain level. So we have working time plans with fixed schedules. However, the works council doesn't acknowledge fixed schedules: that means the employee can, according to the works council, come and go when she wants. When push comes to shove, the works council can say: the employee has flexible time and can go home at 12:00, even though we needed her until 4:00. (Interview, team leader, Oct 2003)

We have to always look and say, now we have a spike in calls, and we have to make sure that if it's the same next week, we can correct for that. When we have extremely high volume in the afternoons, then we can't wait until the next cycle: we have to talk to a team leader, and they have to convince an employee in the framework of their flexible time to stay longer and then work until six P.M. or something. We can only ask and hope that they do it—they always find someone. (Interview, manager, Oct 2003)

This process is quite different from forced overtime rules at U.S. Telecom. Works councils played an important role in making sure agents had some discretion over their own working time, and managers depended on having a good relationship with their employees to keep everything running smoothly. In contrast to the constant struggle over FMLA and flex time at U.S. Telecom, team leaders did not view these rules as rigid policies to work around, but rather constraints that they had to figure out some way to work within.

Other areas of employment practice show a similar pattern. At U.S. Telecom, the union could negotiate some rules around how many times employees were monitored and how this information was used. However, managers set up their own very strict system within these boundaries for measuring individual performance and disciplining employees. Once the union agreed to pay at risk, it lost control over the design of incentives, and management experimented with a variety of different strategies aimed at "getting the incentives right" to promote certain selling behaviors and discourage others. The result was an uneasy mix of carrots and sticks, as managers cracked down on poor performers while paying often exorbitant bonuses to their top sellers, meanwhile trying to build up "team spirit." The contradiction between individual-focused evaluation and the attempt to create more cohesive teams to encourage commitment at U.S. Telecom's centers was striking.

In contrast, Deutsche Telekom's works councils created strong limits on monitoring and evaluating individual employees, and were able to prevent dismissals for poor performance. This meant that there were much stronger incentives for coaching and development, as well as instilling some sense of professionalism among employees. Incentives were likewise team-based, with strong union and works council oversight to make sure they were implemented fairly. The system of human resource practices, incentives, and work design was more internally consistent. There was much more employee buy-in and even (remarkable for Germany) less cynicism about the pervasive focus on team spirit and competitions. Agents were clearly unhappy about growing performance pressures but had some recourse through works councils and the union to build in some greater employee control.

Negotiating Flexibility in a New Sector: U.S. Mobile and German Mobile

U.S. Telecom and Deutsche Telekom are both established companies with strong unions. The second set of matched pair case studies are large wireless companies. Both U.S. Mobile and German Mobile had been covered by union-negotiated collective agreements for only a few years at the time of my research, although German Mobile employees were represented by strong works councils since the early 1990s. Typical of the industry, the two companies had experienced recent mergers that led to growing job insecurity and new bargaining partners. Despite having weaker industrial relations institutions, patterns of outcomes are remarkably similar to those described above: while U.S. Mobile adopted a managerial control model, German Mobile invested in practices that relied on worker skills and discretion.

U.S. Mobile

U.S. Mobile grew rapidly in the late 1990s and early 2000s through mergers and acquisitions. Management then faced the challenge of realizing economies of scale and cutting costs for a vast network of call centers and retail stores with different management practices and pay scales. By 2005, the company had consolidated many of its centers into a smaller number of "megacenters" with between six hundred and eight hundred employees each, often located in rural areas. To staff these centers, it recruited young, high school–educated workers with little job experience of any kind. Similar to U.S. Telecom, consolidation had created new problems: managing a young, high-turnover workforce in a large, impersonal environment where relationships of trust and commitment are more difficult to develop.

The company was also adjusting to its new relationship with the union, which had only negotiated first contracts with the company several years before this study began. Different regional union contracts contributed to some variation in work rules and protections. U.S. Mobile was bringing together customer service work under one job title, including billing, customer support, and first-level technical support; splitting off inbound and outbound sales into another group; and setting up a higher skilled, second-level technical support team. Employees at one center felt that this had eliminated their center's career path, while making customer service jobs too complex and confusing at a time when U.S. Mobile was cutting its training budget. Managers admitted they were still experimenting with different strategies for organizing jobs.

Work organization was similar to that at U.S. Telecom, with a strong focus on the supervisor/employee relationship, only haphazard use of teams, extremely limited employee discretion, and few opportunities for employees to participate in decision making. Employees had little control over their schedules or breaks. Agents chose shifts based on seniority, which were usually set one week in advance, and center managers regularly used mandatory overtime when there were call volume peaks. During busy times of the year, many agents regularly worked two extra hours a day. When call volume declined, managers would ask employees to volunteer to go home without pay. Employees also were allowed four days a year of "excused with pay" time, described as a mental health holiday.

The union contracts achieved some consistency in scheduling. One contract required that the company notify employees forty-eight hours ahead of time when there would be scheduling changes and prohibited split tours, an unpopular practice that allows managers to schedule employees to work an eight-hour shift in two segments, with an hour or more of unpaid downtime in between. However, union representatives complained that managers were unwilling to negotiate creative options for giving employees more attractive or flexible shifts:

> Scheduling could be more creative, but they don't want to do it.... They look at the numbers and forecast each hour. They hire part-time in the sales department instead of full-time positions. But they won't let employees take part-time voluntarily. (Interview, union representative, May 2004)

Employees similarly had little leeway to choose when they would take breaks or leave their desks. They were expected to be in strict compliance with their schedule and were put on progressive discipline if they fell out of compliance.

Tardiness and absenteeism were also punished harshly. For every "occurrence," employees moved through a five-step progressive discipline process that ended in dismissal. Any absence "rolled off" after six months. This meant that an agent could have up to five occurrences within a six-month period before being terminated. If she missed more than three days, two times within the three-month period, she would be put on an accelerated program, "which means you're pretty much out of the door" (Interview, union representative, May 2005).

U.S. Mobile's performance management approach also built in little employee discretion. The company shifted from a strong quality-focused strategy in the early years as it was building up its reputation, to one focused on cutting costs and increasing sales as the industry consolidated and price-based competition grew. The company cut base pay at many locations while increasing bonuses and incentives. For example, U.S. Mobile purchased a company that was paying around $14 an hour starting salary, and after the purchase adjusted this to $9 an hour with more pay at risk. In sales centers, around $7000 of employee pay was conditional on making a quota. If agents went above their quota, they could add additional money on top of that: for example, if they achieved 200 percent of quota, they would add $14,000 to their pay.

U.S. Mobile backed up these incentives with pervasive monitoring and discipline. Coaches used continuous remote monitoring to evaluate quality and catch fraud. Unlike U.S. Telecom, there were no limits on monitoring in the contract. Employees were measured on a range of metrics, from talk time to adherence to schedule, and coaches kept a close watch on any deviance from the schedule. "We expect agents to be at the desks, with the headsets on, 90 percent of the time" (Interview, manager, July 2003). The company had even outsourced monitoring to a third-party firm that was using special technology that collected screen shots and traced key strokes. They quantified this information into a quality score and passed this on to supervisors, who then used it to discipline employees. In some cases, employees had been fired for consistently "over keying" or typing more than was necessary.

In the sales centers, U.S. Mobile had rolled out a new policy to increase sales. If employees did not achieve above 70 percent of their quota, they would be put on progressive discipline, which started with counseling, then went to a written warning, final written warning, and termination. Terminations had been steadily increasing as managers cracked down on poor performers. At several centers, around 80 percent of employees were written up for not meeting objectives. Employees at one center described how managers would humiliate their co-workers by marching to their desks when they were fired and making a big show of putting their things into a box.

Although managers claimed that the company placed a great deal of emphasis on customer service, service ratings had slipped in recent years. U.S. Mobile was ranked close to last in service quality across wireless providers, with complaints on the rise. Managers blamed this on union rules, while the union blamed consolidation and company policies. Fraud was also starting to be a problem, similar to U.S. Telecom, as employees sent phones to friends or charged services that had not been ordered by customers. Turnover was extremely high across call centers, from 30 percent to over 100 percent, and had been climbing.

Managers adopted several new strategies to try to improve dismal turnover rates and customer satisfaction scores. Following the recommendations of a retention study, they put in place a new team initiative to support better communication within work groups. One goal was to overcome the obstacles to knowledge sharing created by individual incentives.

> There's a lot of frustration, because it is a sales environment: if you're helping somebody, that's taking away from your sales. And we found that some people, the "nice" people, were being approached—someone who doesn't bite the employee's head off—it got around among the new employees: well, this person is nice, you can go to her, and so that person's sales would end up suffering because they were too busy being nice and helping the other employees. So that's how the [team] concept was born. (Interview, sales manager, July 2003)

Another set of changes focused on improving agent recruitment and screening, such as putting out new brochures and orientation videos that communicated more accurately what call center jobs involved (sitting answering phones for seven hours straight with few breaks).

However, local managers were for the most part resolved to making do with the tools they had, which meant more monitoring, more discipline, and more targeted individual incentives. Some complained it was impossible to attract motivated workers with low salaries, intense working conditions, and few job perks. One union representative put it more bluntly: "When you're bringing in eighteen-year-old kids and telling them they can't be out of this chair, they're like, screw you, I'm out of here" (Interview, February 2005).

German Mobile

German Mobile's call centers had grown rapidly in the 1990s. Like U.S. Mobile, management had begun to cut costs after the heady years of growth in the wireless industry gave way to consolidation and price competition. Managers had also started reorienting the business to a stronger sales focus. Agents' job title had been changed from customer service representative to sales agent, and employees were put on a new training plan that taught selling techniques and then encouraged employees who did well to train their colleagues.

Unlike Deutsche Telekom, the majority of German Mobile's employees had not gone through a company-sponsored apprenticeship program. However, almost all employees had some form of occupational training, and management tried to recruit employees with a sales background. At one East German location, the manager estimated that close to 70 percent of employees had completed the *Kaufmann* (management assistant) occupational training. Agents were broadly skilled to answer the basic customer service and sales hotline and the credit hotline, while different specialized teams handled second-level technical support or outbound sales. Each employee had a main skill and then was trained to handle overflow from other call types.

Although German Mobile faced similar strategic challenges to U.S. Mobile, the company adopted a very different employment system for its customer service and sales call centers. Employees were on staggered shifts that began every half hour, from 6:00 A.M. until 10:00 P.M. They were able to choose desired shifts, which were then matched with demand and distributed as shift plans eight weeks ahead of time—with a 70 to 80 percent match between requested and actual shifts. An agreement with the works council allowed managers to ask employees to change shifts, but they could not require this. There were also no working time accounts, which works councilors believed would give managers too much control over employees' schedules. The works council in one location also had an agreement to give fixed shifts for ten employees each year, which then rotated among employees. This was seen as particularly desirable for new mothers. Employees had less control over their breaks than at Deutsche Telekom, but were allowed to take regular computer screen "pauses."

These features of work design, staffing, and scheduling were mirrored in the performance management system. The most striking difference from U.S. Mobile was greater employee autonomy and the strong team focus of compensation and evaluation. Inbound agents had no individual-based commission pay. As at Deutsche Telekom, a works agreement required all results to be aggregated to teams of at least five people. Teams had sales goals that they were expected to meet each week and month, and special team competitions and bonuses provided additional incentives to get performance numbers up. Employees saw the team sales numbers on their screens, and these were then posted in rooms with rankings and goals.

Works agreements also placed strict limits on individual evaluation. Quantitative data could not be broken down at the agent level, such as talk times or adherence to schedule. Instead, the team leader kept track of how the team was doing and let the group know when they needed to boost their numbers collectively. An external firm monitored customer service and employee product knowledge through mystery calls, performing fifty to sixty calls per location every fourteen days. Results from these "quality checks" were tallied at the level of the company, the call centers, teams, and individual employees. However, there were clear restrictions on who had access to individual results. Each center had around five trainers who could use this data to give employees feedback and help them improve. No managers or team leaders could look at individual scores, and they could not be used for disciplinary purposes. Management at one location had recently obtained permission from the works council to allow team leaders to do their own individual tests for product knowledge, but again, these could only be used for employee development. There were practically no dismissals, except in a few cases of customer abuse or fraud.

Coaching looked quite different without hard numbers and was described by management as a negotiation rather than evaluation:

> They don't tell them, you're good or bad. Instead, they negotiate with the employee: how they can improve their success. It is an analysis done together, and naturally they know exactly, in this area I'm weak, maybe technical support or product presentation, I can work on that. Or communication, selling. That's decided together between the employee and coach, and there are certain trainings that go along with that. (Interview, manager, July 2004)

Coaching sessions with the trainer were quite involved and could take up to three hours. The team leader was responsible for getting employees together and building "team spirit" through communicating how well the team was doing in meeting its goals and motivating them to meet these goals together. This meant a lot of team meetings, workshops, and group trainings.

Managers viewed absenteeism as a major problem, although again, it was substantially lower than in the United States, running at around 10 percent. The main solution was a *Krankenrückkehrgespräch,* or meeting with employees when they returned after being absent to discuss any issues with work or their health and how to resolve them. Every meeting had to be documented and passed on to the quality manager. Then, when there was a persistent problem, it was "escalated" to the quality manager, who tried to "work out a solution with the employee." This typically meant that both parties would negotiate some course of action to improve attendance. Works councilors felt this had created more stress, leading employees to come in when they were sick, and they would sometimes accompany employees to these meetings to give them support. At the same time, these meetings could not be backed up with hard consequences and attendance problems rarely led to dismissals.

These various policies appeared to contribute to high-quality customer service and low turnover. German Mobile was consistently ranked at the top of service quality ratings and had turnover rates of less than 2 percent.

Comparison

Work organization and performance management strategies again looked quite different in the U.S. and German case studies (see table 3.3). U.S. Mobile gave employees little control over their working time and few opportunities to participate in decision making. Agents were young and inexperienced, scheduling was unpredictable, individual pay at risk was high, monitoring was continuous, and discipline was harsh. In contrast, German Mobile supported its better-educated and older employees with extensive coaching and development, and offered them more predictable schedules. As at Deutsche Telekom, most evaluation and all variable pay was at the work group level, with strict limits on who could see individual performance data. Organizational outcomes also looked better at German Mobile, with lower absenteeism and turnover, and a stronger reputation for high-quality service.

TABLE 3.3 Employment systems at U.S. Mobile and German Mobile

	U.S. Mobile	German Mobile
Staffing and skill		
Typical tenure	• < 2 years	• < 5 years
Typical ed. level	• High school	• Kaufmann/frau apprenticeship
Initial training	• 3 weeks	• 8 weeks
Scheduling		
% part time	• 20–30%	• 10–30% (west); 80% (east)
Scheduling	• Set 2 weeks in advance; 48 hours notice for changes	• Set 8 weeks in advance; 2 weeks notice for changes
	• Limited agent choice and inflexible break times	• Some agent choice
	• Forced overtime; agents asked to leave voluntarily without pay	• No working time accounts; voluntary overtime
Work design		
Breadth of skills	• Universal reps, with division between support and sales	• Specialization in a "primary skill" with training to handle overflow
Use of teams	• Limited use for training	• Strong use for incentives, competitions, and training
Compensation		
Av. Base Pay	• $25,000–30,000	• $35,000
Pay at risk	• 20% for sales reps	• None
Av. % variable pay	• Up to 55%	• 10–15%
Level of variable pay	• Individual-based	• Group-based
Worker rep. influence	• No oversight	• Limited oversight
Coaching		
Basis for coaching	• Individual performance	• Training needs
Discipline	• Steps leading to dismissal if targets not met	• Dismissals for poor performance rare
Monitoring		
Electronic	• Continuous, individual	• None
Other	• No negotiated limits on monitoring	• Mystery calls aggregated to teams and individuals; individual data available to quality trainer
Outcomes		
Absenteeism	• 10–30%	• 10%
Turnover	• 30–100% (50% average)	• 1–2%

One explanation for these different employment systems is, again, workforce skills. Even in this newer, growing industry segment, employees in the German case had more formal education than those in the U.S. case. However, as with the fixed-line cases, management choices exacerbated or reinforced these patterns. U.S. Mobile chose to consolidate smaller locations into megacenters, cut its investments in training and in some cases pay, and created a low-discretion work environment. In many cases, these decisions had led to the loss of a more experienced and skilled workforce.

Differences in collective bargaining institutions between the two companies proved again to play a central role in outcomes, even though unions were substantially weaker than in the fixed-line cases. Worker representatives had uneven influence over management strategies at both U.S. Mobile and German Mobile, in the first case due to multiple bargaining units and the newness of bargaining; in the second case because local works councils often had different agendas and did not have a strong connection with the union. However, it is still possible to describe two very different patterns of labor relations and to map out the effects of bargaining on employment practices. At U.S. Mobile there was a breakdown of partnership at the local level and ongoing conflict over unpopular policies. At German Mobile partnership was more meaningful, backed up by the works councils' stronger participation rights. This allowed them to establish a set of clear rules that restricted monitoring and created incentives for managers to invest in skills.

U.S. Mobile had a formal partnership with its union, but in many locations the relationship had been bad from the beginning. Managers at some centers were used to an earlier union avoidance policy and found it difficult to adjust to working together. One manager described the labor relations climate at her call center as a competition over grievances rather than a partnership:

> (Does the union help you to develop your managers?) No, they hold us totally accountable for that. NO suggestions, NO NOTHING. It a "that's your problem" kind of mentality. There's no sense of partnership, or feeling that they're trying to help us improve. We're supposed to be a strong "labor management partnership" case. But when you get down into it, the smaller picture and the field locations, it's not what it appears and it's a very conflictual relationship. Personally, I have a great relationship with the [union]. You can imagine what a switch that was, going from a union avoidance mentality into a partnership. But you know, I feel like our department has done a really good job of doing that. But for our managers it's really tough. Because for them it's more of a competition: if I give into a grievance, I've lost. So it's very competitive. (Interview, manager, sales center, July 2003)

The union and management established a committee that was supposed to help improve communications around new policies. However, the communication tended to be one way. One manager described this as an opportunity to explain why they have such strict policies, to try to convince the union they were necessary:

> The union does NOT understand our competitive environment; we've got seven or eight competitors and the cell industry is just, they're highly competitive. So we have, as far as progressive discipline, and especially for sales people, we get them out the door if they're not performing, and they're not used to that. And so the biggest thing has been, it's our opportunity to explain to them how we're different from [a traditional Bell company], and it's not going to be the same, it can never be the same or we will die—we will wither on the vine and die if we have some of the policies that [the Bell companies] have. (Interview, manager, sales center, July 2003)

This same manager also complained that since the location was organized, she had less leeway to implement a more professional HR model, which in turn affected employee morale. She and her colleagues looked back wistfully on "the good old days" when they were "more into treating their employees well" and when those employees were more committed to doing a good job. It was not clear why the union was preventing U.S. Mobile from doing these things—in fact, union representatives had also argued for more investments in employees. However, managers associated unionization with other changes that had happened at the same time with the shift to a larger company, such as more bureaucracy and less local control, as well as growing cost pressures in an increasingly price-competitive industry.

From the union's perspective, the company had changed its own position in recent years, moving from an earlier commitment to partnership at the local level to constant conflict. One local representative described this shift:

> Now there is a big change in company philosophy, management styles, everything is changing. The company is a lot less willing to work with the union than they used to be. We used to have monthly meetings with the regional VP and directors, and we would be able to work out any issues within that meeting. Now to get one of those meetings is like pulling teeth and you

have to hound them on a consistent basis to get them to meet. When they do meet, they send a designated person to meet you, who is usually a lower level manager and it's pretty much worthless to meet with them because alright I'll take you up to the director—but then the director won't meet with you, so why bother. We stopped meeting with them for about six months now. We're just filing grievances. The upper-level managers just stopped talking to us, they didn't want to deal with us and we got tired of hounding them to get a meeting. (Interview, union representative, May 2005)

Union representatives felt there was a shift in internal policy to block the union from being effective in the workplace. "When it's benefiting them, they want to deal with us, when it's not benefiting them, they don't want to deal with us" (Interview, union representative, May 2005). I interviewed a group of employees who described an extremely conflictual relationship, where managers obstructed them from filing grievances and created new job titles that they defined as falling outside of the bargaining unit.

The union has to do research to find out if they should be in the union or not. [U.S. Mobile] hides things. They do underhanded, sneaky things. . . . On a variety of different issues, every time we think we are finally getting some-where, something happens that blows it out of the water and we have to start over. Seems the more we try to fight our way out, the more the waters are covering our heads. (Interview, shop steward, May 2005)

In one example, the company and the union worked together to survey employees on how to improve the work environment. Employees were reluctant to fill out the survey, because the company had done this before and nothing came of it, but the union convinced its members that it would work with management this time to come up with solutions. Task forces made recommendations, and the initiative even won a partnership award; but then managers did not implement any of the changes on the basis that they would be too expensive.

Because U.S. Mobile is a national company with multiple bargaining units, communication across union locals was often poor. Union repre-sentatives felt the company was using these divisions to implement new policies unilaterally and then undermine grievances the union filed to chal-lenge these policies. For example, one local tried to file a grievance against sales goals the union felt were unreasonable, but the company argued it was a national policy. Then by chance a local leader was complaining about the new "national policy" with a colleague and found out that her region had a totally different set of goals. Local union leaders were trying to build more systematic communication around the local issues they were encountering. However, the union lacked a clear structure of communication, which frustrated attempts to build a "united front" against management's attempts to marginalize union input.

This distrustful relationship in turn meant that the union took the attitude that everything management tried to implement was done in a sneaky way, with the goal of cutting jobs and worsening working conditions. For example, the company had adopted a flexible working time policy that let agents voluntarily leave without pay when call volume was slack. In some cases, they could take a week or month off. The policy was popular, but the union argued that employees should not take advantage of it because the company was just trying to figure out if it could carry out the same work with fewer employees. Because managers refused to communicate why they were adopting a certain policy, the union was mistrustful of their motives. Because many managers stopped meeting with local union leaders, they felt the only way to influence policies was to file expensive grievances.

At German Mobile, relations between labor and management were more cooperative, backed up by strong collective agreements. It was striking that the framework of rules from works agreements were much more restrictive than the relatively weak contract at U.S. Mobile, and yet managers perceived these as flexible rules they could live with. They implemented employment practices within these bounds. At the same time, the company was clearly trying to shift toward more individually focused evaluation, and similar to U.S. Mobile, managers used local negotiations to open up variation in policies.

Works councils at German Mobile had numerous forums for discussing and resolving issues at different levels of the company. Top management from each division prepared status reports for the central works council and formed working groups with worker representatives to resolve specific issues in areas like scheduling or monitoring.

> We try to find solutions to problems, to negotiate a solution ... that has paid off, we can usually quickly solve any problems that we have. Overall, we have a cooperative relationship—they're ready to work together with us,

to take us seriously. Also, they're afraid to cross us, because we are pretty strong. (Interview, works councilor, March 2004)

Strong codetermination rights meant the works councils were able to obstruct change in different areas and gave them tools to negotiate agreements on a range of issues, from detailed descriptions of when monitoring was allowed and when it was not to employee control over scheduling. Works council representatives also sat on German Mobile's Supervisory Board, which allowed them to have access to up-to-date information on corporate strategy.

One striking difference from U.S. Mobile was managers' attitude toward worker representatives. The way managers described relations with the works council was much more positive: "We have a high and open information exchange," "the relationship is productive and open," and "very cooperative and constructive." As at Deutsche Telekom, they were obligated to bargain on a wide variety of issues, which in turn meant it was in their interest to build trust:

> We have a very good relationship with our works council. It is a productive relationship. Codetermination laws mean that the works council has the ability to block something, which means that it's in our interest to bring the works council in the boat with us. On the one hand to make sure that we follow the law, but also so that the work climate and our relationship with one another isn't disturbed. Of course, sometimes we have different opinions and views and we discuss this, but that lies in the nature of the issues. A trusting relationship is important to build. When it is not there, the firm has problems, on both sides. We could spend years in court over every issue, but that is not in our interest. We want to develop concepts that are in the interest of the employees and the employer. (Interview, manager, July 2004)

The outcomes of bargaining were seen as good for the company, because they built in consistency and ensured there was a two-way communication about policy changes.

At the same time, German Mobile adopted this "high-road" strategy for internal employees while simultaneously increasing its use of call center subcontractors. These subcontractors then employed a lower-cost workforce and adopted a more flexible staffing strategy. Managers complained that scheduling restrictions made it difficult to react quickly to changes in call volume and relied on outsourcers to provide additional flexibility during call peaks. They were also able to experiment with more individual-based incentives and monitoring at subcontractors that their works councils did not let them use in-house. There were growing tensions across local works councils as the company increased its use of outsourcers and increased benchmarking across locations. Works councilors described "saving local jobs" as an important goal that had motivated some changes in formerly tough positions against monitoring. This meant that managers were able to negotiate local works agreements in several areas that were opening up variation and eroding some of the strong protections. Managers would try out new practices in one location and convince the local works council to sign an agreement, then roll it out at other locations if it was successful.

For example, one location agreed to individual-based evaluation of product knowledge. Previously all quality and knowledge checks were anonymous and reported at the group level. However, while quality checks (administered through an outside firm) were regulated through a general works agreement, tests of product knowledge were regulated through local works agreements. Management argued that individual knowledge tests would improve customer service and competitiveness, and succeeded in getting an agreement despite opposition from other works councils. The center manager explained, "We told our works council that they have the challenge to be the best works council in Germany, to motivate them to agree" (Interview, July 2004).

At another location, works councils agreed to "local calls," which allowed management to do their own quality checks, to benchmark results with the external firm. Employees were initially against the plan, but the local works council convinced them it would be in their interest "to secure the location." One works councilor described this as her biggest success, "because they were all against it, now they want to have it" (Interview, November 2004). In some cases, local works councilors were doing the local calls and evaluating employees. German Mobile's works councils were thus also under growing pressure to make concessions that opened up more local variation and changed the team-based focus of evaluation. However, these changes had nowhere near the negative effect on morale and commitment as the unilateral cost-cutting and management control strategy adopted by U.S. Mobile.

Established Subcontractors: Client Help USA
and Client Services Germany

In the four telecommunications cases described above, Germany's stronger codetermination institutions gave unions and works councils leverage in negotiations over work design and performance monitoring, while U.S. unions found their attempts at partnership undermined by consolidation, downsizing, and unilateral cost-cutting strategies. While representing two different sectors, all four cases were in-house workplaces in core firms. Companies in the growing call center subcontractor industry contract with these telecommunications firms and are under even more intense pressure to keep labor costs low and flexibility high. Their clients are more likely to outsource their transactional call center work, and they can easily shift work to another subcontractor if performance metrics slip. Moreover, collective bargaining is typically weaker or nonexistent. Employees in telecommunications firms are benchmarked against subcontractors, and so what happens in these companies matters a great deal for the ability of unions to hold the line on certain regulations in-house.

In this section, I compare human resource management strategies in two large call center subcontractors: Client Help USA and Client Services Germany. Both ranked in the top five in their respective national markets in terms of revenue and employment, and had expanded in other countries. They were established companies in the call center business and had grown rapidly in the past several years through mergers and acquisitions. Both also were outsourcing partners of major telecommunications firms. One important difference is that Client Services Germany had strong works councils and a union contract, while Client Help USA had no collective bargaining. However, Client Services Germany had no works councils or union agreement until the late 1990s, and so it is possible to describe changes in employment practices as the union and works councils became more established. The comparison here thus is structured differently than the previous two cases. Instead of analyzing differences in how collective bargaining affected management decisions in the two countries, I look at whether and how new bargaining institutions made a difference in the German case, relative to its own past practice and to employment practices in the nonunion U.S. case study.

Client Help USA

Client Help USA was a leader in the U.S. and international call center industry, with tens of thousands of employees worldwide. The company was organized in a number of "verticals" that serviced different industry segments, from simple catalogue orders to complex financial services and technical support. However, its largest clients and the largest proportion of its revenues came from the telecommunications and information services industries.

Client Help grew quickly in the late 1990s, as it merged with and bought out smaller call centers. As the company expanded and competition became more intense, top management tried to systematize human resource practices to take advantage of economies of scale and new technologies. Smaller centers were consolidated into sprawling campuses. In one of the larger locations, the company employed some three thousand agents in more than a dozen call centers. It networked its locations and set up new control systems to manage call routing and track agent availability and average handling time in a more systematic way. These centralized control centers then monitored adherence to targets and to service level agreements negotiated with clients that specified the percentage of calls to be answered in a certain amount of time. Client Help also purchased or designed new software to systematize monitoring and measurement. These systems in turn allowed the company to manage performance evaluation, scheduling, and adherence more consistently.

One manager observed that the company had lost its human touch somewhere along the line. "As we have evolved to be more technology driven, the metrics really drive a lot of what we do." The price was low morale, high absenteeism, and turnover rates of more than 100 percent. "The number one reason that employees leave is abandonment, they just don't show up. What that tells you is that there is nothing that connects them to this job—there's no relationship with those around me, no feeling that there would be a need to communicate that they're having a problem." Client Help invested in recruitment and training, sponsored competitions to build team spirit and was constantly inventing new ways to show appreciation of employees, from balloons to parties and prizes. However, these had only marginal effects. Most managers were resigned to leaning heavily on technology and discipline to keep costs low and to keep tight oversight and control over agent performance.

Communications, Inc.   Client Help provided widely diverging services to different clients, and so I focus here on one client-dedicated call center within the company. "Communications, Inc." is a large company in the telecommunications industry, and one of Client Help's largest clients. Several thousand Client Help agents worked for Communications, Inc. in multiple locations across the United States and offshore. The U.S. location that I visited employed more than one thousand agents on this account. Jobs were less complex than those in the telecommunications case studies, with a strong focus on inbound sales (based on customers responding to ad campaigns and calling into the center), but they involved similar tasks. Agents were broadly trained to handle up to sixteen different types of calls, from service and sales to more complex technical support, and could add on products and skills based on tenure. A special project team handled "niche" call volumes, such as second-level technical support. Although these jobs required a broad knowledge of constantly changing products, pay was low, starting at around $8 to $10 an hour and increasing to $14 an hour after seven years. In addition, most of the employees were very young. The majority had only a high school education, and managers estimated that 25 to 30 percent were college students. One manager explained that when someone asked her what she did for a living, she answered: "I facilitate the success of [thousands of] nineteen-year-olds" (Interview, March 2005).

Technology was pervasive in overseeing scheduling, adherence, and break times. Communications, Inc. complicated scheduling considerably when it decided to handle its own forecasting. Because these forecasts were often wrong, managers from Client Help had created their own system and tried to balance the two—sometimes in a rather ad hoc way. Client Help was also obligated to respond quickly to short-term changes in call forecasts by the client. For example, if Communications, Inc. launched a special campaign and failed to inform the Client Help managers or underestimated the call volume this would generate, Client Help had to scramble to find the extra employees, often with very short notice.

To get this flexibility, managers designed a staffing model that used two groups: fixed teams with standard shifts and days off and variable teams that had more unpredictable schedules. Employees were hired into one of the two groups (around 65 percent were in the fixed teams), and then were able to move every sixty days—so most of the new agent openings ended up being in variable teams. While there was some movement between teams, management tried to limit this: "We can't have them moving all the time, or they don't get developed. They don't understand this sometimes, but they need a mother or a father" (Interview, manager, March 2005). Around a third of employees were part time, and placed in dedicated "part-time teams" that provided additional flexibility. As shifts were staggered and space at a premium, the company also adopted "just in time seating" instead of dedicated workstations.

The business had seasonal peaks that created staffing challenges. During the busiest season, Client Help had to ramp up its Communications, Inc. workforce by around a thousand agents and put everyone on overtime. There were also smaller peaks, when managers would match variable teams and request some overtime. "All of our agents really have the expectation that if there are special needs we may ask them to reschedule" (Interview, manager, March 2005). Break times were likewise flexible and could be changed on short notice by management. While full-time employees had two regularly scheduled fifteen-minute breaks and a half hour for lunch, they were expected to stay on the phone to help clear up the queue or come back early if the availability started to slide.

The most striking aspect of management was how intensively employee performance was monitored and measured. All calls were recorded, and then regularly "graded" along a range of quality metrics like friendliness, how well the employee followed the script, how she greeted the customer, and so on. First, a team of quality evaluators graded employee calls across the company. The team leader could listen to the same calls and do her own evaluation, or listen to different calls (four per month). These results were entered in a database that agents were expected to regularly review, make note of areas they needed to work on, and then acknowledge on an online form that they had read and accepted their evaluation. The system also tracked how an agent's performance ranked relative to her peers on a range of metrics, like talk time and availability. This was designed to build a detailed database that tracked how the performance of each agent changed over time, freeing up the team leader to give more targeted coaching and feedback. Employees were expected to internalize the pressure to meet metrics, taking responsibility for monitoring their own adherence to goals. Team leaders would then regularly meet with the client's own quality monitoring team to do "calibration sessions."

The performance evaluation system also gave team leaders tools to track a variety of metrics in real time. This helped them to keep an (electronic) eye on their teams and look for any patterns in behavior that were suspicious. For example, one team leader pointed out that some agents played the "not ready game": if they regularly entered themselves as not ready, they were moved to the back of the queue and so they were less likely to get the calls that came in. When she saw something like this, she could pull up the individual's information, look at trends over time, and see if there was a pattern in the agent's behavior. In addition, a separate group in the "Command Center" monitored adherence and service level and communicated any deviations to team leaders:

> If a particular group is out of adherence by five percent, we start making calls to the managers—we ask what's happening, we figure out what the issues are and try to correct them. So we may see that these certain employees are away from their desk for too long or taking a long break and we inform them of this and the team leaders can start looking for them. (Interview, manager Command Center, March 2005)

The Command Center team dedicated to Communications, Inc. estimated that they made around seventy to a hundred calls per week to team leaders through this system.

If an employee was not meeting performance expectations, there was a process of review and progressive discipline ending in dismissal. This could mean consistently failing to meet metrics like talk time, without following through with recommended steps for improving; or more serious behaviors like committing fraud. However, as with most of the company's clients, the most common reasons for dismissal were tardiness and absenteeism. Managers said the greatest challenge was simply motivating employees to come to work every day.

Center managers tried out a number of strategies to improve morale. The company sponsored regular competitions "to keep things lively." These ran the gamut from quizzes on what the attendance was the day before to special sales promotions from the company. Client Help also tried to build team identification. Team leaders were held accountable for the performance of their teams, backed up by pay at risk. All team leaders were scheduled on the same flexible shifts as their employees, to make sure they were there to coach them and to reinforce tight accountability between the team leader and agents. One manager noted that this was not the policy in many other Client Help call centers, but she insisted on keeping it this way at Communications, Inc. "I think it's key that the team leader is with their team, that they are able to develop their team, that the team has someone they can go to, that there is a relationship, development, accountability" (Interview, March 2005).

Team leaders spoke about trying to build cohesiveness and team spirit. They would often sponsor competitions in their groups "to keep the energy up, to keep it fun." One regularly bought employees pizza or gifts out of her own pocket, or made special meals that she would bring in to reward them for good performance. She also tried to have at least one team activity outside of the workplace every quarter and invited them to her house, "to get to know each other better." This was all intended to sweeten the hard edge of constant monitoring and strengthen a kind of family bond in a huge organization:

> Usually employees want to know how they're doing—when they're good I make sure to thank them for that and they really appreciate it. I usually call them sweetie, and when I don't call one of them sweetie, they'll get concerned and ask, why didn't you call me sweetie today, did I make a mistake? (Interview, Team leader, March 2005)

Team leaders tended to be older, tenured employees, while their agents were on the whole seventeen and eighteen year olds, putting them very much into a parental role.

Not surprisingly, turnover was a huge problem, lingering stubbornly at over 100 percent and recently creeping up to 150 percent. Around 70 percent of this was voluntary. The company was able to get by with a core of more tenured employees, but managers were concerned with the expense of constant recruitment and training for over half of the workforce. Managers blamed poor forecasting for driving this up even more, as scheduling was one of the top three reasons for employee quits. However, Client Help was often not even able to survey employees on their reason for leaving, as 30 percent of turnover consisted of employees simply not showing up for work, with no explanation or notice. Managers and team leaders were trying out different strategies to improve these figures, like rearranging the schedules, trying to create more stability and predictable shifts. However, this had to happen within the framework of the client contract and persistently unpredictable call volume.

Although Client Help USA experienced a number of problems, the company was successful at winning and keeping business from Communications, Inc. The telecommunications company had several other contractors and its own smaller in-house workforce, but had chosen recently to expand Client Help's contract by two thousand agents. Client Help had settled on a competitive model that kept costs low, combining low pay, intensive monitoring, and lean scheduling. Management was experimenting around the edges with policies designed to generate team spirit and improve the working environment, but with limited success.

Client Services Germany

Client Services Germany looked on the surface quite similar to Client Help USA. The company had long been a market leader in Germany's booming call center services industry. It was one of the early telemarketing subcontractors in Germany and quickly grew in the late 1990s and early 2000s through mergers and buyouts. By the mid-2000s, Client Services operated multiple centers in domestic and international locations, with several thousand employees.

However, unlike Client Help USA, Client Services Germany had a works council and a collective agreement. In the late 1990s, after a decade of operating with no collective bargaining, employees successfully organized works council elections, set up general and group-level works councils, and cooperated with ver.di to negotiate a collective agreement. This led to a sharp divergence in the policies adopted by the two companies: while Client Help USA moved toward more pervasive monitoring and measurement, Client Services Germany worked through codetermination to improve predictability and employee discretion.

Client Services' human resource and work design practices changed substantially over time, often driven by client demands as they benchmarked Client Services' performance with other subcontractors and their own internal operations. Many of its clients had accounts with other multinational subcontractors that had either no collective representation or weaker, more poorly coordinated works councils. Clients were closely involved in monitoring and setting performance goals, which changed frequently. Across client accounts, managers met often to discuss performance targets. This demand for flexibility translated into pressure for constant innovation. While client turnover was still relatively low, the threat of losing a contract or losing some portion of a client's business to a competitor was always present. At the same time, Client Services had to respond quickly to changing call volume. Management needed to be prepared to bring in employees to work extra shifts or move employees from other contracts when there were call spikes. Together, this created pressure to keep labor costs low and scheduling lean.

Labor negotiations came to play a more central role as the works councils, supported by the union, sought to move Client Services to more collective regulation of management practices while accommodating diverse, client-driven policies. The outcome was an often uneasy balance between a highly flexible and low-cost service model and new rules that sought to improve job stability, employee discretion, and procedural justice.

Telecom, Etc.   Again, practices varied within Client Services Germany across clients and centers. Because no one client account was as large as Communications, Inc., at Client Help USA, I focus here on one of Client Services' business units that specialized in telecommunications, which I call "Telecom, Etc." Telecom, Etc. had two major call center locations, one in East Germany and the other in West Germany, with close to five hundred employees in each. These had contracts with several major fixed network and wireless telecommunications firms for jobs that ranged from simple directory assistance and outbound telesales to more complex service and sales and technical support. Employees were organized in teams dedicated to a client, although they were sometimes shifted between clients based on need.

Client Services typically trained employees to handle all calls within a client group, and in some cases moved agents between inbound and outbound. The West German location had a much younger workforce, with a large number of university students, while the East German location's employees were older and came from a variety of backgrounds. Fewer employees had the standard *Kaufmann* occupational training compared to the other two German cases described above, although overall education level and experience were higher than in Client Help USA's mostly high school–educated workforce.

Scheduling policies were a major strategic focus for the works councils. Call center subcontractors view scheduling flexibility as their main source of competitive advantage, and works councils have strong codetermination rights over schedules and working time; and so this is an important source of bargaining leverage. At the same time, the works councils were aware (and management continually reinforced the message) that Client Services would not be able to keep work if they raised labor costs and reduced flexibility.

> Our clients only use subcontractors because we can be more flexible. There is no other reason. But sometimes it is difficult to convince the works councils that flexibility is the reason why there are subcontractors. Our condition for [the union] coming in here in the first place was that we would be able to keep this flexibility—otherwise, we wouldn't be able to survive (Interview, manager, June 2004).

Call center managers used two main tools to adjust employment levels to respond to changes in call volume: the design of employee contracts and flexible working time practices. Until 1999, Client Services hired most of its employees as independent contractors, exempting them from making additional social welfare payments and from the legal restrictions of permanent contracts. This gave managers the flexibility to adjust employment quickly. They would send employees home without pay when call volume was low, sometimes for months at a time, and ask them to work extra hours, or hire additional contractors on a short-term basis, when volume was high. At the same time, individuals had a great deal of autonomy over whether they would come in to work or not.

This practice was part of a broader trend, as employers took advantage of a loophole in the law that allowed them to avoid permanent contracts. A coalition of unions and SPD politicians changed the law in 1998, arguing that this practice was undermining employer contributions to the social welfare system. This meant that Client Services was obligated to move its independent contractors to either short-term or permanent contracts.

The uncertainty and discussion surrounding the change in contract status led to the works council organizing drive at Client Services, and the successful election of works councils ensured that they could participate in designing a new model. Within a year, most of the workforce transitioned to permanent contracts. However, management retained the right to adjust working hours. Because employees in many accounts were paid based on the hours they worked and commission pay, their income continued to fluctuate over the year. This income instability was a key concern that the union and central works council sought to address in collective bargaining. They eventually agreed on a plan that set up working time accounts and stable base pay, though managers were uncertain whether the new system represented a positive change.

> On both the employee and employer side, suddenly everything is less flexible than it was before. Because you have to always pay attention to your working time account, when the availability is good enough so that the employees could go home, they don't always want to go home because then their account will build up minus hours. The employee would like to go, but also feel like they can't. It's another form of flexibility: the system is still flexible—you build up hours, then you work them later. But it's not as flexible as it was before. When there was not much going on, the employees were happy to go home. Now it's somehow, they feel: if I go home now, I'll have to work more later—so, the flexibility has already become lower. (Production Manager, July 2004)

Employees voiced similar concerns. While they were able to enjoy a stable salary over the year, they were unsure how much control they would have over their own working time. One works councilor pointed out that even though in theory individuals should be able to ask for time off once they had built up "plus" hours, at busy times of the year supervisors would pressure them to stay. This tension was particularly apparent in the West, where many employees were accustomed to a highly individualized form of negotiated external flexibility. The works councils would fight over implementation issues with managers every month in a meeting to evaluate the working time accounts and tried to provide oversight with team leaders to make sure they were balancing their accounts. Control over working time thus continued to be a struggle, but with ongoing works council input and oversight.

While the new working time accounts required close coordination between the works council and management, scheduling remained much more flexible at Client Services than at most German in-house centers. Managers had a great deal of discretion over employment levels. At Telecom, Etc., center managers tried to be creative by shifting employees between outbound and inbound, or moving them to another part of the business when volume dropped in one client account. Team leaders often negotiated flexible working time with individuals:

> You have to know your own people, how many hours can they work, when can they not work. You have to look at, how flexible can the individual employee be? Some are able to work sixty hours one week and twenty hours another week: these are the people who support the flexibility here. Some have children, and can only work a maximum of one hour later. (Center Manager, February 2004)

At the same time, employees had some control over when they worked and could negotiate changes in schedules with supervisors and their co-workers. Managers set shifts two to three weeks in advance and could change them with up to four days notice.

Scheduling varied across accounts. Shifts were fixed where call volume was more predictable, such as in directory assistance, but could change from week to week for clients with more variation in forecasts. This balance between manager discretion to move employees between jobs or ask them to go home and employees' ability to choose when they would work required considerable communication. While the works council saw its job as improving consistency and transparency, managers still had broad discretion to respond to changing volume in an ad hoc way. At the same time, schedules were not as erratic as at Client Help USA, and employees often had a great deal of control over which shifts they worked.

Break times also affected scheduling flexibility. Another holdover from Client Services' earlier policies was that there were often no fixed breaks: team leaders gave employees permission to leave their desks, based on call volume and service levels. One team leader pointed out that agents knew that there were days when the call volume was bad and it would be difficult to leave their computers. The works councils worked to increase rights to scheduled break time, arguing that because call centers are

Bildschirmarbeitsplätze, or workplaces involving computer screen work, the employer was legally obligated to provide employees with a break every hour. In 2002, the central works council negotiated an agreement that included new rules allowing five minutes off every hour, which was often taken as ten minutes every two hours.

The works councils also saw reducing absenteeism as an area where they could help to cut costs while encouraging investment in health and work climate. In the East German call center, Telecom, Etc.'s works council initiated a partnership with the company's health insurance provider, a local university, and managers to improve ergonomics and employee diet while reducing burnout. As at German Mobile, *Krankenrückkehrgespräche* were introduced to discourage absenteeism, in which the coach would meet with employees when they returned to work to discuss any issues they might have. The works councils also argued that the shift to working time accounts and fixed contracts improved morale and reduced absenteeism. Between 1999 and 2004, absenteeism rates had gone down from 15 percent to around 6 percent at both the East and West German locations.

Performance management strategies focused more on individual metrics than at the other German case studies, but gave agents more discretion and protection from dismissal than at Client Help USA. Client demands drove the metrics used to measure performance, while works agreements regulated how evaluations were carried out and used. Before the works councils were introduced, team leaders monitored and evaluated individual agents. Some of this structure stayed in place in the older West German call center, despite ongoing opposition from the works councils, including a complicated system of commission and variable pay. Employees received two-thirds of their pay in a fixed salary of €6.40 per hour, and then were paid bonuses based on the number of calls completed in an hour, along with additional individual bonuses in sales accounts. On average, employees earned around €10 an hour. The company did not initially transfer this system to the East German location, where agents had a fixed base pay of around €7 an hour. However, the local works council in the East negotiated an additional sales commission for some clients and small individual and team bonuses.

Performance-based pay was another area where there was some conflict between collective regulation and flexibility. This was a particularly contentious issue for a group in the West German center that handled catalogue orders, where premiums differed based on the type of customer. This was a holdover from the older system where employees were treated more as highly flexible contractors. Each client had a different pay rate, and the account supervisor had some control over who was trained to handle which clients, as well as how the calls were distributed among agents daily. Employees felt this was used as a source of pressure and discipline. The works council wanted to adopt a higher fixed wage, as in the East German call centers, but encountered a great deal of resistance.

> There are concerns with employees who feel they're being discriminated against because they are not trained for the higher paying projects. Then, even though you are trained in the higher paying project, your neighbor is getting sent all of the higher paying calls, and you are getting lower paying calls. That's a problem, because employees are dependent on the project leader. The works council can say: we don't have codetermination rights for how much money is divided, but we have the right to help decide how it's divided. We say that this project-based calculation is not good for the employees, and we would rather have another system. That, of course, is sacrosanct: the pope would sooner go in a bordello than [Client Services] would change the system. (Interview, works councilor, February 2004)

Works councilors realized that because the current system was shifting some of the risk to employees, a fixed model would probably reduce the overall pay level. The works council would also have to be given more access to client contracts to negotiate a new system that stayed within contractual and cost constraints.

Management reserved the right to design these variable compensation policies, which it negotiated with clients. However, the works councils could influence the details. For example, a works agreement mandated that at least 30 percent of agents in a project had to be able to meet the goals, and prevented "quotas" that could be used to dismiss or punish employees.

Team-based evaluations had also become more important as the works councils began to regulate individual monitoring. Telecom, Inc. did mystery calls and called customers to ask them to evaluate their calls. On the inbound hotlines, they would average three hundred mystery calls out of eighty thousand calls per month. In addition, many clients did their own mystery calls, typically through another third-party subcontractor. As at

Deutsche Telekom and German Mobile, the works agreement stated that all scores had to be aggregated for groups of five or more and could not be used to fire employees. Teams had sales goals, and when they reached the goal they would get an additional group bonus. In 2004, the group works council negotiated a new four-year agreement that imposed stricter limits. Team leaders could not use coaching to evaluate or discipline individual employees, and remote electronic monitoring was not allowed for any purpose. Before the agreement, managers would often dismiss agents for performance reasons:

> In the [Client Services] world, they were firing employees with the help of mystery calls and monitoring technology. But we disagreed with this, because it was usually based on a *Nasenentscheidung* [gut feeling]: if the employee sounds competent on the telephone or unfriendly. But no one can really evaluate that way. (Interview, works councilor, June 2005)

A more recent challenge was maintaining strict rules against electronic monitoring across the company when these conflicted with client demands. One telecommunications client required voice recordings for a new outbound project, and the works councils were willing to agree to an exception, negotiating a separate works agreement to regulate how Client Services used this data. Another long-time client was rolling out a new monitoring system that would record every key stroke and conversation, and threatened to withdraw the contract with Client Services if the works councils did not agree. Once again, they negotiated a separate agreement that tried to accommodate the client's demands:

> They told [Client Services], when you have problems with the works council, then you don't have the work. Which is a problem for us. We said, let's find a solution. The goal in negotiations is that there will be no consequences for performance monitoring....However, this creates pressure. It's a negotiation, they know that without the works council, they can't do it. But for us it's difficult, because we know that if we don't agree, the work won't be there....One has to meet in the middle, but it's always getting more difficult. (Interview, works councilor, June 2005)

As in the other cases, teams had also become more important. Managers described teams as critical for creating a bond between the employee and the company, and tried to support this in different ways, with Christmas parties and team competitions. However, unlike Client Help USA, Client Services Germany set aside paid time for regular team meetings, which center managers seemed to think were excessive but enormously effective for "blowing off steam," building team spirit, and communicating goals.

Coaching and discipline had a strong individual component, but again the works councils tried to build in more consistency and fairness. Every employee was coached once a month, which involved side-by-side listening and feedback by the supervisor. Then they negotiated goals for the next month, including any training and coaching needed. A major goal of the works councils was to encourage Client Services Germany to focus on "soft" motivation and upgrading skills.

> Team leaders tend to say, you did that well, you did that badly, period. We say, there is a need for training....It was about telling the firm: you have invested so much money in the employees, so you shouldn't fire them. Instead, we encourage them to train them—offer more seminars, do more for them. (Interview, works councilor, November 2003)

Managers complained that it was nearly impossible to fire an employee based on poor performance or service quality because all dismissals had to be agreed on with the works councils. However, if they could prove that they had already tried to train and coach the individual with no improvement, they could eventually get the works councils "in the boat" with them. Works councilors also acted as intermediaries, explaining the importance of meeting quotas and performance targets when an agent consistently fell behind.

The works councils attempted to redefine poor scores as a training quality problem by performing their own mystery calls. They demonstrated that low scores were not the result of individual motivation problems, but instead common knowledge shortfalls. They then used this to argue that managers were not keeping skills up to date. There was some controversy over whether this was the right strategy for worker representatives, who were in the awkward position of monitoring their own members. However, works councilors argued that they then successfully used this in negotiations to get more funds dedicated to training.

The works councils at Client Services Germany were thus able to improve working conditions and promote a more high-involvement

employment model with union support, even in this highly price competitive industry. Employees at Client Services had lower job security,
pay, and discretion than those at Deutsche Telekom or German Mobile.
The prospects for making substantial improvements in these areas were
limited, as the company was forced to compete with other third-party
firms that did not have works councils or collective agreements. Nonetheless, there was a clear trend to increased regulation within these limits,
as works councils learned to use their codetermination rights to improve
job stability and employee discretion. More basically, the works councils played an important role in ensuring the company was following
labor laws:

> We have taken the company to court several times, and we always win, be-
> cause we do our work ahead of time to make sure we're following the law.
> Otherwise we lose credibility. Now they know, when we say something is
> not legal, they know we're right. We had to go to court a few times at first,
> but not any more: now the trust is there, the understanding is there. (Inter-
> view, works councilor, February 2004)

Managers also saw some benefit in the relationship. Greater consistency
improved employee morale and reduced absenteeism and turnover, while
managers could more easily communicate with the workforce through one
contact point. The works councils took credit for reducing turnover from
130 percent in 1999 to 28 percent in 2004 in the West German location.
In the East German location, turnover was extremely low, at 3 percent.
Managers fired on average only one or two employees a year, and to be
dismissed they had to commit fraud or abuse a customer.

At the same time, management was under growing pressures to reduce
labor costs.

> Productivity always has to be better. That wasn't the case here before. Now
> employees feel the pressure. That projects will not be here forever. That
> you have to be ready to change projects quickly. That you always have to
> be alert. That you have to be trained every day. The team coach will come
> and say: you have only made one sale, you need three. We need to keep cus-
> tomers because we have to employ the people. [Client Services] knows this.
> (Interview, works councilor, June 2005)

One of the most difficult challenges for the works councils was maintaining the solidarity necessary for coordinated strategies in the face of this pressure. Client Services had multiple locations and different businesses within locations—some of which shared clients and calls. This meant that works councils were spread out across Germany and were often competing with one another for work. While management sought to create a common culture within the firm, it was still in many ways a fragmented company with different working conditions and worker interests.

The most obvious divisions in the works councils were between the older West German call centers and the newer centers established in the last five or six years. Employees in the major East German location tended to be older and more stable due to high unemployment, while the major West German location had a younger workforce dominated by students. The number of jobs in the West was also cut shortly after the new location was opened, and the lower labor costs and generous subsidies provided a strong incentive to continue to move new contracts to the East. This gave works councils in the West an additional incentive to cooperate with management:

> Management wanted to move more to taking outbound calls, but the employees were not too enthusiastic, so they needed to convince them to move to doing more outbound work. We worked together with the employer to argue that it made sense for them. Or when too few employees are there in evening, we might go and say, think about it, maybe you can work then. It is not to help the employer, but to help the employee or to secure the location. When they can't serve the customers on Saturday, then those calls go to [the East German location]. The people understand that: the fear that [the East German location] will always get more work. (Interview, works councilor, February 2004)
>
> There's the issue of competition between locations that are doing the same work. In the West we've always been more creative in using our *Mitbestimmungsrecht* (codetermination rights), in the East they're still in the dark about how to do this. It's really true. When we have an idea for something that would improve working conditions, then we may give the East an advantage. The tendency is already to move work to the East, so we just further disadvantage ourselves. (Interview, works councilor, February 2004)

These tensions came to a head in 2004 when the East German works council negotiated a separate job security agreement that only applied to their workforce. Ver.di helped with negotiations, based on the logic that these centers were under the most immediate danger of job cuts. In return, employees would work an additional twenty-five hours a year without pay, during which time the employer would have to offer training and qualification.

At the same time, the EU subsidies ran out in 2004, reducing the eastern location's cost advantage. Around that time, Client Services opened a new call center with three hundred agents on the Polish border. It was originally set up to handle calls from truckers who needed assistance paying tolls collected under a new government program. The company established a new subsidiary and again received EU subsidies for the jobs. However, the toll collection system worked unexpectedly well and the calls never materialized. After several months, Client Services had to discontinue the service and started to move some work from its other locations to the new call center. The works councils were not very well informed throughout this process. They did not know about the decision to build the new center until shortly before the company broke ground and had no influence over the movement of work. At the same time, they were helping to set up works councils at the new location and trying to integrate them into the group works council, with ver.di's help.

Despite these challenges, Client Services was widely perceived by ver.di as a model. Growing trust across the works councils created a strong basis for joint work. The 2002 agreement on breaks from the computer screen required solidarity in the face of management resistance, and works councils were generally willing to put aside differences to try to improve working conditions across locations. Ver.di was involved at many levels in supporting the works councils and helping them to coordinate strategies. Works councilors relied on legal support from the union to bring individual complaints before the labor court and sought to recruit union members to support these services and build bargaining leverage. Client Services had a membership rate of around 30 percent, which was low compared to traditional union strongholds like Deutsche Telekom, but quite high for the industry. The combination of a strong union presence and works councils made Client Services an exceptional case of coordinated regulation at firm level, though lacking the support of a binding agreement for the industry as a whole.

Comparison

Client Help USA and Client Services Germany were in many ways similar organizations. Each was an established multinational corporation with a large share of the third-party call center market in their respective countries. Both firms competed in the same markets and secured clients based on their lower labor costs, greater flexibility in responding to fluctuating call volume, and targeted industry expertise. In addition, they both employed university students, and firm-based training investments were similar.

Despite these similarities, Client Services Germany and Client Help USA adopted different human resource management approaches, summarized in table 3.4. Client Help relied on erratic scheduling to meet lean staffing goals and intense performance monitoring to ensure compliance with rules, while making the best of a high-turnover work force. Client Services moved toward greater stability and broader agent discretion, adopting a mixed model that incorporated some degree of employee stability, autonomy, and voice with low pay and intense working conditions.

The different model adopted by Client Services Germany can be directly traced to a series of negotiated compromises between management and the company's new works councils. Client Services' collective and works agreements were relatively weak compared to those at Deutsche Telekom or even German Mobile. There was no agreement on pay at the time of my site visits, there was substantial variation in evaluation and pay practices, and scheduling flexibility was still largely under management control.

At the same time, the company had changed many of its human resource policies to improve consistency and employment stability. Strong German labor laws and union support made it possible to establish a coordinated works council presence. The bargaining power of the works councils had grown as representatives from the different call centers gained experience and expertise in German labor law, established a central works council, and negotiated both establishment-level and corporate-level collective agreements. The relationship with management was not without problems, and the relationship across works councils was still fragile. However, worker representatives clearly had some success in moving toward stronger regulation in one of the most price-competitive sectors.

TABLE 3.4 Employment systems at Client Help USA and Client Services Germany

	Client Help USA Communications, Inc.	Client Services Germany Telecom, Etc.
Staffing and skill		
Typical tenure	• < 1 year	• 2–3 years
Typical ed. level	• High school and university students	• University students (west); mixed vocational training (east)
Initial training	• 2 weeks	• 2–4 weeks
Scheduling		
% part time	• 30%; dedicated part time teams	• 40% (west); 50% (east)
Scheduling	• Fixed teams with standard shifts and variable teams with unpredictable schedules; scheduled breaks • Peaks handled through variable teams, voluntary overtime, and turnover	• Fixed or variable shifts differed across clients; some flexibility negotiated between agents and team leaders • Peaks handled through working time accounts, but with limited agent discretion
Work design		
Breadth of skills	• Separate teams for complex technical support work; most agents trained to answer different call types	• Agents trained to answer different call types
Use of teams	• Limited use of teams for competitions and "building spirit" • No paid meeting time	• Strong use of teams for motivating agents, training, and communicating new policies • Paid time for regular team meetings
Compensation		
Av. base pay	• $8–$14 fixed	• $7.50 fixed ($12 w/ variable) (west); $8.30 fixed (east)
Variable pay	• No pay at risk; small prizes and bonuses determined by client	• Average 30% pay at risk (west); recent introduction of small bonuses in east
Worker rep. influence	• None	• Some works council oversight in design of performance pay and targets
Coaching		
Basis for coaching	• Weekly coaching based on individual performance data	• Monthly coaching, with side-by-side listening and feedback and negotiated goals
Discipline	• Steps leading to dismissal if employee does not meet targets	• Focus on coaching and development, with almost no dismissals for poor performance
Monitoring		
Electronic	• Continuous individual monitoring	• No individual monitoring; negotiated limits on how electronic data is used
Other	• Agent receives frequent electronic updates on performance metrics	• Mystery calls aggregated to the team level and could not be used for discipline
Outcomes		
Absenteeism	15–20%	6%
Turnover	100–150%	28% (west); 3% (east)

Multinational Subcontractor: U.S. Vendotel
and German Vendotel

My final two case studies are the U.S. and German subsidiaries of a multi-national call center subcontractor, which I call here "Vendotel." Vendotel was first established in the United States as a small technical support company in the early 1990s and grew through a series of mergers and acquisitions. By 2003, the company had a global presence, with call centers in more than ten countries across North America, Europe, and Asia. Vendotel also did not have a collective agreement with a union or works council in either the United States or Germany. Thus, compared to the other case studies, it had the fewest formal constraints on management while competing in the most price-conscious segment of the industry.

U.S. Vendotel

I visited one of Vendotel's oldest locations in the United States, with around seven hundred employees who served several clients in dedicated offices. The center was primarily inbound, and roughly half of the agents were in customer service and sales positions while the other half provided technical support. The two largest clients at this location were a multinational information technology firm and a telecommunications firm (which also had a contract with Vendotel's German centers). The customer service positions involved entering information from customers who had just purchased a new product in a database or taking orders for inbound sales. Technical support ranged from helping customers set up home electronics equipment to more complex software support that required some computer science background. Employees were young, and Vendotel relied heavily on community and technical colleges for new recruits.

Scheduling flexibility was a challenge, typical of the industry. Contracts with clients required managers to staff up or down at short notice:

> It can be a pretty intense job in that, you know, if your client bought advertising the night before it's going to run because ABC is running half price because they don't have the commercials lined up, they call you up and tell you that they're running advertising during prime time television, that means obviously you're going to get ten thousand calls at 7:00 tomorrow, so you have to adjust: get all those people in there, and let them know that

there's this ad campaign, this is what they're advertising, be ready, so it's a very intense environment. (Interview, manager, June 2002)

Employees were hired based on their ability to work different shifts and required to have fifty to sixty hours of availability a week. Managers set schedules a week in advance, and then often required agents to work extra hours or go home early based on changes in call volume. It was common to call them at the last minute to come in and help out during an unexpected spike in calls within their "availability window." In addition, all new employees were hired into part-time positions, and then after ninety days were eligible to move to full time based on their interest and average hours worked. Absenteeism often ran between 10 and 15 percent, and so managers regularly overstaffed to make sure service levels did not fall below contractual limits.

Seasonal fluctuations in call volume also created staffing challenges. Because of high turnover, managers were able to hire during busy months and then let attrition take its course. At times they would bring in temps and then transition them to permanent positions, but tended to avoid this because training investments were expensive.

The performance management strategy at U.S. Vendotel was similar to that at Client Help USA. Pay ranged from $7.50 an hour starting salary for simple service jobs to $15 to $20 an hour for the most complex support work. Managers admitted that the pay was low for the local labor market, which made recruitment difficult—particularly for technical support jobs, many of which started at $9 an hour. In addition, clients funded a range of variable pay programs, such as retention bonuses or incentives for high customer satisfaction scores.

Performance evaluation was based on individual outcomes. Coaching occurred through meetings between the agent and her supervisor, and there was no real team structure. Electronic monitoring was continuous, and clients listened in on calls during weekly calibration sessions. One manager described meeting with a client who made a point about poor service quality by dialing in to the remote monitoring line on his mobile phone. Performance stats were fed continuously to agents, and agents were put on progressive discipline leading to dismissal when they performed poorly on talk times or quality scores.

A number of managers at this location had been with the company for years and had observed the changes in Vendotel as it expanded from a local to an international operation. Initially, headquarters was located down the street. If quality began to slide or they were unable to meet call volume, top management would get involved in changing targets or tweaking pay levels. The company also initially invested heavily in agent training and retention, which helped Vendotel to develop a reputation for high-quality service and to attract large accounts from several high-profile clients.

As the company expanded, this focus changed. Headquarters was moved to another city, and management began to benchmark performance across the national network of centers. In the late 1990s, Vendotel centralized its call forecasting and performance tracking in a global operations center. The organization also became more numbers driven as it developed sophisticated measures for talk times and adherence to schedule. "When they started, they were more entrepreneurial, now they're standardized" (Interview, manager, October 2002). This shift away from a quality focus initially drove down costs but also led to declining morale and growing turnover. By the early 2000s, the company began to lose clients.

> We used to see attrition as a good thing. That was how backwards we were in our thinking. Less tenure was associated with more time on the phone. Seems like that should be bad, right? But no: we were compensated by our clients based on the time it was taking to resolve these calls, so we had an incentive to keep those people on the line. The problem was, this was about money for the moment. They didn't think long term; realize that the client can fire you and hire another firm that will keep their costs down. (Interview, HR Director, July 2003)

Vendotel's board of directors realized the company was starting to suffer from poor quality, and in 2002 they fired the CEO and brought in a new human resource director who attempted to shift the focus of the organization toward, in his words, "investing in our people." The new director led an initiative to improve training and agent retention. He described this as a necessary shift in the culture of the organization away from a focus on numbers and discipline and toward empowerment:

> We need to try to give our employees the tools to provide good customer service. Empower them to a degree: I don't mean democracy or anything like that, we can't create a free-for-all. However, we need to solicit input to the extent possible, make sure employees feel that their voice matters, that they

are heard. Rather than just getting them in the door and working them as hard as we can until they quit. (Interview, HR Director, July 2003)

Vendotel also used the Customer Operations Performance Center (COPC) quality certification program to improve measurement and reporting of service quality. COPC is a standard similar to ISO 9000 that was designed for the call center industry and is run by a third-party consulting firm. To meet the standard, centers were required to adopt standard measurement and reporting systems, and to achieve staged goals in areas like reducing attrition and absenteeism and improving employee satisfaction. However, at the same time that the company was trying to shift away from a narrow focus on numbers, the industry was becoming more cost competitive. Clients expected quality to improve but also demanded lower prices, stricter service level agreements, and more flexible contracts.

Local managers at the Vendotel site I visited felt this attempt at a "culture shift" was difficult to implement, given the tight profit margins and need to remain responsive to multiple clients and corporate headquarters. Turnover continued to fluctuate between 80 and 100 percent, around 70 percent of which was from employees who quit. Local managers had adopted several strategies to try to deal with this, in the framework of the broader corporate initiative to invest more in employees.

First, they put in place a scheduling tool that helped make shift planning more predictable. Second, they changed their training strategy to give new recruits more support during their first weeks on the job. Agents were initially put on the floor after two weeks of training, and many were leaving shortly after they started. With the new system, new recruits were placed in a special room with additional supervisor support for the first few weeks after being trained. Third, Vendotel was building a new career path initiative, which trained agents to move to more lucrative accounts, particularly in technical support areas. Managers also tried creating a more formal "map" of progression steps, with additional training at each step.

These changes made a small dent in turnover rates and improved service quality ratings, but did not reduce labor costs. At the same time, Vendotel opened several offshore calls centers in India, Mexico, and Canada. The first Indian center was set up around the time I started my research, in 2002, and over the next few years it took over more of the technical support jobs and all of the written work, such as e-mail and fax. By 2004, the U.S.

center I visited had shrunk to around one-fourth of its peak employment as work was shifted to India and Canada. One of its major clients decided to move all of its work to the company's Indian location by the end of the year, and shortly thereafter the center closed.

German Vendotel

Vendotel expanded into Germany in the late 1990s through buying out two smaller German companies. It continued to operate both locations, although managers in headquarters had serious misgivings about the additional trouble and expense of operating call centers in Europe. The human resource director in the United States described the biggest challenges as fixed contracts and lack of flexibility:

> There are a lot of differences, some of them subtle, some more obvious. The biggest one is the employment agreement we have to enter into with employees there....Here it is employment at will, and so if an employee doesn't work out, we can fire him or her. There, we have to take on a lot of responsibility for the employee once we hire them on a permanent basis, so we need to find ways around these rules....Otherwise, it's like a contract for life, and you put yourself at risk, because in this business there are major fluctuations: what if you lose a client, and then you're stuck with all of those employees? Germany is the worst. We've talked about getting out of there a number of times, because they are so employer unfriendly. But hopefully that is changing. (Interview, HR director, July 2003)

Despite these differences in the U.S. and German regulatory environment, Vendotel had been successful in adopting a common set of practices across the organization. Several layers of management were dedicated to coordinating strategies and "aligning metrics" in the company's European call centers. The German Vendotel human resource managers I interviewed referred often to the six basic Vendotel principles that hung throughout the centers and talked enthusiastically about communicating the company's vision to employees.

While local managers felt there were unique management challenges in Germany, most of the employment practices and outcomes were consistent across locations—although, again, many of these were driven by different client demands. Most of Vendotel's clients were multinational firms that contracted with the subcontractor to service their customers in North America and Europe. This led to intensive benchmarking and communication across "account groups." Vendotel Germany had also recently joined the COPC certification program. This was driving more standardization, and managers were convinced the certification process had had a huge effect on quality.

I visited both of Vendotel's German locations. Each had around 150 employees who serviced several client accounts in dedicated offices, compared to 700 at the U.S. site. One location had several small groups that provided technical support for telecommunications and IT companies, and one large group of close to 100 agents who handled catalogue orders for different clients. The second location had three teams with roughly the same number of agents who handled inbound and outbound sales and provided technical support.

Skill levels varied across these groups. Catalogue orders required the lowest skill level, while the technical support jobs required more specialized training. Catalogue orders also had the most variable call volume, with sharp peaks around holidays, and was more difficult to forecast from week to week due to multiple clients and unpredictable advertising. This had some effect on staffing strategy—for example, around half of the agents in catalogue orders worked in "mini-jobs," a special category of part-time work where employees make €400 or less a month and employers are excused from making social security contributions. Only a minority of agents in both call centers held full-time positions. Agents came from a variety of backgrounds: one account employed almost exclusively teenagers with the equivalent of a high school education, another exclusively travel agents with three years of occupational training.

Schedules were planned with the same software used in the United States, which gave agents limited choice over when they worked. Managers assigned shifts a week ahead of time, but again typical of the industry, they often had problems with unpredictable fluctuations in call volume. There was no working time account, and so when volume peaked the company would try to get agents to come in on their days off or require them to work overtime, while sending them home when volume declined. "Agents must be flexible. They come here knowing this, and learn that some months there is more work, some less" (Interview, manager, June 2004). In addition, around 30 percent of employees were on short-term contracts. The company's policy was to hire all new employees on these contracts for a year, and then move only high-performing agents onto permanent contracts. This also gave managers flexibility to staff up or down, although they had to plan these changes at least a year in advance.

The company had been moving to more lean scheduling practices, which meant increasing the number of part-time agents and putting in place stricter rules. Agents were expected to adhere to fifteen-minute breaks and risked losing a portion of their performance premium if they were "out of compliance." Employees who had held on to their old contracts were able to take more frequent breaks and enjoyed more choice over when they took them—again, a holdover from the German companies Vendotel had bought out. This led to some resentment between groups, and managers complained that Germany's rigid regulatory environment was preventing them from implementing a more consistent policy.

Absenteeism was a more important issue than in the company's U.S. locations because German regulations required paid sick days. This meant local managers put a big emphasis on keeping absences low and would often dismiss employees during their six-month probationary period if there were any attendance issues. They also had adopted *Krankenrückkehrgespräche,* or individual meetings with employees to discuss the reasons they were out sick. As a result of these efforts, absenteeism was lower in Germany than in any other Vendotel location, typically fluctuating between 5 and 10 percent.

Pay was similar across clients, averaging €10.60 per hour, with a range from €7 to €15. Between 20 to 30 percent of pay was "at risk" (depending on the client) and was based solely on individual performance. The outbound sales group had additional quotas and commission pay. These incentives had been put in place under Vendotel and applied primarily to agents who had been hired within the past couple of years, as many of the older employees held on to their old fixed salary contracts.

Team communication and building "team spirit" were more important for coaching at German Vendotel than in the U.S. call center I visited. However, this was not connected to team-based competitions or rewards. Regular team meetings and team breakfasts instead gave agents the opportunity to "blow off steam" and get to know each other. Most coaching was one on one, although there was some attempt to create partnerships between senior agents and new recruits within teams. Agents were also very young—many were students—while supervisors tended to be older employees who had been with the organization for a number of years. One team leader observed, "It is important that someone leads the team who on the private level can be a little motherly, but stern" (Interview, June 2004).

Vendotel had recently implemented routine remote or silent monitoring. Under German management, remote monitoring was not used due to data protection laws, which in theory prohibited recording customer calls or employee conversations. However, U.S.-based subcontractors often got around this by informing customers that their calls would be recorded for quality purposes and by requiring new employees to sign consent forms. This made it easier for multinational clients to develop standardized quality measures and to oversee remote "calibration sessions" of calls across European sites. Employees had been unhappy about the new system when it was first adopted, but had no say in the design or implementation.

German Vendotel had also put in place a new system for evaluating performance. A large proportion of pay was determined by quality scores, and managers were concerned that agents would not view these scores as objective if they were based solely on supervisor ratings. A group of four evaluators met regularly for their own "calibration sessions," in which they listened to five to six calls per employee and graded them in around twenty different areas, such as friendliness, content, active engagement with the customer, use of the customer's name, correct end to the conversation, and so on. The evaluators then discussed their grading for each area and came up with an overall "agent score," which was later discussed between the supervisor and agent, along with strategies for improvement.

Before Vendotel took over, turnover (primarily made up of employees who quit) had been 30 to 50 percent at both locations. One manager quipped, "We used to say that once an employee was here for half a year it made sense to learn their name. With others it didn't pay to try to learn their names because they were likely to be gone the next month" (Interview, June 2004). Under Vendotel management, this had been driven down to around 15 percent, which managers attributed to the stronger focus on service quality, more consistency in employee evaluation and supervisor training, and better selection tools. At the same time, this figure did not include employees whose short-term contracts were allowed to expire, which was a common strategy for dismissing poor performers.

In addition, the company made a concerted effort to solicit employee input through satisfaction surveys and team meetings, and to implement small changes to improve the work environment. Vendotel had successfully avoided works councils or unions. However, managers put in place an alternative form of employee representation, called an "Assistenz Team," or AST. Employees elected two to three representatives, who they could then go to, in the words of one human resource manager, to say "what lay on their hearts." For example, "employees may complain, the monitors hurt their eyes, they are uncomfortable." They brought these concerns to the AST reps, either individually or in monthly meetings, and then reps communicated them to managers. They also set up an online newsletter that provided a discussion forum for employees. This had led to a number of small changes, like buying flat screen monitors and bringing in additional plants. However, managers admitted the committee had no real say over policies like monitoring, pay, evaluation, and scheduling. These practices were centrally decided and had to be consistent across the company, meaning that there was little local flexibility to change them.

Comparison

Vendotel's U.S. and German operations were not identical (see table 3.5). In the United States, there was a strong focus on discipline, dismissals were high, and teams were not used extensively for coaching. The center that I visited had a reputation for low pay, intense working conditions, and high turnover. In the company's German centers, most workers were on permanent contracts, supervisors used teams to motivate workers and build commitment, and the company had set up an elected group of employee representatives to communicate any concerns or suggestions. Turnover and absenteeism were lower, and according to the company's regular surveys, employees were more satisfied.

These differences in management approach were influenced by labor market and industrial relations institutions in each country. Management was committed to avoiding collective bargaining in its European call centers, and had put in place an alternative form of employee participation. The German centers also had somewhat older employees with more formal education than those in the United States, although centers in both countries relied heavily on university students and training was similar.

TABLE 3.5 Employment systems at U.S. Vendotel and German Vendotel

	U.S. Vendotel	German Vendotel
Staffing and skill		
Typical tenure	• 6 months – 1 year	• 2–3 years
Typical ed. level	• High school or community/technical college students	• Varied based on client; many university students & working mothers
Initial training	• 2 weeks	• 2–3 weeks
Scheduling		
% part time	• 30%; all employees part time for the first 90 days	• Over 50%; some "mini-jobs"
Scheduling	• Fixed shifts within a 50–60 hours "availability window" • Changes in call volume handled through asking employees to work overtime in their availability window; and employee turnover	• Variable shifts assigned 1 week in advance • Changes in call volume handled through asking employees to work overtime or come in on their day off; employees sent home without pay when volume slack; and temporary contracts
Work design		
Breadth of skills	• Agents trained to answer all calls within a client group	• Agents trained to answer all calls within a client group
Use of teams	• No use of teams	• Some use of teams for motivating agents, with regular paid meetings
Compensation		
Av. Base Pay	• $7.50–$20 fixed hourly pay; $8–$9 average	• $8–$18 hourly pay; $12.50 average
Variable pay	• No pay at risk, but small bonuses based on client	• 20–30% pay at risk based on client
Coaching		
Basis for coaching	• Team leader provides weekly coaching based on individual performance data	• Team leader provides monthly coaching based on quantitative metrics and a formal quality appraisal by 4 evaluators
Discipline	• Steps leading to dismissal if employee does not meet targets	• Mix of development and discipline; fixed-term contracts allowed to run out if performance low
Monitoring	• Continuous electronic monitoring by managers and clients	• Daily electronic monitoring by managers and clients
Outcomes		
Absenteeism	• 15–20%	• 5–10%
Turnover	• 80–100%	• 15% (plus around 10% 'nonrenewal' of fixed-term contracts)

The option to offshore work was also not as immediate a threat in Germany—a factor that created additional cost pressures in the U.S. location I visited and eventually led to the company's decision to close the center.

At the same time, these differences were relatively minor when compared to the other three matched pairs. Vendotel had developed a global strategy and culture that it imported to its German location, and management was committed to creating a standardized product for its multinational clients. This meant intensive electronic monitoring, individual-based evaluation and pay, and extremely flexible staffing practices—none of which were subject to codetermination by employees. Compared to the other German case studies, Vendotel had taken the most unilateral approach to work reorganization, and "employee participation" was used to make minor changes in work climate rather than shape an alternative approach to management.

Discussion

These eight case studies do not show uniform low-road convergence. Managers adopted different approaches to organizing and managing similar call center jobs. These differences map to some extent onto national setting. The German companies tended to adopt a more high-involvement or professional employment model that made use of teams to train and motivate agents, gave employees some opportunities to participate in decision making, and used performance evaluation to develop skills rather than to discipline poor performers. In the U.S. cases, teams were primarily used to raise morale, discretion and participation were low, monitoring was intense, and poor performance often led to discipline or dismissal.

A comparison of negotiations over work reorganization showed that worker participation at the local level played a central role in these outcomes. The union and works councils at Deutsche Telekom, German Mobile, and Client Services Germany were able to use codetermination rights to substantively influence the design of scheduling, compensation, and monitoring practices. Employment systems were not identical across the three companies, but had some common elements. First, scheduling practices built in employee discretion over shifts and breaks. Deutsche Telekom had given employees the most autonomy due to works agreements that required supervisors to negotiate with the members of their teams to manage call peaks and working time accounts. Client Services had more constraints due to tight margins and client contracts, but nonetheless had improved scheduling predictability and agent choice over shifts through recent agreements with the works councils and the union.

Second, all three German companies built a team-focused structure for training and developing employees, which was closely linked to a performance management system that limited individual evaluation and monitoring. Again, Deutsche Telekom had the most elaborate negotiated protections against direct supervisor control of individual performance, but worker representatives had negotiated similar checks and balances at German Mobile and Client Services. As the two telecommunications companies adopted performance-based pay and sales competitions, collective agreements also did not allow managers to base incentives on individual performance, strengthening the role of teams. German Vendotel was an anomaly, with unpredictable scheduling and much more individually focused monitoring and performance appraisal practices.

Union leverage over these kinds of decisions was more limited in the United States. Even at U.S. Telecom, which had a strong union with a long history of partnership over work design, management had moved unilaterally toward a managerial control employment model. Supervisors used forced overtime to deal with fluctuations in call volume and created rigid rules to encourage attendance and adherence to schedule. The union negotiated some flexibility for employees through paid FMLA and flex time, but these contract provisions were resented by managers, who viewed them as an obstacle to meeting performance goals. The union was able to negotiate limits on how many times a month employees were monitored and to establish some general guidelines concerning how that information was used. However, it lacked the rights to bargain over the design of the performance management system. U.S. Mobile's union had no input in scheduling or incentives, and watched helplessly as managers increased monitoring and tightened discipline. The union in both cases simply did not have the legal rights or bargaining power to participate in the design of new practices. Instead, union representatives tried to negotiate rules that protected employees, which managers in turn tried to work around. As a result, employment practices had increasingly come to resemble those in the two U.S.-based call center subcontractors, albeit with more job security, better pay, and more consistent and transparent work rules.

Taken together, the case comparisons demonstrate that strong institutional supports for workplace democracy were crucial in encouraging management to adopt high-road approaches to reorganizing jobs and motivating workers. This held in two industries—telecommunications and call center subcontractors—that were experiencing growing competitive pressures and increasingly fragmented and decentralized bargaining. However, the case studies also showed large gaps in pay and working conditions between these two industries, which are increasingly linked through contracting relations. A further question is thus how stable distinctive employment systems are in the face of broader pressures to cut costs. This is the subject of the following chapter.

4

Losing Power in the Networked Firm

The case studies in chapter 3 compared the employment systems adopted by U.S. and German telecommunications call centers and their subcontractors. In this chapter, I shift the focus from work reorganization to organizational restructuring. Organizational restructuring is defined as the reconfiguration of an organization's administrative structure (McKinley and Scherer 2000; Bowman and Singh 1993). It can include changes in the boundaries of organizations, such as the externalization of work through subcontracting and the internalization of new business units through insourcing. Restructuring also includes changes to the structure of the firm that affect job and department classifications, such as decentralization or segmentation of work functions across operating units or subsidiaries.

In the telecommunications firms considered here, managers face decisions concerning how to organize work across networks of internal and external call centers. Three kinds of measures are commonly used to restructure these networks: consolidating small centers into large national in-house call centers, creating new subsidiaries for certain categories of call center work, and outsourcing work to third-party subcontractors. The consolidation of work allows employers to achieve scale economies and further automate and rationalize jobs; and employees must either move to the new location or be laid off. Nonetheless, the company's collective agreement still governs pay and working conditions. When firms establish subsidiaries, their collective agreements often no longer apply, but unions find it easier to organize and negotiate with these subsidiaries than with independent subcontractors because they can leverage bargaining power in the parent firms. However, managers can also refuse to cooperate with unions and almost always introduce different pay and employment practices. Unions find it particularly difficult to represent workers at subcontractors, because they are under more intense pressure to reduce labor costs and typically do not have a history of collective agreements.

Worker representatives are understandably interested in these kinds of decisions and have tried with varying success to negotiate over them. In the following case studies, I compare the strategies that unions and works councils at major telecommunications firms have adopted toward organizational restructuring, and their effects on management strategy and worker outcomes. I focus on firms with unions and/or works councils, representing all of the major fixed-line and wireless companies with a significant union presence in 2003–4, when I conducted the bulk of my interviews. In the United States, these included AT&T, four former RBOCs (Verizon, Bell-South, SBC, and Qwest), and Cingular; and in Germany, the three major subsidiaries of Deutsche Telekom (T-Com, T-Mobile, T-Online), Arcor, Vodafone, and E-Plus. AT&T, the former RBOCs, T-Com, and Arcor competed mainly in the local and long-distance fixed-line sector, while Cingular, Vodafone, and E-Plus were all wireless companies. At T-Online and E-Plus, I also examine negotiations over organizational restructuring at subcontractors following their take over of each company's call centers.

Findings show that unions had some influence over organizational restructuring decisions in both countries, using resources that varied at the firm rather than the national level. However, they became increasingly defensive in their responses over time, negotiating wide-ranging concessions in exchange for job security and the return of outsourced jobs to in-house centers. These trends resulted in downward pressure on pay and working conditions, and were undermining company and workplace-level bargaining power.

United States

In the United States, incumbent telecommunications firms went through several waves of restructuring following divestiture. AT&T cut close to 60 percent of its union represented workforce between 1984 and 1994, while employment in the regional Bells' regulated telephone business declined 28 percent on average between 1984 and 1992 (Keefe and Batt 1997: 48–52). Incumbent firms also began to segment customers according to market segment (residential, small business, and large business) and their revenue profile (from high value to low value), often setting up distinct business units for these groups (Keefe and Batt 1997: 79; Batt 2001).

Both downsizing and the redesign of call center jobs were important issues for the CWA and its members in the 1990s, and the union had some influence over these decisions through job security provisions in contracts and the legal right to negotiate over salary levels for new job titles (Katz, Batt, and Keefe 2003; Keefe and Batt 1997; Boroff and Keefe 1994; Darbishire 2005). While these are ongoing concerns, I focus here on three related restructuring measures that have been a focus of bargaining over the past decade: consolidation, outsourcing, and subsidiary creation.

In the following sections, I compare union strategies toward organizational restructuring at AT&T, SBC, and BellSouth (which were integrated into one company, AT&T, following a series of mergers in the mid-2000s), Cingular Wireless (which became AT&T Mobility following these same mergers), Verizon, and Qwest. The CWA had the most success in influencing outcomes at Verizon's eastern bargaining units due to a history of strong contracts, strategic campaigning, and union militancy. However, union representatives most often responded with concessions, introducing new job classifications and pay scales to halt or reverse outsourcing, or to prevent work from being shifted to nonunion subsidiaries. This has led to growing inequality in pay and working conditions within and across call centers.

AT&T

AT&T has faced intense competition in the long-distance market since the 1980s and responded by aggressively cutting costs. Not coincidentally, it was also the first company to rationalize and outsource its call center work. AT&T operator services came under early pressure for concessions. Between 1950 and 1996 technological changes such as complex switching systems for long- distance calling, Operator Service Position Station, and voice recognition technology reduced the number of operators employed by AT&T by 75 percent (Rechenbach and Cohen 2002: 79–80).

In the late 1980s, AT&T consolidated its long-distance operator centers from 120 to 60 locations and approached the CWA asking for help coming up with a more cost-effective strategy. The union agreed to a new job classification of "term employees" who could be hired for a specific project on a two- to three-year contract. While the salary did not change, these employees had no termination pay or relocation rights. After consolidation, term employees in the offices that remained open gained permanent status. However, it soon became standard policy to bring in all new hires under the "term" title, and then hire a new group of terms after their contracts expired.

In 1997, AT&T management approached the CWA to discuss performing some of its directory assistance work in-house, as part of a plan to expand these services and reduce subcontracting. The company "had a vision of...having well-trained folks who would give you such an experience that you would want to come back" (Interview, CWA representative, September 2005). The union eventually agreed to a new job title with a much lower pay scale for this project, starting at $6.30 an hour at a time when other operators in the company were making more than $20 an hour. AT&T planned to staff the new centers with a disposable workforce and chose two locations near colleges and military bases. However, the job's good benefits attracted a stable workforce, and low turnover drove up wages while demand for the new service never materialized. Eventually in 2004, the company closed one of the centers and converted the second center to a "dual party relay center" that helped hearing impaired customers. The conversion of work resulted in an increase in pay for the workers who were able to qualify, but at a level that was still considerably lower than that in traditional operator services.

Telemarketing also came under early cost-cutting pressure. AT&T established the nonunion subsidiary American Transtech in 1983 to provide financial services for its shareholder accounts. Following divestiture, Transtech began to handle the company's telemarketing and customer service jobs, as well as to sell outsourced services to other companies. Hourly wages ranged from $6 to $12, roughly half the equivalent pay for union members. In 1995, one of the company's largest call centers in Jacksonville, Florida, employed three thousand temps out of a workforce of five thousand, most of whom had been working at the company for three to five years (Bahr 1998). The CWA attempted to organize Transtech in the early to mid-1990s but failed due to high employee turnover and union busting campaigns led by local management (Bahr 1998: 110–11). In 1995, the CWA convinced a majority of Transtech's Jacksonville workers to sign union cards, but AT&T opposed the union (violating a neutrality pledge), and the union lost the election.

AT&T also outsourced a growing share of its sales and service work. Before 1997, the company defined a number of customer segments that were routed to different groups of employees or centers, based on value added. At first, only "low-value" customers were routed to a subcontractor. Then in the late 1990s, AT&T began a major drive to outsource and offshore most remaining long-distance work, keeping a few domestic call centers open to benchmark subcontractor performance. By 2004, AT&T was outsourcing 45 percent of its calls, including two-thirds of its long-distance calls and around one-fifth of calls from its local customers. Between January 1999 and December 2003, the number of in-house customer care employees dropped from 7,500 to 3,300, while the number of employees at subcontractors on AT&T's accounts grew from 830 to around 3,500 (Interview, CWA representative, April 2005).

The CWA also used a number of different tactics to try to keep work in-house and extend "wall-to-wall" bargaining at AT&T. One strategy was to set up partnership and neutrality agreements. The 1992 Workplace of the Future Agreement (WPOF) extended management neutrality to nonunion subsidiaries in union organizing elections, improved job security, and made it easier for redundant workers to be transferred to subsidiaries (like Transtech). The agreement created Business Unit and Division Planning Councils, which were supposed to give union representatives more say in "medium-term" business decisions like investment, subcontracting, closures, and introduction of new technology (Boroff and Keefe 1994). CWA president Morty Bahr (1998: 231) wrote, "WPOF has…been the forum through which CWA communicated our intense commitment to management that union members wanted access to all jobs within the company, including jobs that had been 'designated' nonunion."

The union's optimism soon gave way to frustration. By 1998 only eight Planning Councils had been established, and they remained weak and underfunded. The neutrality agreement failed to stop management from waging an antiunion campaign at Transtech and opposing other union organizing attempts at its subsidiaries. Over the next five years, the partnership became increasingly irrelevant as the company cut close to 60,000 jobs, with little consultation. WPOF finally collapsed in 1999.

AT&T's contract with the CWA has language that prohibits contracting if it would involve layoffs or part-time work. However, the company was able to get around this by moving work outside of the "Geographic Service Area" of thirty-five miles—strictly speaking, if none of the work was being subcontracted in that thirty-five-mile radius, the company did not violate the contract. At the same time, a series of consolidations and layoffs coincided with skyrocketing attrition and dismissals, as the company set new difficult-to-achieve targets and started cracking down on absenteeism and tardiness. The union found it difficult in the midst of all this fluctuating employment to figure out where the work was going. AT&T would close a center in one location, and tell the CWA they were moving the work to several different locations, which then was next to impossible to verify.

The CWA attempted another partnership in 2001—this time to try to address the problem of outsourcing. The union formed a committee with AT&T, using leverage over the regulatory approval that the company needed to divest itself of wireless, broadband, and manufacturing equipment. AT&T provided detailed information on its outsourcing activities and data on the cost difference between the in-house and outsourced workforce, which it estimated at around 40 percent. After recalculating this figure to account for higher quality, productivity, and sales at union centers, the CWA narrowed the cost differential to 15 percent for domestic outsourcing and 30 percent for outsourcing to India. The union then put forward a proposal to reduce the costs of performing work in-house that involved creating a new job title for employees handling lower revenue work and allowing more temporary work. The CWA and AT&T also formed a joint committee to address absenteeism at in-house call centers, which resulted in a pilot project to redesign jobs by introducing job rotation and greater scheduling flexibility. The pilot was a success, proving higher employee morale and better productivity. And so the committee got approval to roll out a larger study at more call centers.

These projects were cut short in 2004 when a regulatory change made it expensive for AT&T to remain in residential long distance. AT&T responded by pulling out of the long-distance consumer market. One consultant involved in the committee described the poor communication around this decision:

> We actually met to plan to do the whole thing, and then got a call, the company is pulling out of it. We didn't know what was happening, but for some reason they pulled out of it completely. The union talked to them some more, we got them back into it, they signed a purchase order, I mean literally the vice president of AT&T signed this purchase order saying yes, we're definitely going to do this. The next day AT&T did their press conference, we are no longer going to pursue residential long-distance service. It's such an AT&T thing to do. It was very shocking, nobody could figure out what was going on. So of course, the whole thing was over, done. (Interview, October 2004)

By 2005, AT&T had closed several of its domestic call centers, leading to a loss of about 550 union jobs, and cut a thousand subcontractor jobs. Although the CWA tried to use an array of strategies to influence these decisions—partnership agreements, wage concessions, and limits on layoffs—the company successfully pursued a unilateral strategy of outsourcing and consolidation.

In 2005, AT&T was purchased by SBC Communications, which adopted the AT&T name. In 2006, the new AT&T merged with BellSouth and became the sole owner of Cingular Wireless (now AT&T Mobility). All three of these case studies are discussed in more detail below.

SBC Communications

SBC was formed through mergers between several smaller RBOCs with different histories. The original Southwestern Bell region covered five Southwestern states. In 1997, it merged with Pacific Telesis, bringing Nevada and California into the fold, and between 1998 and 1999 it acquired Southern New England Telecommunications (SNET) in Connecticut and Ameritech in the Midwest.

The companies that made up SBC had different contracts and labor relations environments. SNET was represented by the independent union

Connecticut Union of Telephone Workers until it joined the CWA in 1998, and had a tradition of strong agreements. Connecticut was also slowest to consolidate its call centers, holding on to a number of smaller locations. Ameritech went through a major consolidation in the Midwest between 1995 and 1996, reducing its centers by more than half. The company kept most jobs within the region but was beginning to route call overflow and put in place a "follow the sun" policy of routing late night calls to the West Coast and early morning calls to the East Coast. Differences in labor costs across regions also increased incentives for moving jobs. In the early 2000s, for example, SBC closed down centers in California and moved the work to lower-cost locations in the Southwest.

SBC introduced lower-tier agreements for directory assistance—a common trend across the former RBOCs. This happened in individual companies at different times prior to the mergers. In 1995, the Connecticut Union of Telephone Workers negotiated a new title for operators at SNET that paid between $6 and $10 an hour, or around $8 an hour less than traditional employees. The company set up a separate subsidiary for this group, which by the mid-2000s had expanded to around six hundred employees, with only around a hundred left in the old operator services jobs. Over time the union was able to improve contracts, with average pay rising to $16 an hour. However, in other parts of SBC, the company gradually introduced a range of new job titles for operators with different pay and working times.

SNET also set up a subsidiary in 1998 to sell outsourced call center services to other companies. The original focus was outbound sales, but over time it began marketing itself as a high-end inbound customer service provider. The union cooperated with this effort and was able to represent employees, although at a wage that was around two-thirds that of in-house customer service and sales representatives.

The CWA supported SBC's various mergers and used its leverage over regulatory approval for these mergers to set up one of its strongest partnerships. This allowed it to win card check neutrality across the company, as well as an agreement to bring much coveted technical support work in-house. One of the sticking points in 2004 contract negotiations was insourcing around three thousand Tier 1 DSL help desk jobs that had been contracted out to Accenture. The new agreement guaranteed that the work would be brought back somewhere in the thirteen-state SBC region after the contract with Accenture expired in 2007, but obligated the union to negotiate a competitive price for that work. Management also agreed that SBC employees would handle sales of new products like DSL, long distance, and video, and agreed to "discuss expanding outbound telemarketing jobs within the workplace."

By the time the contract expired, SBC had merged with AT&T. The CWA did succeed in negotiating a new job title under what was at the time called the "AT&T Internet Services" contract, which covered technicians in California and Texas. A separate "Tier 1" title was rolled into this contract at a pay scale starting at $21,000 a year, and the subcontracted jobs were moved to five new call centers in cities with high unemployment. The new company also negotiated a new "leveraged" customer service title for core fixed-line call center employees in 2009, in which 40 percent of pay was based on commission from sales. Under the agreement, employees were given the option to move to the new title—which gave them the possibility to earn additional money—but were able to move back to the old title if they were dissatisfied. According to union representatives, the company was having difficulty convincing the regular workforce to move to the title; and in some regions, temporary representatives were placed in the new jobs.

The new management of the merged company had begun taking a less cooperative approach to bargaining, as the "long-term Bell-head" managers were replaced by a new generation who took more of a "take it or leave it" attitude in negotiations (Interview, CWA representative, April 2010). The new leveraged job title was becoming one source of conflicts with local representatives concerning the basis for incentives (e.g., sales or other performance measures), and enforcement of other companywide rules and objectives. In autumn 2010, employees rejected a settlement the CWA had reached over the summer with management. The union was working to improve the contract but faced new pressures as the company again began to subcontract portions of this work. "I guess they got the PR value of bringing the work back from overseas and now they're just looking for the cheapest solution again" (Interview, CWA representative, November 2010).

BellSouth

BellSouth was a regionally based telecommunications company that provided local telephone and Internet services. The core of its business was fixed-line services, housed in BellSouth Communications. It also owned a minority share of Cingular Wireless (together with SBC), which is now part of AT&T Mobility. Until 2006, BellSouth was the only RBOC that had not merged with another "baby Bell," staying in its traditional nine state region in the Southeast, and the CWA continued to represent the majority of its core workforce. Several waves of restructuring, downsizing, and outsourcing reduced this core from around 88,000 in 1995 to 63,000 in 2004. In 2006, as discussed above, BellSouth merged with AT&T.

BellSouth's call center operations had become increasingly centralized over time. In the 1970s and early 1980s, the company had a large network of call centers with an average size of around thirty employees. Over time, the company introduced some call routing and combined locations, reducing the number of centers from several hundred to around eighty, which ranged in size from twelve to one hundred employees. Like Bell Atlantic and NYNEX, BellSouth remained organized along regional lines at a time when many telecommunications firms were creating "megacenters" and introducing national call routing.

BellSouth management put in place a committee in 1995 to study alternatives for consolidating call center operations. The company brought in consultants and initiated fourteen major reengineering work streams, all focused on "driving costs out of the business." A project group responsible for restructuring the call centers recommended consolidating to seven locations and downsizing. In the end, the company decided this was too costly, due to the high expected displacement of workers and union resistance.

Beginning in the late 1990s management also began an aggressive push to outsource call center work. BellSouth informed the union in 1997 that it intended to outsource directory assistance and "toll direct" jobs, and the CWA responded by offering to discuss strategies to keep the work in-house under a union agreement. Eventually, the company created a new business unit called National Directory and Customer Assistance (NDA/CA) that performed directory assistance services for BellSouth and other clients. CWA negotiated a new contract for the business unit with different benefits and a lower pay scale, starting at $7 an hour and topping out at $8.50. The union was faced with, "lose it all or try to build a new bargaining unit" (Interview, CWA representative, February 2005). In 2005, they were in the third round of negotiations and working conditions had been steadily improving. In addition, NDA/CA had the only contract at BellSouth that prohibited subcontracting. BellSouth also agreed that any operator work that had been done in-house could not be transferred to the new company.

In the meantime, the company started outsourcing new call center work. Outbound telemarketing was outsourced in 1998 and outbound collections for "high-risk" customers in 2000. Subcontractors were encouraged to be more aggressive in collecting from customers who had bad credit ratings, while the in-house workforce continued to focus on providing quality service for less risky customers. At the same time, the in-house workforce was expected to transition to a "revenue-driven" organization that could effectively compete with the subcontractors. Employees in collections were aware that the company was looking for ways to outsource more of their "lower-skilled" jobs and felt added pressure to increase performance. The CWA and BellSouth discussed the possibility of bringing outbound work in-house under a lower-paying contract, but the company refused to consider this until the union agreed to substantial pay at risk and very low base pay.

In January 2002, BellSouth announced a major reorganization and consolidation of consumer operations. A telecommunications slump had followed the dot.com bust in 2000, and the company suffered financial losses and a falling stock price. Management began looking for new ways to reduce costs and improve operating efficiencies, including cuts of five thousand jobs, or 5 percent of its workforce. The consolidation strategy involved flattening the corporate hierarchy, reorganizing departments under a smaller number of central divisions, reducing the number of centers by two-thirds (from seventy-nine to twenty-eight), and cutting total employment by close to a thousand. Call centers grew from an average of fifty or sixty agents to around two hundred. At the same time, territorial was replaced by regional call routing. Prior to consolidation, each territory had developed its own systems and policies for tracking performance. A key goal of the new structure was holding management accountable to standardized metrics and operating procedures.

Consolidation was a major blow to the CWA, which had not been informed of this plan during 2001 bargaining. The union filed multiple grievances but was unable to influence restructuring measures. While the CWA negotiated an agreement that allowed employees to follow their work, only a small number of "veterans" were willing to move, and consumer services had to hire around a thousand new employees. Many employees were also reshuffled, requiring training to learn new skill sets.

Despite the animosity generated during the consolidation process, the CWA continued to partner with BellSouth over other restructuring measures, with some success. In the early 2000s, management was starting to outsource online customer support. When the union found out, it was able to use political pressure to convince management to instead create 125 "web rep" jobs in a separate in-house center, under the traditional customer service contract. In 2004 bargaining, the company signed a letter of agreement with the CWA agreeing to work together to move other "jobs of the future" into the bargaining unit. Voice over Internet protocol, wireless Internet, and video sales and support were moved to union centers, and the CWA and BellSouth began to work together to bring DSL help desk work back from contractors. These initiatives were put on hold during the 2006 merger with AT&T.

Cingular Wireless/AT&T Mobility

Cingular Wireless (now AT&T Mobility) is a unique case because it was only recently organized by the CWA and is still the only major U.S. wireless company with a substantial union presence. Cingular was jointly owned by SBC and BellSouth, as it brought together BellSouth's subsidiary BellSouth Mobility and a number of regional mobile companies that merged or were bought out by SBC in the late 1990s. The CWA partnered with SBC to get legislation passed in the late 1990s that was favorable to the company, and in return, SBC agreed to card check neutrality for its wireless subsidiary. This allowed the union to form a bargaining unit once the majority of employees had signed cards signaling their support, while committing management to refrain from campaigning against the union. The union faced initial resistance from BellSouth when it collaborated with SBC to create Cingular, but eventually the CWA secured a card check agreement across the company. This was one of the few examples of true management neutrality toward union organizing in telecommunications.

By the mid-2000s, the CWA represented employees in three large bargaining units: one that encompassed the southeastern states, a second in the Southwest, and a third "National" agreement covering the remaining states. Three-fourths of the union's members were concentrated in right-to-work states in the Southeast and Southwest, where "union shops," in which every employee in a bargaining unit is obligated to be a union member, are illegal. Contracts remained relatively weak and provided the company with a lot of flexibility, with no negotiated restrictions on moving work or outsourcing. However, management agreed to notify the union prior to layoffs, to lay off temporary workers and contractors before regular employees, and to transfer rights and relocation allowance when work was moved to a new location. Cingular also had a longstanding policy of keeping all of its customer service and telemarketing work in-house, so there was initially no threat of outsourcing. The company was using a nonunion subcontractor for operator services, but CWA reached an agreement to move this work to BellSouth's and SBC's union represented subsidiaries.

Cingular substantially consolidated its service and sales jobs in the early 2000s. The company moved most of its call center work from northern states to southern states, where the pay was typically lower and labor regulations weaker. In 2001, around forty-two hundred jobs in inbound and outbound customer service, collections, credit and activation, roaming and technical support were transferred to six regional centers in the Southeast. Cingular adopted a "megacenter" approach for the new centers, which typically housed around eight hundred employees and had turnover rates of between 30 and 50 percent.

The location of call center work became a much more important strategic issue when the company merged with AT&T Mobility in 2004. Cingular was almost 100 percent organized, but after bringing in 20,000 new AT&T employees, union density dropped to around 45 percent. The company quickly networked its Cingular and AT&T call centers, and as it consolidated these centers, the union was concerned that work would be moved to the nonbargained AT&T units. The decision of where to perform the work was based on where there was the most capacity and whose statistics were best in an area, and AT&T centers began to be used as "backup centers" for call overflow.

One troubling outcome of the merger from CWA's perspective was management's new willingness to consider outsourcing. AT&T Mobility had outsourced a substantial proportion of its call center work, and these contracts transferred to the new merged company. For example, AT&T had already signed a contract with a subcontractor in Monterrey, Mexico.

After the merger, a Cingular manager went there to help set up the center, and the company started sending calls from former Cingular locations to the new center with no plans to bring the work back to the United States. One CWA representative noted there were fears that as Cingular management got used to working with subcontractors, there would be a gradual shift in policy to make more use of outsourcing. "They're getting a little more comfortable with it, and that's getting quite concerning" (Interview, May 2005). Because there was no contract language around outsourcing of work, the union had very little leverage over these decisions.

At the same time, the CWA was successful in getting the agreement of SBC to extend card check neutrality to the AT&T sites. By 2010, the CWA had incorporated all former AT&T workers into its three existing collective agreements.

Verizon

Verizon Communications is one of the largest U.S.-based telecommunications companies. In 2005, Verizon's fixed-line business had more than 55 million access lines in twenty-nine states. The company also jointly owned Verizon Wireless with the UK-based Vodafone group.

Verizon was formed in 2000 when the former RBOC Bell Atlantic merged with the independent telecommunications company GTE. Bell Atlantic traditionally served the Mid-Atlantic states, but expanded into the New York and New England markets in 1997 when it merged with NYNEX. These mergers brought together companies with very different collective agreements and bargaining histories. GTE did not have a strong union legacy from the former Bell system and had negotiated a patchwork of weak collective agreements with the CWA. NYNEX had stronger agreements, due in part to its location in a region with high union density and strong labor laws as well as its militant local unions, who were known for having the highest strike rates of any CWA district.

By the mid-2000s, Verizon had multiple agreements with the CWA and IBEW. Verizon East, encompassing the former NYNEX and Bell Atlantic territories, had two regional bargaining tables and twenty-seven separate collective agreements that covered around 80,000 employees, while Verizon West in the former GTE territories had sixty separate agreements covering 37,000 employees. Smaller contracts also covered several of the company's subsidiaries.

The CWA continued to be strongest in the company's eastern bargaining units and had the most success in influencing restructuring in these units. When the three companies merged, GTE had gone furthest in consolidating its call centers and outsourcing customer service and sales work. One of the CWA's concerns was that jobs would be moved to lower-cost regions. The Verizon Northeast and Mid-Atlantic contracts stated that the company could not route calls if it would "directly result in the layoff, downgrading or part-timing of service representatives." They also prohibited the permanent transfer of more than 0.7 percent of CWA represented jobs from the "defined universe" (defined as the county in New York, the region in New England, and the state elsewhere). These were the clearest limits on moving work in any of CWA's contracts.

In addition, the union negotiated rules in New York and New England that prevented consolidation of call centers across "Interdepartment Transfer Areas." In New York, the company could not close down locations if employees would have to commute more than thirty-five miles from their original work location. This forced Verizon to improve efficiency by networking smaller locations and sharing overhead across these locations. When the company decided to close a center, management had to do a painstaking analysis of where employees lived and how far they would have to commute to prove there would not be undue hardship. Management tried to change these rules in 2003 bargaining, but the CWA succeeded in keeping the limits in place, which were further strengthened by a "no layoff" provision in the contract. The CWA won an arbitration case prior to 2003 bargaining that forced Verizon to uphold this provision for New York and New England.

These limits give Verizon incentives to find creative ways of using its higher-cost, lower-turnover eastern workforce. For example, as call volumes fell in New York, its call centers had a surplus of workers. Verizon management was able to bring some work in from New Jersey and Pennsylvania to keep agents busy—which involved difficult negotiations among the unions in all three states. In addition, local managers succeeded in bringing outsourced campaign work back in-house on a trial basis. Verizon eventually decided to permanently in-source this work when employees proved they could sell at a higher rate than subcontractors. In New

England, the CWA partnered with management in 2003 to reduce absenteeism and improve productivity. Committees found new ways to reduce costs, and managers agreed to in-source DSL campaign and billing work. As a result, the company's New England call centers hired more than two hundred new representatives between 2004 and 2005, despite losing customers in the region.

Verizon West undertook more substantial consolidation. In the mid-1990s, GTE consolidated its billing and order work in a few megacenters in each state. California and Texas had the largest centers, with between four hundred and eight hundred employees, while others averaged around two hundred. The centers were also networked to handle calls for other states. There were no negotiated limits on moving work, although contract language on severance pay and moving allowances made consolidation across states expensive.

Bell Atlantic, NYNEX, and GTE kept their directory assistance work in-house. As traditional operators were displaced, companies built up directory assistance call centers, often consolidating them into megacenters. In the mid-1990s the CWA negotiated a second-tier operator title across the three companies, but this was implemented differently. For example, in GTE's California centers, the CWA prevented the company from hiring into the second-tier title for several years. However, in the early 2000s, IBEW agreed to adopt the title in the union's bargaining units. Under the threat of losing members to IBEW centers, the CWA allowed Verizon to hire employees servicing new customers under the new title, with a top wage cap at $13.19 compared to $21.72 in the traditional title. Over several years, the number of employees in the traditional operator title shrunk to around half of the workforce.

The CWA also negotiated local contracts in the former NYNEX and Bell Atlantic regions that limited or prohibited outsourcing of certain jobs, like telemarketing or inbound calls. The union won these provisions through a series of campaigns. In the mid-1990s, Bell Atlantic formed a nonunion subsidiary called Bell Atlantic Plus and began moving customer service and sales work to the new company at lower pay. In 1998 bargaining, the CWA made this a key issue. During the ensuing strike, the union organized a public campaign that highlighted poor customer service at the new subsidiary. Bell Atlantic eventually agreed to bring all of the work in-house and to limit future outsourcing. At Verizon West, most contracts did not limit outsourcing, and the kinds of jobs that were outsourced varied by state. For example, Arizona used subcontractors to handle overflow of call disconnects, but this was not possible in California where the contract stated that only 5 percent of "traditional" work could be handled by subcontractors.

The outsourcing of "new work" also proved to be a contentious issue, including service and sales for new telecommunications products, technical support, and telemarketing. When Verizon first started selling DSL, it outsourced inbound sales. CWA successfully organized a campaign to bring this work back in-house, arguing that because it was bundled with traditional phone services it fell under "protected" work. The CWA has also tried to make the case that Verizon employees should sell wireless products when they are bundled with residential service. In August 2004, wireless was moved out of the centers to Verizon's nonunion wireless subsidiary. The merger with GTE created new incentives for the company to pull some of its sales work in-house, although mostly to its western call centers where wages were more competitive with those of subcontractors.

The union had less success in convincing the company to in-source higher-skilled DSL technical support jobs. One CWA representative estimated that around three thousand of these jobs were handled by subcontractors in seven locations in the US, and two thousand jobs were offshored (Interview, April 2005).

Qwest

Qwest Communications is a telecommunications carrier based in the western states. In 1995, Southern Pacific Rail, which operated a large fiber optic network in the Southwestern US, acquired the smaller Qwest, took on its name, and proceeded to expand its network. It grew through a series of acquisitions that allowed it to compete in Internet Protocol (IP) telephony and long distance. In 2000, the company acquired US West, the smallest of the RBOCs, giving it access to more than 25 million customers in fourteen states in the Western and Midwestern United States.

At divestiture, US West brought together Mountain Bell, Northwestern Bell, and Pacific Northwest Bell, which remained under three separate contracts until 1992. The company suffered from low growth rates because it was concentrated in sparsely populated states and was one of the first RBOCs to push for deregulation and later to diversify into cable. US West also had the worst customer service record of the Bells, which led to millions of dollars in fines between 1993 and 1995. The CWA partnered with management to improve customer service in the mid-1990s, but the quality of the partnership changed along with the company's leadership and economic fortunes. After Qwest acquired US West, the new company cut 16 percent of its workforce and then another 25 percent following the telecommunications bust. In 2002, Qwest was further plagued by negative publicity due to allegations of improper accounting practices, leading to a formal review by the SEC. By the mid-2000s, the CWA represented 28,000 employees across the company but had been unable to organize the locations belonging to Qwest's long-distance operations.

Restructuring of call center work at US West (and then Qwest) followed a similar pattern to the other RBOCs. Operator services was the first area to come under pressure for rationalization and restructuring. The original three Bell companies had more than six thousand operators who were scattered in small, local offices and protected by contract provisions that gave them shorter shifts and special differentials. In the early 1990s, US West started trying to change some of these provisions to introduce standard eight-hour shifts, but this was resisted by the CWA. Then in the mid-1990s, again following a national trend, positions declined due to rationalization, and the company consolidated its remaining operators in a few remote locations. The CWA negotiated a new operator title with lower pay and job security for "agent services." Similar to SNET and BellSouth, US West was handling operator work for outside clients, and management argued that because it was paying union wages the company could not compete with lower-cost providers. The CWA hoped to pick up new work for members and stem job loss to nonunion companies. At first, agent services and traditional operator services were separated, with agent services handling most of the contract work from other companies. These traditional positions continued to decline in the late 1990s, and the CWA negotiated an agreement to transition the remaining employees from operator services into the agent services contract. The workforce was relatively stable between the late 1990s and mid-2000s, with around a thousand employees in seven agent services centers.

In customer service and sales centers, consolidation occurred in several waves in the 1990s, and then again during the layoffs following the Qwest merger and the telecommunications bust. The union had little influence over these decisions and no contractual limits on moving work, bargaining instead over provisions such as relocation assistance to lessen the impact on the workforce. In one example, US West decided to consolidate its customer service and technical monitoring centers in the early 1990s, and the CWA asked to participate in developing a consolidation plan. They worked on a joint plan with the help of outside consultants, but shortly before it was set to be implemented, management changed course and adopted its own unilateral strategy that involved closing more than five hundred offices and cutting nine thousand jobs. The remaining eighteen megacenters were concentrated in thirteen cities, and jobs were eliminated entirely from Montana, Wyoming, North Dakota, and South Dakota (Boyle and Pisha 1995).

Outsourcing was similarly controversial. The original contract with US West prohibited outsourcing if it would involve layoffs or part-time work. However, this was relatively easy to get around due to high turnover rates and the possibility of using voluntary redundancy to downsize. US West and then Qwest initially outsourced jobs like call overflow and final collections. The company began contracting out more jobs in the late 1990s, such as customer retention and billing inquiries. Then in 2003, Qwest management informed the CWA that it was outsourcing around three thousand customer service and sales jobs. The company came to the union with figures showing a huge cost gap: it was paying subcontractors $21 to $24 an hour for work that in-house employees were performing for $40 to $45 an hour. Following heated debates, the CWA eventually decided to allow a lower-tier job title for new employees. The union negotiated a letter of agreement in the fall of 2004, and then incorporated the new job title into the 2005 contract. New employees started at $8.50 with a maximum salary of $10 an hour but kept the same benefits.

In return, Qwest brought around half of the jobs back in-house and began discussions on the other subcontractor jobs. Management also agreed to keep all existing centers open until the end of 2005. Although the CWA was unable to get this extended in 2005 contract negotiations, the company had no plans to consolidate and was expanding its workforce in several new locations. This agreement also led to closer partnership over outsourcing decisions. The CWA formed a special committee to meet quarterly with management, and Qwest began sharing more information in formal reports to the union.

Summary

These case studies show that organizational restructuring became an increasingly important strategic issue for the CWA across its major employers. The union consistently used different forms of bargaining leverage to influence consolidation decisions and fight employer attempts to move call center work out of its core firms. The CWA was most successful at Verizon's eastern bargaining units, where it was able to combine strong contractual protections, member mobilization, and partnership in the legislative arena. However, the union was forced to make concessions across the case studies to keep work in-house or in subsidiaries covered by a union contract. Many companies were reluctant to give the union access to their subsidiaries and outsourced work to avoid the constraints of collective bargaining agreements. Union representatives agreed to lower-tier titles to make their workforce competitive with the third-party subcontractors from which they sought to recover jobs. This contributed over time to reduced pay levels for certain jobs and greater diversity in employment conditions within firms.

Germany

German unions faced similar pressures and conflicts associated with organizational restructuring from the mid-1990s. Consolidation was primarily a concern at Deutsche Telekom (DT), due to its legacy of smaller, geographically dispersed call centers. Similar to the CWA, worker representatives at DT fought the movement of work, with some success. However, the fragmentation of collective bargaining and the "newness" of call centers in Germany meant that unions and works councils had difficulty developing a consistent strategy toward outsourcing. Both ver.di and IG Metall originally allowed some outsourcing to alleviate pressure to cut labor costs and increase flexibility in-house, while trying to organize the subcontractor industry. Although both unions organized works councils in these third-party firms, intense price competition and employer resistance limited their ability to improve working conditions.

At the same time, core employers increasingly used outsourcing, subsidiary creation, and variation in collectively negotiated rules across their internal networks of call centers to demand concessions. As a result, unions and works councils started to focus more attention on keeping work in their core firms and in some cases adopted more militant, conflict-based strategies to protect member interests—with mixed success.

In the following sections, I compare changing union and works council strategies toward organizational restructuring at the major national telecommunications companies: Deutsche Telekom, Arcor, Vodafone, and E-Plus. Ver.di initially had the most influence over call center consolidation and outsourcing at Deutsche Telekom's core fixed-line subsidiary T-Com, due to residual bargaining power and strong works councils. However, this had weakened by the mid-2000s, leading to growing convergence in outcomes.

Deutsche Telekom

Deutsche Telekom shifted to a divisional structure in the late 1990s based on its four market "pillars" of T-Com (fixed-line), T-Mobile (wireless), T-Systems (business and IT), and T-Online (internet services). T-Com was the only one of the four divisions that remained legally within the parent company, along with headquarters and shared services (such as billing and printing). It employed the largest proportion of the workforce (64 percent) and had the most continuity in employment contracts from the old state monopoly.

T-Com also was also the base of union strength in the DT corporate group. Membership density was close to 70 percent, and around 30 percent of employees were still *Beamten,* or civil servants, with lifetime job security. The Post Reforms allowed DT to continue to employ civil servants, which made up around half of the workforce when the company was privatized. However, employees gave up their civil servant status when they transferred to DT's subsidiaries, where the workforce also tended to be younger and less likely to join the union. T-Systems had around 25 percent membership density, T-Mobile had 15 percent, and T-Online was long the "weakest link," with 5 percent union density. Not coincidentally, ver.di was unable to conclude an agreement with T-Online, despite years of negotiation. Negotiations were cut short when DT decided to bring the subsidiary back into the parent company in 2005 to take advantage of growing synergies between internet and network services, creating a new business unit "T-Home." While works councils were strong across the corporate group and most works councilors were ver.di members, they did not always communicate with their colleagues at other subsidiaries or with the union.

Strong job security protections were the Deutsche Post Gewerkschaft's (DPG) and then ver.di's best bargaining chip as they tried to influence organizational restructuring at DT. The DPG succeeded in extending contract provisions after privatization to employees in both West and East Germany, which included guaranteed employment security at the age of forty for those with fifteen years of service. These protections placed constraints on DT management as it sought to reinvent itself as a lean, profitable company. Between 1995 and 2004, 110,000 positions were cut in DT's core operations. Network services experienced the most severe job losses, as the telephone network was digitalized and many service technicians became redundant. Because the collective agreement prohibited business-related layoffs, management used early retirement, voluntary buy-outs, and natural turnover. Around 90,000 employees left through these programs between 1995 and 2000, and a further 24,000 transferred voluntarily into other divisions in the DT group (Sako and Jackson 2006: 17).

Despite these expensive measures, a large number of workers decided to remain with the company after having been made redundant. In 2002, ver.di and DT negotiated an agreement that allowed the company to move these employees into a new subsidiary Vivento Personal Service Agentur (PSA), a "temporary employment and qualification company" (*Beschäftigungsgesellschaft*). These employees were then placed in different divisions for short-term projects, or recruited to fill the occasional permanent job opening. Vivento was set up as a temporary agency that would also offer services on the private market, but this segment grew too slowly to employ the thousands of redundant workers. Because DT was obligated to maintain these employees' former pay level when they moved to Vivento, job cuts did not lead to the hoped for payroll cuts. The company found itself in the awkward position of paying a growing number of employees to sit at home while trying to make do with a leaner workforce across the company.

At the same time that Deutsche Telekom was downsizing, it had begun to restructure its call centers. Each subsidiary had its own network of centers under separate management. In 2003 there were around 31,000 call center employees in T-Com, 2,200 in T-Mobile, 650 in T-Online, and 400 in T-Systems.[1]

T-Com and Vivento Customer Services   At T-Com, there has been constant pressure to reduce the number of customer service and sales centers. T-Com initially did not consolidate centers to the same extent as many U.S. companies, due to strong union opposition and the expense of relocating employees. While it closed some smaller centers, T-Com mostly sought to improve economies of scale by rearranging administrative units, downsizing management, and improving networking within regions. In 2001, the company drastically restructured its administrative regions: seventy-nine regions with "mixed" business and mass market customer segments were split into seventeen consumer regions and eight business regions. Two years later the structure was changed again, and consumer was consolidated into eight regions. The company cut around two-thirds of upper management, creating a much leaner system of reporting and accountability while increasing performance pressure. Managers' pay was also gradually tied more closely to center performance, and their job security came to depend on meeting stricter metrics and performance goals.

As the number of administrative units decreased, local managers became responsible for multiple centers in different locations. However, a *Standortsicherungsvertrag,* or location security agreement, across T-Com initially protected the smaller call centers from substantial consolidation. Within this general framework, regional works councils had the right to negotiate over consolidation within their territories. During the process of restructuring the administrative regions, or *Niederlassungen* (NL), in the early 2000s, union and works councils set up local committees that discussed what form restructuring would take and sought to influence the location of work. In one example, telemarketing was originally handled in three separate locations in a NL. T-Com concentrated the work in one city with the agreement of the works councils, meaning employees either had to follow their work or work in another call center in the area. However, gradually the regional works council was successful in getting back offices reopened in the two locations that had been closed.

Our first job is to bring work to the people. That means we have certain employees at each location, and with constant restructuring at Telekom there is always the danger that this work will be taken away. We try to prevent that—when we have well-trained employees at a location, we argue that they can move work to those locations. It doesn't matter where they sit, the work can come to them. (Works councilor, July 2004)

As local works councils are ultimately responsible for negotiating over how downsizing is accomplished (through closing locations or downsizing across the organization), committees at all levels were important for making sure different interests were represented. Close coordination across the works councils also prevented the closing of call centers in East Germany where the unemployment rate was already high.

As in the United States, new CTI technologies that allowed companies to route calls between centers made it easier to move work and increased competition between locations. In the late 1990s, T-Com management and the central works council signed a collective agreement on call routing stating that all calls that originated in a region had to first go to agents in that region, as long as they answered them within a certain time period. After that, calls were routed to other regions where agents were free. This was similar to the agreement at Verizon East, where all calls had to stay in the state or county. However, it built in some additional flexibility that increased performance pressure and competition across regions. In some cases call forecasts for certain regions were inaccurate, leading to under- or overstaffing. These forecasts were made at corporate headquarters, with limited local input. However, the costs were born locally, as certain understaffed centers routinely "lost" their calls to another area.

The possibility of a region's calls being routed due to low productivity was used to put additional performance pressure on agents. "Keeping our calls" became a sort of rallying cry for local management to improve talk times, playing on fears that jobs would be permanently lost if call centers in other regions were more efficient. One local works councilor observed, "Before we were always glad to give up work when we didn't have enough people to answer the calls, now there's fear that we'll never get the calls back" (Interview, March 2004). Worker representatives generally agreed that management would like to put in place nationwide routing, and it was not clear whether call routing was a business decision that was *Mitbestimmungsfähig,* or a subject of mandatory codetermination.

These changes increased competition at all levels of the organization. One manager from a region known for its militant works councils pointed out that its reputation could prevent them from getting work: "The problem that we always anticipated, that's now starting to come up, is that they are trying to keep [this region] as small as possible, and to not give us more work, which would help secure our jobs" (Interview, October 2003). Growing competition across local works councils made it more difficult for the central works councils and union to coordinate strategies for keeping certain work rules the same across regions.

One major point of contention was opening time rules, which are negotiated with local works councils. For several years, calls after 10:00 P.M. were routed from each region to two central call centers after hours. Opening hours were changed a few years later to 8:00 A.M.–11:00 P.M. Monday through Friday and 8:00 A.M.–10:00 P.M. Saturdays and Sundays, and certain call centers in each region were dedicated to working late evenings and weekends. However, this was implemented differently across regions based on negotiations with the regional and local works councils: some operated only Monday through Friday and some evenings; some only until 8:00 P.M., others until 10:00 P.M.

Works councilors and unionists felt that frequent changes in these rules were used to play locations off each other. For example, one region's works councils would agree to keep its call centers open half an hour later without discussing this with other works councils, and this would create pressure across the company to negotiate a new closing time to remain "competitive."

> It has gone so far that of course every employer tells their works council: when we don't have this model, then there will be consequences—they act as if…others are doing this, the work will go to them, and the work will be lost in this region. That means the employer plays regional interests off one another. This kind of thing happens on a higher level, at the regional level, but also at the local level.…They try to use *Standortpolitik* [the politics of location]—like with this working time theme. It's not always in the local interest to play along, because they don't see what the whole firm strategy is—how this plays into it. And they have succeeded, at the level of the firm, in worsening working conditions. If the works councils were unified, they would be able to stop this from happening. (Interview, ver.di representative, July 2004)

At the same time, ver.di was successful at keeping pay levels the same across T-Com, which meant this was not a factor in benchmarking or concessions. During privatization, the DPG negotiated identical pay scales for East and West Germany, which was unusual at the time. This is an important difference between T-Com and most of the US RBOCs, where large differences in pay across regions were creating growing pressure for moving work.

Outsourcing at T-Com progressed slowly and focused on lower skilled jobs. In 1998, DT conducted a benchmarking study that showed large cost savings from outsourcing directory assistance work. After presenting various options, managers gave the union and works councils a choice to either agree to a lower pay scale or allow management to outsource the work. In the end, they agreed to outsourcing. One member of the bargaining committee described how difficult it was to make this decision:

> We had placed a lot of value on keeping the jobs ergonomic, making sure they were good for the employee's health, which was expensive. This cost situation was definitely there. That's where the pressure originally came from. In the 1990s, we looked for solutions with the employer. They came to us and decided to try to bring the level of the call center work up: keep the more complicated work in-house, but with the knowledge that simpler call-center work would go out, be outsourced. Our first demand was of course that the work would stay in-house and all be at the same level. But the employer said, that won't work, we can't do that, so this was the other solution. It was not an alternative for us to create worse working conditions, to take money away from the employees. The other option, then, was to move these simpler jobs. So we tried to get higher value jobs for those employees who remained. The result was the development we see: the simpler work was outsourced. (ver.di representative, July 2004)

T-Com outsourced twenty-eight hundred of thirty-five hundred directory assistance jobs to Walter Telemedien, one of the oldest third-party subcontractors in Germany, which at the time had no works councils and no collective agreement. The employees who had formerly performed this work were then moved to other call centers in T-Com and DT's subsidiaries. Around the same time, T-Com faced an unexpected spike in calls when it began offering a new DSL product and was able to retrain many of the employees whose jobs had just been outsourced to handle these calls.

Parallel to this, the company reorganized special campaign work, remaining directory assistance work, and late night work into a new group of six "Aktions call centers" in 2000. While T-Com's service and sales centers were divided into a number of separate regions (*Niederlassungen*) that only took calls from customers in those regions, the new Aktions call centers were organized in a nationally networked "special region"— Niederlassung Spezial, or NL Spezial. These centers had begun taking calls for other firms on a contract basis, but DT was losing money because it was unable to charge the full cost of service due to its more expensive workforce. The company decided to develop the NL Spezial as an internal support network that provided a short-term solution to the joint problems of unpredictable call volume and the difficulty in moving work across regions at T-Com.

These call centers took over the five hundred or so remaining directory assistance jobs, and employees were retrained to support the service and sales centers when call volume was too high, as well as during late evenings and weekend hours. So, for example, if one region found that it needed a thousand employees to service its calls, but only employed eight hundred, two hundred employees from the NL Spezial would be assigned to support them. The NL Spezial also served as an internal outsourcer for DT's subsidiaries, handling short-term project work, directory service, call peaks, or simple service and sales jobs. T-Com outsourced some of its outbound telesales work to third-party subcontractors, keeping the rest in-house or sending it to the NL Spezial.

These various arrangements were awkward solutions to problems associated with changing market strategies and unpredictable call volumes. Meanwhile, a growing number of well-paid and underemployed workers were sitting in its temporary agency Vivento PSA, with more job cuts looming. In January 2004, DT established a new subsidiary called Vivento Customer Services (VCS) to handle the corporate group's lower-skilled call center work, with plans to bring some work that had been outsourced back in-house and expand into the third-party call center market. Around four thousand employees from the NL Spezial were taken over by VCS, and DT began moving five hundred employees from Vivento PSA into the new company.

At the same time that this was happening, ver.di was negotiating a new collective agreement with DT. The union was under a great deal of pressure to help the company cut its labor costs and come up with alternative ways to employ the Vivento PSA workforce. DT had announced future cuts of up to forty thousand jobs and made it clear that without concessions, management would not extend job security. Around 20 percent of employees were protected from *Betriebsbedingte Kündigung,* or layoffs for economic reasons, while the rest were either civil servants with lifetime job security or fell under rules carried over from before privatization that prevented layoffs if employees were forty years old or had fifteen years of service. While the final two categories of protections were pretty much impossible to change, *Betriebsbedingte Kündigung* was up for renegotiation in 2004 and overwhelmingly would affect the East German workforce. Ver.di was also interested in playing a part in negotiations over the pay and working conditions for the new Vivento call center subsidiary.

In March 2004, DT and ver.di concluded an employment pact (*Beschäftigungsbündnis*) that reduced working time from thirty-eight to thirty-four hours, with only partial wage compensation—meaning employees would be paid for the equivalent of a 35.5 hour work week. Civil servants also had their weekly working time cut, even though they were not officially covered by the agreement, but retained their full pay. In return, management extended job security protections until the end of 2008. Employees in Vivento PSA retained their full salary when placed in a job, but pay was cut to 85 percent of their former salary when they were not working. Ver.di also was able to keep the new call center subsidiary Vivento CS under the DT collective agreement with guaranteed job security through the end of 2008, but the union agreed to a reduction in pay of 8.75 percent. The employment pact was estimated to have saved the company around €300 million (Dribbusch 2004).

Ver.di saw the creation of Vivento CS as a positive development that would allow the company to take back thousands of jobs that had been outsourced, as well as to compete as the only call center subcontractor in Germany with a strong union contract. The union was thus willing to make some concessions to make the workforce "competitive" in this market segment. One ver.di official stated, "Our main motivation for cooperating with the plan to set up VCS was to bring back work that had been outsourced. This work was sent out to firms with bad working conditions, and that puts pressure on us to lower our working conditions. We want to help to build up good jobs in this sector, before they all sink to a low level" (Interview, July 2004).

Works councils were more divided, as they feared that more work would be moved out of "core business" areas and into Vivento CS, where costs were lower. In addition, management soon made it clear that it intended to sell the new subsidiaries. Between 2006 and 2008, DT transferred twelve of its nineteen VCS establishments, representing around eighteen hundred employees, to the subcontractors Walter Services and Arvato. These measures shifted former DT workers to firms with weaker or no collective agreements. This presented a new set of challenges for ver.di's telecommunications department, as it sought to support its members who now worked for call center subcontractors. Those employees who moved to Arvato (owned by the notoriously antiunion conglomerate Bertelsmann) had the terms of their existing collective agreement secured through 2009, at which time managers informed employees that they were required to sign individual contracts at a lower level. Pay would initially average €25,000 a year, with more than a third of that amount paid directly by Deutsche Telekom; however, this "top-up" was secured only for five years. In addition, working time was increased to forty hours from thirty-eight, and other former perks, such as vacation time, were cut.

Ver.di initially encouraged employees not to sign the new contracts, and instead sought to pressure Arvato to negotiate a collective agreement, using leverage from its members in the former VCS locations where membership density remained at around 40 percent. Predictably, the union faced steep resistance from management, which informally threatened to move work to other locations if employees refused to sign individual contracts. This appeared to be a credible threat when Arvato announced that it would close former Vivento centers in Potsdam and Freiburg (and lay off their eighty employees) by the end of 2009—a decision that also diverted union attention from avoiding the downgrading of working conditions to saving jobs.

Ver.di faced a different set of challenges at the VCS locations that were transferred to Walter Telemedien. Walter was the only major call center subcontractor to negotiate a collective agreement with ver.di, but the price for this was a "competitive" wage rate for the industry: the agreement set minimum hourly pay at €5.11, with an additional performance-based component of €1 to €2. When Walter purchased the new locations from

DT, the employees were automatically transferred to this existing agreement, based on a provision in German law that provides an exception to transfer of undertakings rules when both firms are covered by agreements with the same union. Walter's agreement had been negotiated and administered by a different department within ver.di (FB13), under terms that ver.di representatives in the telecommunications department (FB9) felt were unacceptable. This meant that employees who had formerly earned an average annual salary of €33,000 saw their pay cut by around a third.

Walter's collective agreement expired at the end of 2007, at which time ver.di sought a new agreement at its preferred minimum wage of €7.50 an hour. Walter initially refused to consider an agreement at this level. However, in 2009, after a series of warning strikes (*warnstreiks*), they eventually succeeded in getting an agreement, with provisions for regular pay increases with seniority and higher pay rates for evening and Sunday work. While this was an important victory for ver.di, it did not bring pay and working conditions up to the level that employees enjoyed in their former jobs at DT.

T-Mobile   Meanwhile, DT's two other major subsidiaries, T-Mobile and T-Online, had also been restructuring their call centers. Call volume steadily grew at T-Mobile in the 1990s, which allowed the company to expand its use of subcontractors without cutting jobs. Works councils at T-Mobile originally saw outsourcing as a useful tool for improving job security and avoiding unsocial working times. Employees were reluctant to work late hours and vacations, or agree to erratic scheduling plans, and subcontractors stepped in to offer this flexibility.

By the mid-2000s, subcontractors handled late hours, peak times, vacations, night shifts, and outbound campaigns. In early 2000, T-Mobile closed one of its call centers and began outsourcing more of its core work. As a result, job security was a major issue in 2002–3 negotiations. Management eventually agreed to a location security agreement (*Standortsicherungsvertrag*), stating that no locations would be closed until 2008. However, extra call volume could still be subcontracted as long as no jobs were lost. In return, the works councils approved a more flexible working time model that they had previously opposed, and ver.di agreed to a lower pay raise of 1 percent instead of the original 2.1 percent the union had demanded. In addition, they gave up calls during "unsocial" working hours to subcontractors. Previously, work had been organized in fixed shifts, and employees got paid overtime when they worked certain shifts, like nights or weekends. Now during these times the work was sent to the cheaper subcontractors, but T-Mobile could not lay off its in-house workforce and had to bring back work during regular hours. A job security agreement also protected employees from layoffs.

These negotiations required close coordination across the union and works councils:

> We were able to accomplish this because we can work together with the works councils. They can put the employer under pressure, because they need their agreement for certain things.... For example, in the 2002–3 bargaining, the works council refused to agree to extending working time to holidays. The employer said they wanted to close locations and outsource the work, and the works council said they would block the shift plan the employer wanted. So they started to negotiate. This is the first level of pressure before a strike, to demonstrate our power, show solidarity, protest an unpopular position the employer has taken. (Interview, ver.di representative, November 2004)

As at T-Com, job security had become a key bargaining issue. As ver.di and the works councils tried to make the in-house workforce more competitive, they were forced to hold down pay and allow more flexibility.

Then in 2006, the ugly specter of outsourcing came up again. Ver.di agreed not to strike during negotiations, because they were "open result," meaning that both parties did not have to come to agreement. Management demanded large pay concessions and the introduction of pay at risk, which the union opposed. Management then went directly to the employees with their offer and told them that if ver.di did not agree to it they would outsource the work.

> Then they said to the employees, "listen everyone, if you don't accept this, when you don't want this—or ver.di doesn't want this—then we will sell this part of the business, outsource the work to external subcontractors. There you will get fifteen percent less pay and have to work longer." As a result, people had an incredible amount of fear. There are women whose husbands are unemployed, people who had built houses and had to make payments. Less money would ruin these people. They had such fear that

they put an enormous amount of pressure on us—sent us endless emails
and circulated petitions saying, "Please agree to these terms. The agreement
they've put on the table is not great, but better than being outsourced and
losing pay." (Interview, ver.di representative, August 2007)

In the end, ver.di signed the agreement, leading to substantial concessions.

T-Online   T-Online was the only subsidiary in the group that did not have
a collective agreement with ver.di. Employees transferred to T-Online from
DT were able to keep their former working conditions, but new employees were brought in under a variety of pay scales. Several attempts to negotiate with ver.di broke down. The bargaining commission was in more or
less continuous negotiations between 2001 and 2003. In the middle of this,
the company outsourced a number of jobs, which distracted the attention
of the works councils and the union. Then after talks resumed, the parties
reached an impasse over working time: while management insisted on at
least a forty-hour week, ver.di demanded a thirty-eight-hour week. Negotiations started up again in 2004 and the two parties were close to a compromise agreement at the beginning of 2005, but then DT announced its
decision to bring T-Online into the parent company. Management agreed
to integrate the T-Online employees into the DT collective agreement by
the end of September 2006, conditional on separate negotiations.

Like T-Mobile, T-Online took over call center locations from DT as the
online business expanded. For example, Oldenburg was formerly a directory assistance location, and as T-Com outsourced these jobs, employees
transferred to T-Online. In the late 1990s, the company first began focusing on improving customer service in response to skyrocketing calls and
complaints, and in the space of a few years grew to five locations with
between 300 to 350 employees in each. Then in 2002, T-Online sold three
of these locations to different call center subcontractors—Bertelsmann/
Arvato, Walter Telemedien, and Sykes. Managers kept around 10 percent
of first-level technical support in-house to benchmark subcontractor performance, but subcontracted the other 90 percent.

The decision to sell the company's call centers was resisted by the works
councils at locations that were sold as well as from ver.di. However, lacking a collective agreement, ver.di had weak leverage. Ver.di and T-Online's
central works council went through four rounds of negotiations, with a

final agreement that pay and working conditions would remain the same for eighteen months after the new companies took over, along with full job security and extension of previous works agreements. There was little solidarity among the works councils at the time of the decision. Works councilors at one of the transferred locations described feeling "abandoned" by the central works council and the works councils at the call centers that remained within the company.

Workers had varied experiences after the sale. Siegen, which was bought by the U.S. firm Sykes, probably experienced the most dramatic changes in working conditions. This story was summarized in the introduction to this book: after the center was sold in 2001, the new management began to tighten rules and demand concessions. The works council was initially successful in preventing changes such as the elimination of breaks from the computer screen and an attempted rule prohibiting employees from decorating their cubicles. However, the pace of work became notably more intense, as calls per employee per day nearly doubled. After initially resisting variable pay, the works council agreed to a new bonus system of between €100 and €200 a month based on targets that changed frequently. Initial training was reduced from six to two weeks, and most new employees were hired under short-term contracts with lower pay. The works council successfully retained team-based evaluation, but team meetings were cut back because they took too much time away from the phones. Sykes managers stopped meeting with the works council, and works councilors began filing a string of lawsuits to enforce their contract and contest violations of labor law. Eventually the center was closed and the work moved to the company's northern German call centers.

Works councils at the different Sykes locations tried to work more closely together to improve working conditions across the company, but most of these attempts were frustrated by employer opposition. In the early 2000s, the local works councils discussed the possibility of establishing a corporate group-level works council, or *Konzernbetriebsrat,* that would have more bargaining leverage. However, management asked works councilors to sign a statement that they would not join or take part in the founding of a Konzernbetriebsrat and threatened to close the locations that did not sign. Works councilors admitted it would be difficult legally to set up consultation at the national level because headquarters was located in the United States, and continued to be divided over whether to press the issue or make do with more informal means of coordination.

As a result of these changes, a large gap began to open up in working rules and working conditions between T-Online's in-house and outsourced centers. The T-Online works council held the line on preventing silent monitoring and individual evaluation of employees. However, the in-house workforce faced the problem that based on most metrics, such as efficiency and quality, they were at the same level or fell behind the outsourced partners. Management increasingly held them to the same quality standards and transferred management practices they learned from their subcontractors. Often they would try out new ideas on the subcontractors, and then try to use this to get the same change adopted in-house. For example, T-Online started piloting a silent monitoring program, and eventually rolled it out to all subcontractors. The in-house works council continued to resist silent monitoring, but there was growing pressure from the workforce to change the rules. One works councilor described being attacked by employees at the annual meeting for threatening their jobs by not giving in to employer demands.

The decision to bring T-Online into the parent company in 2005 triggered a new round of negotiations with ver.di. The original agreement between T-Online and DT laying out the conditions of the merger included a plan to outsource the Kiel and Oldenburg locations, but ver.di succeeded in getting an agreement to integrate all locations and employees into DT. Managers also agreed to a thirty-eight-hour week across T-Online, and were not able to lay off employees or close locations until a new collective agreement was negotiated.

T-Service   The growing differences across DT's subsidiaries fed fears that T-Online's outsourcing strategy would become the model across the company.

> The company will say: at T-Online they can do this, they can run a call center with these working conditions, and we can't, so let's move this work to T-Online. Then the people will immediately have problems with a different payment system. This is the biggest problem that we have right now. When we don't try to help improve performance and lower costs in T-Com, the same thing will happen that has happened in T-Online. More work will go out, with lower pay. (Interview, ver.di representative, July 2004)

Managers talked about the need to become more market oriented and competitive. They used benchmarking with subcontractors, across business units, and across call center locations to make the case for changing collective agreements. One manager noted, "The works council says, well, you're always threatening to close down locations. We say, that's not the point: the market is moving in a certain way, we can't ignore the market, we have to go with the flow, and that's the way it is" (Interview, July 2004). Works councilors talked about growing fear among employees that their jobs were constantly threatened. Internal employee surveys at T-Com showed a huge spike in insecurity following downsizing.

This meant that ver.di was under more pressure to negotiate job security and location security agreements—like those in T-Com and T-Mobile—or to figure out ways to work with the company to in-source work, such as agreements to reduce pay at the subsidiary Vivento Customer Service. This pressure also made it more difficult to coordinate the activities of local works councils, particularly across more weakly organized T-Online locations, as employees feared if they did not agree to concessions they would lose their jobs. There were also conflicts within the different subsidiaries over moving work to Vivento CS. For example, T-Mobile had originally planned to move its sales work to Vivento, but the works council was able to negotiate an agreement that committed management to retain these jobs in-house. At the same time, the company insisted on moving more of its telemarketing and business hotline work to Vivento. While T-Mobile management promised not to cut jobs through this strategy, this was not secured in a collective agreement.

Then in 2007, DT announced that it planned to shift 50,000 of its technical service, technical infrastructure, and call center jobs to three new subsidiaries, under the name "T-Service," and demanded that ver.di renegotiate pay and working conditions. Ver.di responded by leading a six-week strike—the first in the history of the company—with strong support from its membership. Despite this show of strength, the union faced a number of challenges to building bargaining power in negotiations. Ver.di's members initially sought to use their position on the DT supervisory board to oppose the creation of the subsidiaries, but were unsuccessful. Once management decided to go ahead with the planned restructuring measures, the union was unable to strike to oppose these measures: under

German law, it could legally strike only to protest the *consequences* of such measures for employees. In addition, managers planned to move employees from both T-Mobile and T-Com into the subsidiaries, which they argued gave them the legal right to adopt the less favorable T-Mobile agreement without further negotiation (particularly for the new call center subsidiary). One union official noted, "I suspected that what they tried to implement earlier at T-Mobile, they wanted to extend later across the company, but it wasn't explicit at the time" (Interview, August 2007). Finally, DT publicly threatened to sell the service subsidiaries if it was unable to get a favorable agreement. This put ver.di in a weak, and largely defensive, bargaining position.

Under the agreement eventually reached by both parties, wage levels for former T-Com employees moved to T-Service were reduced by 6.5 percent over forty-two months, and weekly working time increased from thirty-four to thirty-eight hours without pay compensation, amounting to an overall reduction in compensation of more than 10 percent. In addition, new employees were to earn 30 percent below the former level; the use of variable pay increased, with 15 percent of base pay tied to DT's organizational performance and individual and team performance targets; and the regular working week was lengthened to include Saturdays in call center operations. Management agreed to extend protection against compulsory layoffs until 2012, to refrain from selling the new service subsidiaries until 2010, and to offer 4,150 jobs at T-Service to DT apprentices.

In one controversial initiative, ver.di established a fund targeted at T-Service employees that only its members could access. Around €50 million was put in this joint fund, financed by DT and ver.di; and ver.di created a nonprofit organization to administer it. Ver.di members could apply to the fund for a wage supplement equivalent to the difference between their current and former wage. A competing union, DPV-Kom, challenged this in the courts, on the basis that it is illegal to negotiate a collective agreement that only members can benefit from. However, the courts upheld ver.di's right to administer such a fund (which was set up as a complicated legal construction that could not be classified as a collective agreement). One union official noted that the fund had been bogged down in a number of problems, as union representatives sought to create a transparent system for informing eligible members that they could apply, and then assisting them with a complicated application process.

In 2008, DT created further upheaval when it announced a plan to close thirty of the new Deutsche Telekom Kundenservice (DTKS) call centers by 2011 and consolidate the jobs in a smaller number of centers. Ver.di led a series of protests, and management eventually agreed to keep its thirty-three remaining centers open through 2012 and to maintain job security provisions.

Arcor

Outside of Deutsche Telekom, union and works council influence over call center restructuring was much weaker due to more fragmented collective bargaining institutions and lower union density. Arcor was Deutsche Telekom's major competitor in fixed-line services in the 2000s. It was established in 1997 as Mannesmann Arcor, a joint venture of the consortium CNI Communications Network International, led by Mannesmann, and the Deutsche Bahn subsidiary DBKom Gesellschaft für Telekommunikation. After the telecommunications market was liberalized in 1998, Mannesmann Arcor started competing in residential fixed-line services. The company grew through a number of mergers, including the takeover of o.tel.o, the third largest competitor in the fixed-line market; the online service germany.net; and a number of smaller city carriers. In 2001, Vodafone acquired Mannesmann through a hostile takeover, and continued as the majority shareholder in the company until 2008, when it acquired the remaining shares from Deutsche Bahn and Deutsche Bank.

The different firms that were brought together through these mergers and joint ventures were originally represented by different unions, which remained involved in bargaining. The main unions were IG Metall and Transnet, the union of the Deutsche Bahn. Both were cosignatories to collective agreements (with Transnet taking a lead role), and each advised different local works councils, based on which company a location belonged to previously.[2] The mining, chemical, and energy union (IG BCE) and the public sector union ötv (now part of ver.di) had negotiated a framework agreement at o.tel.o in 1998 before it merged with Arcor, and IG BCE continued to play a minor role at some locations. While these unions had generally cooperative relations, there was some competition for members. One IG Metall representative described a meeting he attended at o.tel.o, in which works councilors invited representatives from each union to present their case and then voted on which they would rather work with.

Arcor built up its customer service and sales centers quickly as the market expanded in the late 1990s. When Arcor and o.tel.o merged, Arcor brought together the call centers of both companies into a new subsidiary, Mannesmann Customer Operations (MCO). In 2000, there were six hundred employees in the new company: four hundred in Essen at the former o.tel.o site and two hundred in Eschborn, who had previously been transferred from Mannesmann. At that time, MCO moved some work to Essen, where unemployment was higher. Eschborn's works council felt they had no influence over this decision, and employees were afraid their location would be shut down. The two works councils also had to work together to harmonize their different collective agreements. Arcor had an agreement with Transnet, while o.tel.o had only a framework agreement with ötv and IG BCE but very detailed works agreements. Bargaining leverage was also weak due to low union membership:

> The negotiation process was very difficult. On the one hand, they're used to having a collective agreement. On the other hand, they don't want to be bound by a collective agreement as an independent telecommunications provider. The union organization rate is not very high, not enough to force the employer to negotiate a collective agreement. A strike was out of the question. (Interview, IG Metall representative, February 2004)

Another challenge was creating a common framework of pay and working time rules. When MCO was originally formed, there were sixteen different employment contracts, and the works councils faced the daunting task of figuring out how to bring these together into two contracts.

IG Metall and Transnet finally negotiated a separate agreement for the subsidiary in 2003 that included a new job classification system. Then a few months later, Arcor decided to bring customer service back into the parent company to improve "synergies" and communication across departments. MCO's works councils were made up almost exclusively of call center employees, but after being brought into Arcor the much larger company works council became responsible for all negotiations. Works councilors were concerned that call center issues would get less attention under the new structure.

In areas like IT they can protect their own rights. There are more conflicts here: when working time starts, when employees can go home, the way the call queue works....It will be different now that we are in the firm— now the works council represents all employees, and they have different problems and priorities. So I'm interested to see if they use this to weaken our agreement and working conditions. This probably wasn't the reason for bringing MCO back in to the firm, but is an important side effect. (Interview, works councilor, May 2004)

The company also downsized the call centers through natural attrition, dropping from 240 to 80 employees in Eschborn. While the works councils tried to work with the union to influence this, they did not have a lot of leverage. Union membership in the call centers was only between 5 and 10 percent, and high turnover made it easy to cut jobs without layoffs.

Segmentation of work also changed over this period. Originally employees were multiskilled, handling all billing and support questions. In 1999 work was split between technical support and sales, and in 2001 the company created more specializations to help service more complex products. For example, certain teams would advise new customers, others advised regular customers on ISDN and DSL, yet another answered billing questions, and so forth. At the same time, employment practices and pay stayed roughly the same across these segments. In 2003, Eschborn became specialized in handling small business customers, while the Essen location continued to focus on residential customer service and sales.

Arcor outsourced call volume peaks, late nights, some outbound campaigns, and all directory assistance work. When o.tel.o first started building up its call centers in 1999, it tried staying open twenty-four hours. This proved too expensive, and management decided to start outsourcing late night and weekend calls, with works council approval. After the merger, the company immediately outsourced all of its directory assistance and a portion of telesales and customer win back as it expanded its marketing efforts. Works councilors felt that outsourcing was not used explicitly to threaten the jobs of in-house workers, but could often be a subtle prod to improve performance:

There is a danger of more outsourcing when we don't have better quality than the outsourced call center. Employees are afraid of this, because they know it is cheaper. It is not directly said, but there is identical performance.

The quality is a problem here, and they are working on that. (Interview, works councilor, May 2004)

Work councilors felt that the higher-skilled work would stay in the company, and the best strategy for securing jobs was to work together on developing more value-added business services and improving the skills of the workforce. Over the next few years, Arcor management outsourced all remaining consumer call center jobs, retaining a smaller in-house workforce that was dedicated to large business customers.

Mannesmann/Vodafone

The steel and engineering group Mannesmann was granted the first license for a competing mobile communications network in 1989 (the D2 network), and took the lead role in the consortium Mannesmann Mobilfunk GmbH. It retained 51 percent of the new subsidiary, with minority shares owned by Dutch, British, and French companies. Mannesmann Mobilfunk quickly became T-Mobile's major competitor and has vied with the former monopolist for the place of market leader over the past decade.

Mannesmann was a lead firm in the metal industry employers association, with a strong central works council and close relationship with IG Metall. However, the union found that it was not so easy to extend collective bargaining to the new mobile company. Union membership remained extremely low, averaging between 5 and 10 percent across the firm. At the same time, the works councils were strong, well organized, and almost all works councilors were members of IG Metall (92 percent). Steady growth in the mobile industry and Mannesmann's strong market position contributed to expanding employment and profits, and the company developed a cooperative relationship with its works councils that secured steady gains for employees.

We have a pretty low organization rate, but because of good working conditions or social conditions, people don't really see the need to join the union. Works councils are relatively strong in the firm—so they say, why do we need a union, the works council looks out for my interests. (Interview, works councilor, March 2004)

There was also a lot of variation in the relationship between IG Metall and the local works councils in different regions. In some cities, such as Hannover, the union was an accepted bargaining partner and union membership was higher; while in others, like Berlin, relations bordered on conflict and IG Metall representatives had very little contact with works councilors. Throughout the 1990s the union tried unsuccessfully to negotiate a collective agreement, facing resistance from management and lukewarm support from employees.

Then in 2000, the U.K.-based multinational Vodafone launched a bid to take over Mannesmann. The works councils initially opposed the takeover, fearing it would lead to job cuts and weaken their influence over policies. As the takeover began to look inevitable, the central works council pushed for a collective agreement with the union. Management still refused to negotiate, and so the works council used the threat of negative publicity to force a compromise.

> We had a meeting with the responsible work director on the *Aufsichtsrat* [Supervisory Board] and said, pay attention, we need to negotiate a collective agreement. They said, we don't want that. We said, should we give the news some information about this? The next day five camera teams were here for our protest against Vodafone. They didn't find that very funny, but we did it. Their fear of this image thing was always there....Somehow we succeeded in getting almost every employee with us on the street to protest against the takeover. (Interview, Works councilor, March 2004)

Management eventually agreed to reopen negotiations, and IG Metall concluded bargaining in 2001. Vodafone initially tried to get the mobile company E-Plus on board for a sector-level agreement, but was unsuccessful. As a compromise, the union set up a framework agreement that was "open" for other firms to join—but Vodafone remained the only signatory. The main success was to formalize the gains the works council had built up over the years in works agreements. The new collective agreement secured rules on issues such as part-time work, training, vacation days, monitoring, and scheduling, and reduced working time from forty to thirty-eight hours per week. However, they could not agree on a new compensation structure, and so the union set up a separate commission to negotiate an *Entgelttarifvertrag,* or collective agreement on pay.

Mannesmann/Vodafone built up its call centers over time, growing from twelve employees at the first call center in 1992 to more than two thousand employees across Germany in 2004. The fastest growth occurred in the late 1990s, when some locations tripled or quadrupled in size. Vodafone kept all of its directory assistance work in-house at two of its centers under separate management. Large business was handled through another department organized around regions with individuals assigned to service clients, although one of the centers had employees trained to answer more routine requests from business customers.

Location of call center work became a more important issue after the takeover. In the early 2000s, Vodafone opened a new location in Bautzen, in East Germany. The company received subsidies from the local government to build the new center and originally planned to pay the new workforce substantially lower wages, or in the words of one union official, "create a dumping price." However, the central works council helped to set up local works council elections and was able to build a relatively solidaristic position across the company to prevent competition for work. Simpler call center jobs servicing prepaid mobile customers were moved to the new location, weakening the possibility of benchmarking against "core" service and sales jobs. The works councils agreed to a lower pay scale: while employees were usually moved to a higher pay grade after six months, employees in Bautzen stayed at the lower pay grade for a year and were placed on temporary contracts. However, after two years they had the opportunity to move up to the same level as in the West. In collective negotiations, an important demand of the union was to eliminate this difference: "The location advantage that they've been able to use, in my opinion, needs to be gotten rid of. The firm has profited from this for three years, but it's time to stop, because this could mean that jobs will be moved from Rattingen or Hannover to Bautzen" (Interview, works councilor, March 2004). As in the other firms, the works council used leverage in other areas to influence these business decisions:

> As a works council we have the possibility to take part in some management decisions, and we have definitely used that. Even though there is no

Mitbestimmungsrecht [codetermination rights], they wanted to have our agreement in other areas, to quickly build up call centers with a certain flexibility and working conditions, so they had to give us something in other areas that were important to us. (Interview, works councilor, March 2004)

At the same time, this had opened up variation in working conditions within the company. Union membership at the new center was also extremely low, as around 80 percent of employees were part time and thus found it more difficult to pay dues.

Vodafone began outsourcing calls in 2003. Growth in the wireless industry had slowed, and in 2001 the company faced the problem of a sudden drop in call volume, leaving a surplus of around five hundred more call center agents than were needed. For the first time after a steady expansion, employees faced the possibility that their jobs could be cut. They got over a rocky few months by shifting employees within the company, and then over the next several years the growing complexity of services and products led to expanding call volume. However, management anticipated that more erratic and unpredictable demand would continue to create staffing problems. In 2000, the works council agreed to let Vodafone outsource peaks in call volume and some telemarketing campaigns in exchange for strong job security protections. The works council also negotiated a *Beschäftigungssicherung* agreement, that there would be no layoffs for economic reasons. One works councilor described outsourcing as a useful tool, because it allowed call center employees to have fixed schedules, and ensured that as call volume changed over the year the company would not have to hire employees on short-term contracts or lay off its core workforce.

We can't do the peaks anymore: these are given over to other call centers. The reasoning is not to have to hire more employees who can't be kept, to be more flexible. So this is a good instrument, also for the works council: we give some calls up, but we have an agreement for job security so the works councilors don't experience this as threatening—all calls can't be outsourced. (Interview, works councilor, June 2004)

Because Vodafone was uncertain about the future of the market, management decided not to expand the in-house workforce. Any new growth in call volume (in 2005, around 4 percent per year) was outsourced, totaling about 20 percent of calls. Only high-value customers and special niche jobs like second-level technical support were exclusively handled in-house. Works councils began to feel the pinch of competition as they were benchmarked against the subcontractor:

> We know that more calls are going to [the subcontractor], that is the fear: that more calls will be taken up by them. We try to hold as much as possible here. Through different projects we try to hold everything in our own customer service area. Management communicates to us that what we are not able to answer goes to [the subcontractor], and of course we try to avoid that. Their quality is now exactly as good as our own customer service representatives. (Interview, works councilor, July 2004)

Local works councilors felt they had only limited means of influencing these decisions, outside of improving their center's performance. Works councilors and employees described the most important issue in negotiations as job security and keeping call centers open.

This was made worse by the perception that because central decision-making had shifted to the United Kingdom, the works council would have less leverage over future investment decisions. Integration across Vodafone's international operations had moved slowly. Local management was given a great deal of autonomy, as the company was performing well in Germany. Vodafone was also expanding internationally through buyouts and joint ventures, and had not yet turned its attention to consolidation. However, works councilors anticipated that this was a looming threat, as the company started realizing synergies across its European operations.

IG Metall meanwhile had a difficult time establishing a strong role in the company or a cooperative relationship with the works councils. Although the union concluded an agreement in 2001, it was unable to boost membership. Vodafone was viewed as strategically important to build up IG Metall's fledgling IT and telecommunications department, and so the union put additional resources into supporting staff and organizing campaigns. It started several programs to try to improve services for members, including offering rebates at local fitness centers or sponsoring employee soccer games. The union also set up a larger training program, Ich Starte Durch, that provided career coaching and seminars for union members, such as English language classes or training in communication and leadership techniques. Local union officials tried to partner with works councils on a program for "Family and Career" aimed at women, who were concentrated in call centers. However, these were not successful in raising membership, and attendance in training seminars was so low that many regions discontinued them.

IG Metall hoped to strengthen its role by successfully negotiating a collective agreement on pay. There were only two main pay groups in the call centers, which provided little opportunity for advancement. A major goal of the union and works council was to build in more levels that would reward employees for skill or experience, as well as create clearer job descriptions and rules on performance-based and overtime pay. The job security agreements for Vodafone locations were running out, and IG Metall hoped to secure a longer-term limit on layoffs. However, these negotiations broke off in 2005 in part because of growing splits within the works councils. A number of call center employees opposed continuing negotiation, based on the fear that this would cost them their jobs:

> The locations with big call centers had the strongest opinion against going on with negotiations.... There's also an east-west divide—the pressure is stronger here [in the East], and they are more likely to give up money to save jobs. But the problem is, there's no negotiation over this—there is no agreement where if they will give up money they get job security. The problem is that the union hasn't really gotten established here—we can't come in. They could have an action, push for these things, but they won't. That means we can't get a foot in the door, because we are not negotiating, and employees say: IG Metall doesn't do anything for us. It's a vicious circle. (Interview, IG Metall representative, June 2005)

E-Plus

E-Plus was the third largest mobile phone company in Germany, with around 13 percent of the market in the mid-2000s. E-Plus built up its call centers quickly, and by 2001 it employed 1,430 call center agents. Employees elected works councils across the company between 1996 and 1997. They initially faced resistance from management, but gradually established a decent working relationship. The DPG also started a campaign to improve working conditions in E-Plus, as part of its project to organize new telecommunications firms and call center subcontractors. The union focused on the company's call centers, because these had the largest number of people who had similar problems with working conditions. They first organized to get equal pay for part-time workers, based on new regulations from an EU directive. The union brought the issue to court and succeeded in convincing the company to change its policy, which in turn helped it to build a working relationship with the company's works councils. Almost all works councilors were ver.di members, although among the employees membership stayed under 10 percent. IG Metall also advised some works councils, as E-Plus was initially owned by a metal industry firm. Following an agreement with the DGB, IG Metall agreed to turn over responsibility to ver.di, although it continued to have members in the company.

Then in 2002, E-Plus sold all three of its call center locations to the Dutch subcontractor SNT. There was already a close relationship between the two companies: E-Plus's parent company KPN owned a 51 percent stake in the SNT group. After SNT took over close to fourteen hundred E-Plus employees, it became the second largest call center subcontractor in Germany, with fourteen locations and more than three thousand employees. There were no layoffs, and employees were able to formally hold on to their old contracts for twelve months. However, after four months the new management asked employees to accept a new contract with SNT, and around 90 percent of employees agreed. This led to a series of changes, including increased performance-based pay and monitoring.

The works councils agreed to these changes, due in part to growing fears that their jobs could be moved. SNT was structured in such a way that every location was a separate company (GmbH and CoKG). This meant that each call center was responsible for turning a profit. Among the E-Plus centers, calls were routed based on agent availability and each center was paid according to the number of calls answered. If one center was less efficient, this cut immediately into its profit and could threaten its continued viability. This led to new pressures on the works council to help improve efficiency and intensified competition across centers. A works councilor at SNT described the new constraints they were under:

> Earlier with E-Plus, with time we learned that we can work together. That is a learning process. That has begun again with us at SNT. But the economic situation is very different. With E-Plus, we could try out different

things. With SNT, it could directly cost jobs. It is difficult for the works council to take that kind of risk, when hundreds of jobs could be lost. (Interview, works councilor, May 2004)

The integration of the E-Plus call centers created new tensions within SNT, as well. Pay was substantially different across locations—for example, some of the company's call centers in eastern Germany paid around half of what E-Plus employees made—and working conditions were generally better at the E-Plus sites. IG Metall also advised some of the SNT works councils, while ver.di primarily advised old E-Plus works councils. A group works council (*Konzernbetriebsrat*) negotiated collective agreements for all sites. However, only six of the company's fourteen centers had local works councils, and because each location was legally a separate company, there was no central works council, or *Gesamtbetriebsrat*. SNT had grown rapidly, and many of the smaller call centers it bought out had no tradition of collective bargaining. This meant that decisions on company policies did not have the full participation of all locations—a problem exacerbated by the large differences in working conditions.

SNT began to have problems with declining call quality, due to high turnover and poor investments in training. Management developed a new program called "40+3": employees worked for forty hours a week, and then received three additional hours of qualification, but were not paid for the extra three hours which added up to more than one hundred hours a year. Managers told their works councils that they expected the majority of employees at every location to sign on to the new agreement. However, several works councils were not sure they wanted to go along with the new plan, including a Berlin call center that was being advised by IG Metall. The local works council said they would give the group works council the ability to negotiate over the plan, but did not want to give them the *Abschlussmandat,* or mandate to finalize the agreement. At that point, management threatened to close centers that did not agree to the new program, and eventually the Berlin works council voted to accept it. Employees working under temporary contracts who continued to oppose the new working time arrangement did not have their contracts extended.

IG Metall representatives had little leverage in these conflicts because there was no collective agreement. They helped the works councils to oversee the new plan, to make sure that the extra three hours were actually used for training. Works councils were also trying to make sure that employees got something in return for participating in the program, such as better job security and limits on short-term contracts. In the end, the new working time arrangement was pushed through because of fears that jobs would be moved and lack of solidarity across works councilors.

Summary

Restructuring of call center work in German telecommunications companies introduced new forms of worker-to-worker competition: between locations within a corporate network and between the in-house and outsourced workforce. In some cases, as at T-Online and E-Plus, whole locations were sold off, precipitating a dramatic change in working conditions. At other firms, like T-Mobile, Arcor, and Vodafone, works councilors initially agreed to outsourcing during call volume peaks or "unsocial" working times, but eventually discovered that this undermined their bargaining leverage and created new pressures to improve performance.

The success of worker representatives in influencing these strategies and their effects on employees was uneven. T-Com initially represented a "best case" where ver.di and works councilors used strong job and location security agreements to keep most core work in-house at high pay, and to slow the consolidation of call center jobs. However, over time management succeeded in expanding outsourcing through selling its subsidiary Vivento Customer Services to subcontractors, and in reducing pay and the number of call centers following its establishment of the new subsidiary T-Service. At the other companies, unions and works councils found themselves in a largely defensive position due to low membership, weak coordination across locations, and a pervasive fear of job loss.

Comparison

The case studies presented in the previous chapter showed clear differences in the institutional resources unions and works councils in the United States and Germany were able to draw on in negotiations over work reorganization. Worker representatives had more uneven success in influencing organizational restructuring, with less of an obvious national pattern in outcomes. Union strategies toward consolidation were similar, with unions in both countries trying to limit employee relocation and job loss—albeit using distinctive resources such as "legacy" contract provisions in the United States and coordinated bargaining across works councils in Germany. In contrast, strategies toward outsourcing initially diverged. The CWA consistently fought outsourcing, which it was confident would lead to layoffs, shrinking membership, and declining job quality. In the United States, the large pay gap between in-house and outsourced call centers was long the most important issue driving outsourcing decisions; and closing this gap became central to negotiations about in-sourcing call center work.

The DPG (now ver.di) and its works councils did not have to fight to hold on to institutional security until recently and were able to protect job security through strong collective agreements. Outside of Deutsche Telekom's core fixed-line business unit T-Com, telecommunications companies were expanding their call centers in the late 1990s as companies like Arcor entered the newly liberalized fixed-line market, and companies like Mannesmann took advantage of booming demand for mobile services. These conditions meant that German worker representatives were more concerned about pressures from management to cut costs, increase working time flexibility, and extend working hours: these problems could be outsourced along with some of the work, often in exchange for job security guarantees.

However, strategies began to look more similar as competition increased and employers increased their use of subcontractors for a range of jobs (see table 4.1). Ver.di's willingness to negotiate a lower pay scale for DT's new call center subsidiary Vivento Customer Services marked a shift in position, from opposing internal pay differentiation to cooperating reluctantly with it in order to bring work back in-house. Across the German cases, unions and works councils were becoming more concerned about job security and willing to make some compromises to reduce costs and improve performance relative to subcontractors. Ver.di held down salary increases at T-Mobile and agreed to wage concessions at T-Service. The CWA agreed to a lower-tier wage for its service and sales workforce at Qwest after the company started outsourcing core work, and negotiated a new title at AT&T in order to bring work back in-house.

Despite growing similarities, certain aspects of union strategies continued to diverge. German unions negotiated provisions similar to those in

TABLE 4.1 Comparison of union strategies toward organizational restructuring

	United States	Germany
Strategy toward consolidation	Limit movement of work through: • Expensive relocation provisions • Negotiated limits on amount of work moved out of the region • Job security agreements • Pressure through regulatory authorities and local politicians	Limit movement of work through: • Expensive relocation provisions • Negotiated limits on amount of work moved out of the region • Location security and job security agreements • Solidarity across local works councils used to keep pay and working conditions similar
Strategy toward outsourcing	Consistent opposition to outsourcing through: • Enforcing "legacy" contracts prohibiting outsourcing if it would involve layoffs or part-time work • Negotiating limits on outsourcing certain jobs • Organizing public campaigns, regulatory leverage, and partnerships aimed at convincing companies to in-source work • Negotiating second tier wages or moving work into subsidiaries at lower pay	Change in strategy from allowing some outsourcing to trying to limit it through: • Negotiating location security agreements and job security protections • Organizing works councils and negotiating collective agreements at call center subcontractors • Negotiating flexible working time rules, second tier wages, and concessions on pay levels and pay increases

the United States that limited outsourcing, such as location and job security agreements. However, concessions were more often targeted at improving flexibility in core firms through new practices like flexible working time and performance-based pay—practices over which German works councils had more substantial control compared to U.S. unions. Probably the most important difference was that German unions were slower to adopt the kinds of public campaigns popular in the United States and approached regulatory policy as a way to support core employers rather than secure agreements. This was linked to their stronger comanagement role at the corporate level in firms like Deutsche Telekom, Arcor, and Vodafone through participation on supervisory boards, and a reluctance to campaign against major unionized employers. This was changing, as ver.di became more willing to organize strikes and public protests in response to announced restructuring measures. However, the focus of union strategy continued to be on maintaining influence through their traditional, institutionalized role in core companies.

Variation in actual union effects on organizational restructuring decisions was most obvious at the company or regional level. Unions initially
had the most success at Deutsche Telekom and Verizon's eastern bargaining units, both in limiting consolidation, preventing or reversing outsourcing, and preventing substantial variation in working conditions across
locations. This was due to their long history of strong and, in the case of
Verizon, often militant unions. Firms with newer, weaker collective agreements, such as Arcor and Cingular, or those that faced intense price competition, such as AT&T and Qwest, unilaterally consolidated and outsourced
call center work. However, by 2008 DT management was similarly able to
substantially downgrade pay and working conditions through these kinds
of strategies—including the sale of Vivento Customer Service locations to
subcontractors and the decision to move all call center work to the new
subsidiary T-Service under a new collective agreement. Formal contractual protections, high membership density, and even the ability to organize
a strike with strong support from the workforce did not supply the bargaining power necessary to halt these restructuring decisions—or even to
substantially lessen their negative effects on the workforce—in the face of
a management determined to cut labor costs.

Across the case study companies, outsourcing and consolidation weakened bargaining leverage and moved job security to the top of unions' and
works councils' agendas. Movement of work between regions and organizations increased competition based on pay and working conditions.
In Germany, the largest regional movement was from West to East; in
the United States from North to West and South. Regional and sectoral
variation in working conditions and union strength meant that employers
had a greater ability to play locations off one another. At the same time
that worker representatives in both countries began taking these kinds of
restructuring decisions more seriously, their success in influencing them
declined precipitously.

Effects of Organizational Restructuring on Pay Levels and Inequality

A final point of comparison between the two countries is the effects of the
organizational restructuring strategies described above on patterns of pay

differentiation for call center jobs. The case studies showed that in both the United States and Germany, similar restructuring measures contributed to the downgrading of pay and working conditions. In the tables and figures below, I present data on changes in pay levels and pay inequality associated with these measures in the largest case study firms: AT&T in the United States and Deutsche Telekom in Germany. Table 4.2 compares call center pay scales for the six AT&T fixed-line contracts (including former AT&T, SBC, and BellSouth call centers) and the three AT&T Mobility contracts (including former Cingular and AT&T wireless centers) in 2009–10. At all companies, pay scales were based on seniority—thus, all employees started at the same level, based on the title, and were able to progress to the top salary level after eight to ten years with the company.

Within AT&T fixed-line call centers, there were some differences by region; for example, starting salaries ranged from $13,624 in the Southwest to $34,736 in the Southeast (based on a forty hour week). However, average salaries were in a similar range and typically close to the top of the pay scale due to high seniority, with most regions falling between $50,000–$55,000. A larger difference can be seen between these contracts and AT&T's new Internet Services "Customer Assistant" title, which was created as a concession by the CWA to bring back 'Tier 1' work that had been subcontracted under SBC (discussed above). Here the starting salary is $21,008, in the same range as the fixed-line contracts, but the scale only goes up to $29,120. High turnover in these centers means that most employees were at the bottom of the scale, earning less than half of the average for other fixed-line centers. Call center workers at AT&T Mobility had a lower starting salary than the new Customer Assistant title, but were able to progress to a higher top salary: between $31,000–$33,000 for the standard customer service agent.

Figure 4.1 illustrates differences between pay spread and average salaries for the different contracts and job titles summarized above. This gives a clearer picture of the large differences between the AT&T fixed-line contracts, on the left, which had a large spread and high average salary; and the new Internet Services Customer Assistant Title and AT&T Mobility contracts, on the right, which had a much smaller spread and lower "top" salary level.

Table 4.3 compares past and current pay rates for call center jobs within Deutsche Telekom and at its two major subcontractors, Walter Services

TABLE 4.2 Pay levels at AT&T call centers, 2009–10

	No. of agents	Starting salary ($)	Average salary ($)	Top salary ($)
AT&T fixed-line				
East	688	30,438	55,187	55,318
Legacy	843	18,720	55,594	62,244
Midwest	2,669	16,354	52,619	63,778
Southeast	1,082	34,736	48,966	52,416
Southwest	4,349	13,624	50,618	54,392
West	1,959	22,854	58,457	62,608
Internet services				
Technical support rep I	N/A	34,216	N/A	59,065
Technical support rep II	459	36,140	54,652	62,044
Customer assistant*	3,634	21,008	26,104	29,120
Average (unweighted)		25,343	50,275	55,665
AT&T Mobility				
Mobility Ntl: CSR1	4,923	19,136	24,586	33,410
CSR2	126	19,396	38,181	39,104
Mobility SE: CSR1	5,111	18,382	28,225	31,148
CSR2	93	18,564	36,509	36,166
Mobility SW: CSR1	N/A	19,734	N/A	32,474
CSR2	N/A	23,686	N/A	34,658
Average (unweighted)		19,816	31,875	34,493

*The customer assistant position was created in 2007 to handle "Tier 1" calls that had formerly been subcontracted.
Source: Communications Workers of America.

and Arvato. The first three columns to the left illustrate starting pay rates and average pay rates for call center workers at T-Com, T-Mobile, and Vivento Customer Services, based on 2006 collective agreements. This already shows the large gap that had opened up between groups of call center employees in the companies: customer service representatives at the fixed-line business unit T-Com earned a starting salary of €34,620 and an average salary of €37,392 (based on a thirty-four-hour work week), compared to €24,888 starting and €27,660 average at the Group's wireless subsidiary T-Mobile (based on a thirty-eight-hour work week).

Employees transferred to Vivento Customer Services initially saw their former salaries reduced by 8.75 percent. However, these call centers were later sold to the two subcontractors, Walter Services and Arvato (far right columns) between 2007 and 2009. Employees were guaranteed some continuity in their salary in the short term but in the long term would be moved to the subcontractors' typical pay rates. At Walter, the recent collective agreement with ver.di set starting hourly pay at €7.50 (approximately

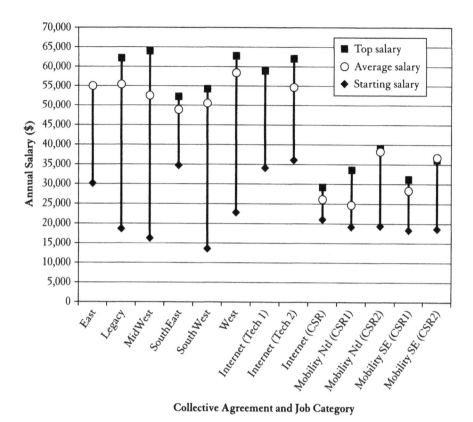

Figure 4.1 Call center pay levels for AT&T fixed-line and AT&T Mobility, 2009–10
Source: Communications Workers of America

€16,000 annual salary, based on a forty-hour week). Data on starting pay was not available for Arvato, but works councilors estimated average pay at €18,000—similar to the average at Walter.

As described above, all of the call center jobs from T-Com and T-Mobile were moved to the new subsidiary T-Service in 2007. Existing employees experienced an effective reduction of their salaries by more than 10 percent, while overall salaries were reduced by 30 percent—with starting salary for customer service representatives of €23,490 and an average salary of €25,839. In addition, 15 percent of base pay was tied to Deutsche Telekom's organizational performance and individual and team performance targets, introducing "at risk" variable pay for the first time.

TABLE 4.3 Pay levels at Deutsche Telekom call centers and major subcontractors, 2006–8

	Deutsche Telekom AG				DT's major call center subcontractors	
	T-Com (2006)	T-Mobile (2006)	Vivento Customer Services (VCS) (2006)	T-Service, DT Kundenservice (2007)	Walter Services (2007)	Arvato Services (CC/CRM) (2007)
Employment in CCs	~18,000	~3,000	~3,000	~22,000	~7,000	~10,000
Starting salary					~€16,000	Not Available
Dir. assistance	€23,772			€20,435		
Service (simple)	€29,646	€24,888		€20,435		
Cust. service	€34,620			€23,490		
Large business	€31,374	€32,088		€26,545		
Average salary			Transferred employees had a reduction in their previous salary level of 8.75%		~€18,000	~€18,000 (€25,000 planned, former VCS)
Dir. assistance	€28,470			€22,478		
Service (simple)	€33,264			€22,478		
Cust. service	€37,392	€27,660		€25,839		
Large business	€35,564	€28,872		€29,199		
Variable pay					~15–20%	Not Available
Service and sales	7%	10%		15%		
Large business	€5323 (100%) €7985 (150%)	€7260 (100%) €12,375 (150%)		15%		
Working hours	34	38	38	38	40	40

Source: Pay data from the DT companies and Walter Services are based on collective agreements and estimated averages from ver.di and works council representatives. Pay data from Arvato are based on estimated averages from works councilors.

Thus, all of the jobs from the left three columns in table 4.2 had moved to the companies represented in the right three columns by 2007. Existing employees' salaries were protected for several years, with reductions "phased in" at both T-Service and the subcontractors. However, this shift of work will involve substantial long-term declines in salary levels for all call center employees at Deutsche Telekom.

Figure 4.2 illustrates the changes that the movement of call center work from T-Com (2006) to T-Service (2007) introduced in the overall pay spread and average pay levels for different job categories—directory assistance, simple services, customer service representatives, and large business representatives. For each pair of job categories, the left-hand line represents the starting, top, and average salaries under the 2006 T-Com agreement for that category, and the right-hand line represents the equivalent salary

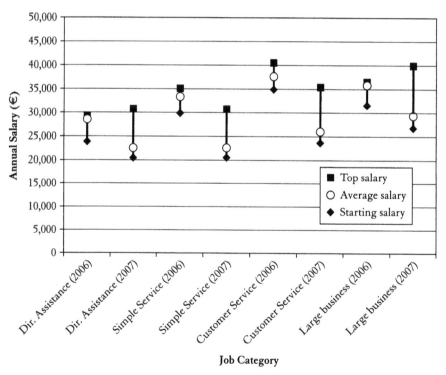

Figure 4.2 Changes in pay levels following the movement of call center work from T-Com (2006) to T-Service (2007)
Source: ver.di

for the same category of work under the 2007 T-Service agreement. In all cases, the average drops substantially, from between €5000 to €10,000; the starting salary declines; and the possible pay spread increases.

The salary figures presented above demonstrate large, and growing, pay inequality between different categories of call center work in both countries. Both the CWA and ver.di have negotiated concessionary agreements that permit lower pay scales for certain categories of call center jobs. However, the CWA appears to have been more successful at avoiding pay concessions for its core members. This may reflect the more recent and dramatic growth of outsourcing in Germany, a weaker tradition of union militancy, as well as broader acceptance by the workforce and union of the need to keep Deutsche Telekom's call centers "competitive" in order to retain jobs in-house. Whatever the explanation for these outcomes, they provide evidence that Germany's strong industrial relations institutions are insufficient to stave off large concessions, resulting here in a major degradation of job quality for thousands of service workers.

Discussion

The case studies in this chapter show substantial cross-national convergence in both management strategies and worker outcomes. As with work reorganization, the impetus for and goals of organizational restructuring were similar in the United States and Germany. Telecommunications companies consolidated and outsourced call center work in response to pressures from growing market competition and using resources provided by new technologies and a booming sector of low-cost subcontractors. Management decisions were not made in an institutional vacuum. Negotiations with unions and works councils influenced how firms pursued these similar goals in each country. Unions had success in leveraging different forms of bargaining power to slow or reverse consolidation and outsourcing, and to win agreements that protected job security and working conditions.

However, both the substance of restructuring strategies and their effects look much more similar between firms and countries. Employers were able to use these strategies to escape collective agreements and to introduce growing differentiation in pay and working conditions. In the United States, low bargaining coverage and variation in collective bargaining institutions across sectors and regions have long been problems for unions. In Germany, these challenges have only recently emerged, as institutions become much less encompassing than in the past. In the telecommunications and subcontractor industries, unions and works councils have been forced to make compromises due to increased competition for jobs across locations and between in-house and outsourced workplaces. Organizational restructuring has thus not only had a disorganizing effect on industrial relations institutions in traditional sectors like telecommunications, but also has made it more difficult for unions to establish new institutions across the more decentralized "production networks" that are now typical of how companies organize their call center work. As bargaining becomes less encompassing and coordinated in Germany, there is growing convergence with the United States on differentiation in pay and working conditions within and across firms.

5

Broadening the Comparison

The previous chapters discussed three related trends in the U.S. and German telecommunications industries: changes in markets and industrial relations, work reorganization and employment systems, and organizational restructuring. In this chapter, I ask how generalizable these case study findings are to a broader set of workplaces and countries. First, I compare collective bargaining institutions, employment practices, and pay inequality in U.S. and German call centers, using data from matched establishment-level surveys of call centers.[1] Similar surveys were administered in each country between 2003 and 2004, as part of the Global Call Center Project, a twenty-country study of management practices and employment relations in call centers from a range of industries. Second, I summarize comparative findings from a broader set of countries, based on survey and case study data from the Global Call Center Project and other international studies of these workplaces.

Survey Findings from the United States and Germany

Collective Bargaining Institutions

Table 5.1 compares the percentage of call center workplaces and the total customer contact workforce that were covered by different collective bargaining arrangements in the United States and Germany, broken down by industry segment. For the German sample, the first three rows compare the level at which unions negotiate collective agreements; and the final four rows compare bargaining structures, based on whether there was a union agreement and/or works council present. The German survey also included three categories of ownership—in-house, independent subcontractor, and outsourced subsidiary—while the U.S. survey only distinguished between in-house and outsourced firms.

This comparison shows that collective bargaining covered a minority of call center workplaces in both countries. In the United States, more than 90 percent of establishments and 84 percent of the workforce had no collective agreement; compared to 74 percent of establishments and 55 percent of the workforce in Germany. Furthermore, 14 percent of German establishments and 42 percent of the workforce had company agreements, with only 4 percent of workers under an industry agreement. Bargaining was thus overwhelmingly based on decentralized, company-level negotiations. In addition, a similar proportion of call centers had dual bargaining to those having only a works council, with close to 40 percent of the workforce covered by each. A very small number of establishments were covered by a union agreement with no works council (only five of the call centers surveyed).

In both countries, a higher share of in-house call centers was covered by collective bargaining. This difference was particularly stark in the United States, where only 1.5 percent of subcontractors had a union agreement. In Germany, the picture is more mixed: 54 percent of in-house centers had no collective agreement, compared to 85 percent of subcontractors and 80 percent of outsourced subsidiaries. However, 67 percent of the in-house workforce was not covered by an agreement. Bargaining was also more likely to occur at the industry level for in-house firms and was almost exclusively at company level in subcontractors, with even distribution for outsourced subsidiaries.

TABLE 5.1 Collective bargaining coverage and structure, U.S. and German call centers

	Total	In-house	Subcontractor	Outsourced subsidiary
United States				
Union				
% establishments	9.1	10.3	1.6	N/A
% workforce*	16.2	20.4	1.4	N/A
Establishments in survey	**455**	**393**	**62**	**N/A**
Total workforce covered	**82,587**	**64,331**	**18,256**	**N/A**
Germany				
Industry-level agreement				
% establishments	11.8	31	1	10
% workforce	4	19.9	0.5	2.9
Company-level agreement				
% establishments	13.8	15	14	10
% workforce	41.5	13.6	50.4	17.9
No collective agreement				
% establishments	74.3	54	85	80
% workforce	54.6	66.5	49.1	79.2
Union + works council				
% establishments	22.4	45.8	11.1	10
% workforce	42.5	33.5	47.3	17.1
Works council only				
% establishments	23	35.4	16	35
% workforce	36.6	47.3	33	46.7
Union agreement only				
% establishments	3.3	0	3.7	10
% workforce	2.9	0	3.6	3.7
No union or works council				
% establishments	51.3	18.8	74.1	45
% workforce	18.0	19.8	16.1	32.6
Establishments in survey	**152**	**48**	**81**	**20**
Total workforce covered	**17,827**	**2956**	**12,503**	**1898**

* Figures for % workforce are based on weighting the establishment data by the number of employees in each establishment.
Source: Global Call Center Project survey

A much larger proportion of Germany's in-house call centers (46 percent) had dual bargaining compared to subcontractors (11 percent) or subsidiaries (10 percent). However, the proportion of the workforce covered by these arrangements was again higher in subcontractors, reflecting their larger size. Meanwhile, 47 percent of the in-house and outsourced subsidiary workforce had a works council only, compared to 33 percent in subcontractors. Outsourced subsidiaries thus appear to have been particularly successful at avoiding collective bargaining with a union but did continue to have a works council presence.

These statistics are consistent with case study findings. Overall, union density and bargaining coverage were lower in the United States. However, collective bargaining was fragmented and decentralized in Germany. In this environment, works councils are often the sole form of worker representation. Meanwhile, subcontractors were almost a completely union-free zone in the United States, and in Germany different categories of outsourced call centers had lower bargaining coverage or more decentralized bargaining institutions compared to in-house centers.

Employment Systems

A central argument in this book is that participation rights and union bargaining power are important supports for the adoption of high-involvement employment systems. The U.S. and German survey data can be used to examine whether patterns found in the case studies are present across a larger sample of workplaces. It is important to note that the call centers surveyed were not identical in terms of the markets they served and the profiles of their employees (see appendix B). One of the most significant differences is the high proportion of subcontractors and outsourced subsidiaries in the German sample, representing 100 out of 150 establishments surveyed, compared to 64 subcontractors out of 464 establishments surveyed in the United States. In both countries, in-house centers were typically established earlier, while outsourcers tended to be larger, employing more customer contact employees. Due to differences between these two market segments, it makes sense to analyze them separately. In addition, compared to German centers, U.S. call centers tended to be older, larger, focus on inbound rather than outbound calls, and have longer average call handling times—differences which hold across segments. Thus we might expect German centers to have adopted *more* of a constrained employment model, on average, based solely on typical task complexity or skill requirements by call type.

Education levels and experience also differed between countries and segments. In-house call centers in the United States were twice as likely as those in Germany to report the typical education level of employees as "university degree," while proportions were similar in outsourced centers.

In Germany, a separate question was asked concerning the proportion of employees who had completed dual apprenticeship training. On average, 78 percent of agents in in-house call centers had this training, with only slightly smaller figures in outsourced centers. U.S. call centers also reported having a larger proportion of very low-tenure (less than one year) employees. This suggests that overall, human capital was higher in German centers.

Figures 5.1 and 5.2 present comparative data on work organization, performance monitoring, and outcomes for in-house and outsourced call centers.

First, a comparison of work organization shows that German call centers were more likely to adopt high-involvement practices than those in the United States (figure 5.1). A larger proportion had in place self-managed teams, flexible job descriptions, and flexible scheduling arrangements for a majority of their workforce. Close to twice as many German in-house centers reported high use of flexible scheduling arrangements compared to those in the United States. Employee discretion levels were also generally higher in Germany. The largest difference here is in employee discretion over their break times: around 75 percent of both in-house and outsourced centers in Germany reported high discretion over breaks, compared to 37 percent of in-house centers and 25 percent of subcontractors in the United States. Overall, outsourced centers gave workers less discretion than in-house centers and were less likely to adopt practices like self-managed teams; however, these differences were larger in the United States.

Figure 5.2 compares performance monitoring practices, as well as outcomes such as absenteeism and turnover. Here, differences are even larger between the two countries. German in-house centers continuously monitored a higher proportion of calls compared to U.S. centers. However, they communicated performance statistics less frequently to employees (a practice associated with work intensification) and used significantly less supervisor monitoring. The high rate of continuous monitoring in Germany may be related to the practice of using "mystery calls" to evaluate service quality, which do not involve recording call data. In addition, as the case studies showed, recording of performance data in Germany is often coupled with tight restrictions on who has access to that data and how it is used. There is some evidence of this here, in that the use of performance data for purposes of disciplining employees was much more common in

In-house centers

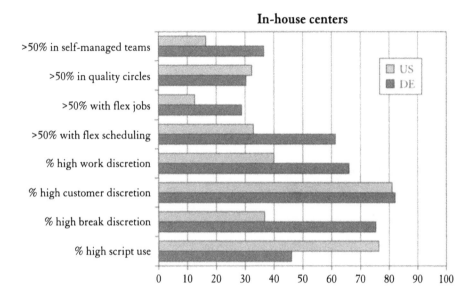

Outsourced centers

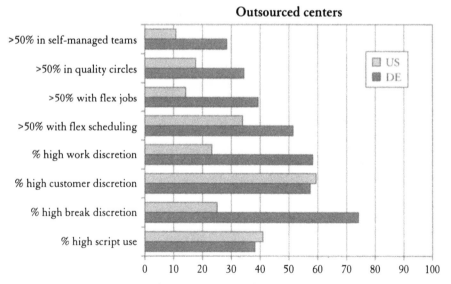

Figure 5.1 Work organization by country, in-house and outsourced centers
Source: Global Call Center Project survey

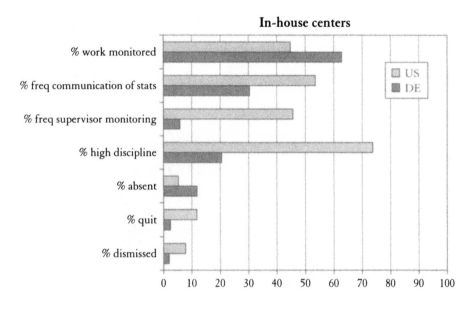

In-house centers

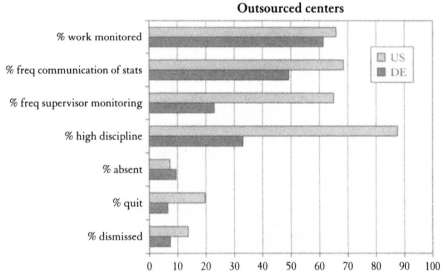

Outsourced centers

Figure 5.2 Performance monitoring and outcomes by country, in-house and outsourced centers
Source: Global Call Center Project survey

the United States, with 74 percent of in-house centers and 88 percent of subcontractors reporting high use, compared to 20 percent and 33 percent in Germany.

Finally, the United States had higher quit and dismissal rates, but similar or lower absenteeism rates—likely an outcome of a more discipline-focused set of employment practices. In both countries, outsourced centers monitored work more frequently, were more likely to use this data to discipline workers, and had close to twice as high turnover rates compared to in-house centers.

Collective Bargaining and Employment Systems

A further question is how these practices differ across call centers with different collective bargaining arrangements. Based on case study findings, we would expect centers with dual bargaining arrangements in Germany to make more use of high-involvement practices compared to those with no collective bargaining; but to find more mixed outcomes where only works councils are present. In the United States, unions have fewer formal means to influence practices such as work design and monitoring. However, union presence should be associated with higher pay and more secure jobs, as these are both areas where they have traditionally had bargaining rights and power.

Figures 5.3 and 5.4 compare the same set of employment practices and outcomes as those discussed above—work organization, performance monitoring, and absenteeism and turnover. Here the comparison is between union and nonunion call centers in the United States, and German centers with both a union agreement and a works council; a works council but no union agreement; and no union agreement or works council. Again, the different characteristics of call centers in each group caution care when interpreting results (see appendix C). Workplaces with union agreements in both countries tended to be older, to handle in-bound calls, and to employ a more skilled or experienced workforce.

A comparison of work organization (figure 5.3) shows that union presence was associated with lower use of high-involvement practices in the United States, but with more mixed outcomes in Germany. Nonunion call centers in the United States on average had a higher take-up of flexible scheduling practices, self-managed teams, quality circles, and flexible job descriptions; gave employees more discretion over their working methods and breaks; and monitored a smaller percentage of their work continuously—although customer discretion and script use were similar.

In Germany, call centers with both a union agreement and a works council more often adopted flexible scheduling for the majority of their workforce, and had (somewhat) higher levels of work discretion. However, centers with no collective bargaining were more frequent users of self-managed teams and quality circles (if only marginally); and flexible job descriptions and script use were similar. Call centers with works councils but no union agreement fall between or below centers with dual bargaining and those with no collective bargaining across many measures. However, several measures of discretion were comparatively high.

Figure 5.4 shows a similar set of comparisons based on performance monitoring practices and outcomes. Here, outcomes are more mixed for the United States, where unionized centers monitored a larger proportion of work, but made less intensive use of supervisor monitoring and were less likely to use performance information to discipline employees. In addition, quit and dismissal rates were much higher in nonunion call centers. This is consistent with the notion that unions provide job security protections or encourage employees to remain in their jobs due to higher pay and protection from arbitrary management decisions.

In Germany, call centers with dual bargaining also monitored a higher percentage of employee calls. However, communication of performance statistics and supervisor monitoring were much less frequent, while performance data were less often used to discipline employees. For example, 6 percent of centers with dual bargaining reported frequent supervisor monitoring (once a week to daily), compared to 27 percent of centers with no collective bargaining. Centers with works councils only were again in the middle or higher on most measures of monitoring, with the exception of supervisor monitoring where rates were at a similarly low level to those with dual bargaining. Finally, collective bargaining was also associated with lower quit and dismissal rates, similar to the United States.

Taken together, this comparison of descriptive statistics shows some support for the generalizability of case study findings. The most substantial differences were found between U.S. and German in-house centers—though outsourced centers in Germany also appeared to offer better working conditions than their U.S. counterparts. Patterns for collective bargaining

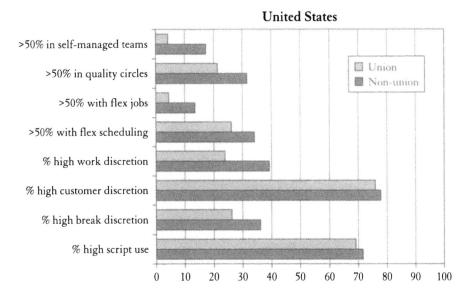

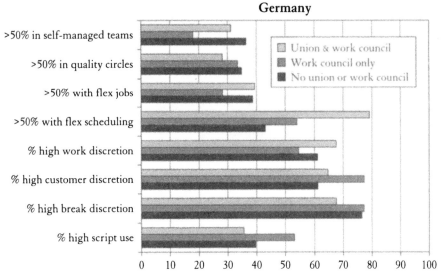

Figure 5.3 Work organization by collective bargaining arrangements, United States and Germany
Source: Global Call Center Project survey

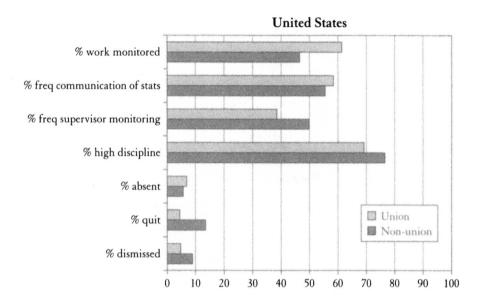

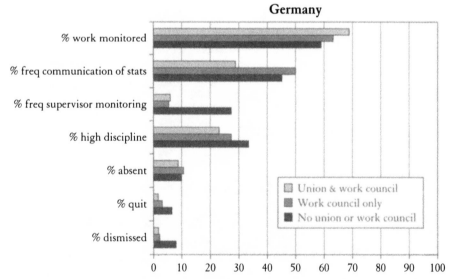

Figure 5.4 Performance monitoring by collective bargaining arrangements, United States and Germany
Source: Global Call Center Project survey

are more difficult to interpret, with a moderate use of different participatory practices in nonunion centers in both the United States and Germany, as well as possible limits on monitoring intensity in centers with collective bargaining in both countries. As mentioned above, it is difficult to interpret these findings because other characteristics of each group may affect outcomes—such as, for example, human capital, task type, industry, and center size.

To test whether collective bargaining in each country was associated with different employment practices and outcomes (controlling for these other variables), I conducted a series of multivariate analyses (Doellgast 2008a).[2] I constructed two scales, based on the groups of measures described above: (1) a "high-involvement work organization" scale, including the percentage of the workforce in self-managed teams, in quality circles, and with flexible job descriptions; as well as a measure of overall discretion; and (2) a "high-discretion performance management" scale, including measures of the frequency of supervisor monitoring, how often employees were given statistical information on their performance, how often employees were given feedback on their phone technique, and the extent to which information from performance monitoring was used to discipline employees. Because these are additive indexes, they should measure the extent to which employers adopted multiple practices at high intensity.

Findings showed that, first, German call centers were significantly more likely to adopt high-involvement work organization and high-discretion performance management compared to U.S. call centers. This held when comparing centers with no collective bargaining in both countries. Second, union and works council presence in Germany was only significantly associated with the performance management index; and centers with works councils did not use more of these practices. Third, United States call centers with union agreements were lower adopters of high-involvement work organization compared to those with no agreements, but there were no differences in performance management. In both countries, outsourced centers monitored workers more intensively than in-house centers, but work practices were similar.

I also looked at the relationship between collective bargaining, employment practices, and quit rates. Here, again, the strongest results were by country, with lower quit rates in German call centers than those in the United States, even across centers with no collective bargaining. These differences were only partially explained by differences in management practices. Collective bargaining was also associated with lower quit rates in both countries. However, here the effect of dual bargaining in Germany was no longer significant when accounting for differences in management practices, while union presence in the United States remained strongly significant.

These findings are broadly consistent with patterns in the descriptive data discussed above. The largest differences in employment systems were between countries, with German firms more likely to adopt a "high-involvement" model of call center management compared to those in the United States. At the same time, collective bargaining also made a difference for practices and outcomes, reducing quit rates in the United States and lessening the intensity of performance monitoring in Germany. Of course, these data are based on very rough measures. As the case studies showed, often the biggest differences between centers concerned the ways in which practices were implemented, such as who had access to performance data or the particular ways in which scheduling flexibility was managed. However, they do provide evidence that the case study findings reflect broader trends in both countries: national and workplace institutions were associated with different employment practices in call centers.

Pay Levels and Inequality

A final set of comparisons concerns patterns of pay levels and differences in pay between workplaces. Table 5.2 compares median pay levels in each country, based on the reported "typical" agent salary at the center level; as well as degree of pay dispersion for centers in different industries and with or without union agreements. Pay dispersion is measured here as the coefficient of variation, or the ratio of the standard deviation to the mean. Median pay in call centers was above the national median in both countries: in the United States, the median in call centers was $29,000 compared to a national median of $27,000; in Germany the dollar equivalent was $26,208 compared to a national median of $21,000.[3] A comparison of coefficients of variation show that wage dispersion in call centers was also substantially higher in the United States than in Germany.

The data also show some evidence of union effects on pay. Having a collective agreement was associated with a 36 percent wage premium in

TABLE 5.2 Pay levels and pay inequality, U.S. and German call centers

	United States		Germany	
	Median	Coefficient of variation	Median	Coefficient of variation
All	$29,000	0.51	$26,208	0.33
Union agreement	$36,000	0.38	$35,728	0.31
No union agreement	$28,000	0.52	$26,208	0.31
% difference	28.6		36.3	
In-house	$30,000	0.52	$33,264	0.30
Outsourced	$25,000	0.32	$26,208	0.32
% difference	20		26.9	

Source: Global Call Center Project survey

Germany and a 29 percent wage premium in the United States. In-house centers also paid higher wages compared to outsourced centers. The median typical wage for in-house centers was on average 20 percent higher compared to subcontractors in the United States, and 27 percent higher in Germany. Coefficients of variation show overall high pay dispersion within these groups. However, differences are largest among U.S. nonunion call centers and in-house call centers.

Again, these findings are broadly consistent with the case studies. Both the United States and Germany show high levels of pay dispersion, with overall higher wage levels in call centers negotiating union agreements and operating in-house compared to their nonunion, outsourced counterparts. The level and characteristics of pay inequality within and between these segments in Germany were similar to patterns in the United States. This provides further evidence that increased pay dispersion is a converging trend. Moreover, this trend appears to be associated with both subcontracting and escape from (or avoidance of) collective bargaining.

Beyond the United States and Germany: International Findings

The United States and Germany are often held up as representative of "liberal" and "coordinated" market economies—characterized by the extent to which economic activity is coordinated through the market or through nonmarket institutions (Hall and Soskice 2001). However, they are also unique in their respective categories. The United States arguably has the most weakly regulated labor markets and weakest unions of the liberal countries. Meanwhile, Germany stands out within social Europe for the extent of recent erosion in these same institutions.

Comparative survey and case study research can be used to ask to what extent national and collective bargaining institutions influence outcomes in a wider range of countries in each group. The U.S. and German surveys analyzed above were conducted as part of a larger study, the Global Call Center (GCC) Project. Teams in twenty countries carried out identical establishment-level surveys, stakeholder interviews, and case studies in call centers (Batt, Holman, and Holtgrewe 2009). A complementary study on "Low Wage Work in Europe" (with some of the same team members) examined call centers as one of five typically low-wage occupations (Gautié and Schmitt 2009; Lloyd, Weinkopf, and Batt 2009). I summarize below a few key findings to come out of this research that relate to the arguments presented in this book.

Collective Bargaining Institutions

Figure 5.5 presents GCC data on patterns of union and works council representation.

Call centers were more likely to be covered by some form of collective agreement in the European coordinated economies. However, they show different patterns of coverage, which can be traced to distinct institutions that support the incorporation of new workplaces and industries into collective agreements. Spain and Sweden have 100 percent coverage by union agreements, while France and the Netherlands have a very low proportion of workplaces with no collective bargaining, particularly among in-house call centers. The governments in France, the Netherlands, and Spain pursue policies of extending collective agreements to all firms in a sector, provided they are negotiated by what are deemed to be "representative" unions and employers' associations. In Austria, employers are required to join the *Wirtschaftskammer,* or business chambers that negotiate on behalf of employers, which serve a similar purpose. Sweden and Denmark do not have traditions of statutory extension, but in practice high union membership rates and strong employer norms of complying

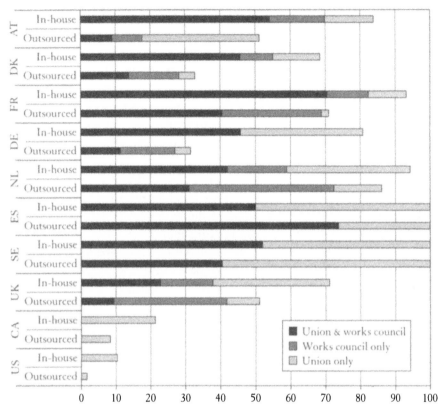

Figure 5.5 Collective bargaining arrangements coverage and structure, coordinated European and liberal countries
Source: Global Call Center Project survey

with agreements have kept bargaining coverage high. Thus, in all of these countries data showing lower rates of coverage by union agreements in call centers probably underestimate the proportion of firms that adhere to the minimum terms of sectoral agreements. Germany is an exceptional case within Europe where statutory extension is rarely used and unions have a declining ability to enforce agreements due to falling membership, leading to dramatic declines in bargaining coverage—mirrored here in the low rates of union coverage.

Across the liberal countries, Canada and the United States have very low bargaining coverage in call centers; while the UK more closely re-sembles patterns in other European countries that lack formal extension mechanisms. All three have a decentralized structure of collective bargaining, with most agreements concluded at the company or establishment level. The United States stands out, however, for weak labor law enforcement and low coverage of collective agreements. In the UK, unions have fewer formal legal protections for organizing and bargaining compared to the United States and are encouraged to seek voluntary recognition by employers before following a (more recently established) statutory recognition procedure. However, they have maintained higher membership rates and a stronger public role. The legal framework of collective bargaining in Canada is more similar to that in the United States. However, union organizing in Canada has not encountered the kind of concerted employer resistance observed in the United States, due to stronger protection for and enforcement of union recognition and bargaining rights (Godard 2009).

The data in figure 5.5 also show interesting differences in bargaining structure and presence between in-house and outsourced call centers. Across in-house call centers, on average around half of all workplaces negotiated collective agreements with both a union and a works council. France stands out for its particularly high rates of dual bargaining (71 percent), while Germany is unique for having a high proportion of call centers with works councils but no union agreement (35 percent). In nearly all countries, with the exception of Sweden and Spain, coverage by union agreements and dual bargaining were lower in subcontractors. These differences were particularly stark in Germany, Denmark, and Austria, where less than 15 percent of subcontractors were covered by dual bargaining. In the United States, only one subcontractor surveyed had a collective agreement, while the UK had a high proportion of subcontractors with works councils, which represent a weak form of consultation under British law.

Case study findings show that industrial relations institutions in each country have provided different resources for unions to establish collective bargaining in the newer subcontractor sector. In Austria, France, the Netherlands, and Spain, unions have taken advantage of extension provisions to negotiate new binding agreements with call center subcontractors or to extend existing sectoral agreements to these groups (Doellgast, Batt, and Sørensen 2009). In Denmark, there was no designated sectoral agreement, but subcontractors often followed the terms of other agreements or adhered to the Salaried Employees Act (*Funktionærlov*), which sets pay and working conditions for white collar workers (Sørensen 2008). Germany again stands out as the one country that had no sectoral institutions and very few company agreements regulating pay and working conditions in subcontractors (Weinkopf 2009).

At the same time, unions in all of these countries have had difficulty negotiating and enforcing strong terms and conditions in subcontractors. The Netherlands is an interesting case because it was the first country in which unions negotiated a separate agreement specifically for this sector. However, it has been plagued by problems, with employers refusing to accept certain key union demands and withdrawing briefly from negotiations to sign a more favorable agreement with a smaller union (Van Jaarsveld, De Grip, and Sieben 2009; Klaveren and Sprenger 2008).

Similar patterns can be seen in other European countries. In Spain, unions negotiated a national agreement for call centers, in with better wages, dismissal protections, and scheduling rules than those in other national service sector agreements. However, many subcontractors instead chose to follow these weaker service agreements, despite concerted union efforts to enforce the stronger call center agreement (Shire, Schönauer et al. 2009). The Austrian trade union confederation (ÖGB) succeeded in incorporating subcontractors into the national agreement for miscellaneous business services in the late 1990s (Holst 2008). However, many subcontractors successfully avoided its provisions through hiring workers on freelance contracts (Shire, Schönauer et al. 2009). Under Austrian law, freelancers were exempted from sick leave and vacation pay, and were not covered by the terms of collective agreements or able to vote in works council elections.

Employment Systems

Comparative case studies and survey findings showed that high-involvement employment systems were more common in Germany than in the United States. Data from the GCC surveys show that in this respect German firms are to some extent typical of other "coordinated market countries." Call centers in these countries tended to make more use of high-involvement work design, have lower dismissal rates, give employees more discretion, and use less intense performance monitoring compared to those in liberal market countries (Doellgast, Holtgrewe, and Deery 2009; Holman et al. 2009).

At the same time, the data show some substantial differences between countries typically grouped in these two categories. France showed lower rates of job discretion and more intensive monitoring compared to the other coordinated countries; while UK managers monitored workers less intensively than those in other liberal countries (ibid). Denmark had higher dismissal rates than other coordinated economies, while the UK and Canada had lower dismissal rates than the United States (Doellgast, Holtgrewe, and Deery 2009; van Jaarsveld, Kwon, and Frost 2009). Thus, overall, call centers in countries with stronger traditions of social regulation tended to offer higher quality jobs; but nationally specific institutions appeared to play some role in shaping these outcomes.

I have argued that variation in collective bargaining institutions was an important factor explaining differences in the take-up of high-involvement practices between the United States and Germany, as well as between firms in Germany. The international data give some support for this argument: in the coordinated countries of Europe, dual union and works council representation was associated with greater use of high-involvement practices, while centers with works councils monitored workers less intensively compared to those with no collective bargaining institutions (Doellgast, Holtgrewe, and Deery 2009). Meanwhile, in the liberal countries, union presence either made no difference for work design and performance monitoring or was negatively associated with these practices; but did lower dismissal rates (Doellgast, Holtgrewe, and Deery 2009; van Jaarsveld, Kwon, and Frost 2009).

In addition, across both groups, subcontractors had weaker collective bargaining institutions and tended to adopt more low-road or Taylorist employment practices. They monitored workers more often and gave them less discretion in their jobs (Doellgast, Holtgrewe, and Deery 2009; Holman et al. 2009), had higher dismissal rates (Doellgast, Holtgrewe, and Deery 2009), and paid lower wages (Batt and Nohara 2009). Subcontractors also used more part-time workers in the liberal countries (van Jaarsveld, Kwon, and Frost 2009) and employed a higher proportion of temporary workers in coordinated countries (Shire, Mottweiler et al. 2009). This sector thus most represented a trend of "low-road convergence." Only German and Austrian subcontractors used more high-involvement practices compared to those in the United States; and the presence of collective bargaining in subcontractors was more weakly associated with these practices in coordinated countries and had no effect in liberal countries (Doellgast, Holtgrewe, and Deery 2009).

A high-involvement model was also associated with better outcomes for workers. Batt et al. (2010) found that centers that used high-involvement work design and less intensive performance monitoring had higher wage levels in both liberal and coordinated countries. Van Jaarsveld et al. (2009) also found lower dismissal rates in call centers that had higher levels of job discretion in liberal market countries. Call center workers thus not only enjoyed the "soft" benefits associated with more discretion, more flexible schedules, and opportunities to participate in decision-making, but also gained economically through higher salaries and more stable jobs.

These quantitative results give an overall picture of national differences in practices and outcomes. Qualitative findings help to shed light on the particular role that collective bargaining institutions played in shaping management strategies. For example, France stood out in the data for having higher rates of monitoring and lower discretion compared to other European countries. Case studies in French banking, utilities, and subcontractor call centers also found strong trends of Taylorization and work intensification (Beraud, Colin, and Grasser 2008). This may be due to France's weak participation rights and workplace-level collective bargaining institutions, which mean that management typically has broad discretion over work redesign. Denmark is an interesting counterexample, where case study research found a high take-up of high-involvement practices, typically developed through close partnership with worker representatives (Sørensen 2008). Sørensen and Weinkopf (2009) argue that the combination of high union density, workplace bargaining institutions, and strong employer norms of conforming to agreements supported high-involvement models.

Pay Levels and Inequality

The case studies in this book showed that strong participation structures at the workplace level in Germany were being weakened by bargaining decentralization and opportunities to exit collective bargaining arrangements, contributing to concession bargaining and growing pay inequality. International survey data and case studies provide further evidence that institutions setting minimum terms and conditions of employment can have a substantial influence on pay levels and distribution. Again, the GCC data show variation between liberal and coordinated countries, but also within each group (table 5.3).

First, median pay in call centers differed across countries. Austrian and Dutch agents were paid well below the national median; while Danish and Swedish workers were paid well above average. In the other countries, call center wages were on par with or slightly above the national median. Lloyd et al. (2009) evaluated cross-national differences in the incidence of low-wage work, or the proportion of call center jobs that fall below two-thirds of the national median wage level. Here, Germany and the Netherlands stood out, with each having over 35 percent of the workforce in "low-wage" jobs—notably, at a higher rate than the United Kingdom (28 percent) or the United States (19 percent); and much higher than Denmark (5 percent) or France (4 percent).

Second, there were large cross-national differences in patterns of pay inequality between centers. Austria, Germany, the Netherlands, Spain, Canada, and the United States showed moderate to high inequality; while Denmark, France, Sweden, and the UK were moderate to low. Based on descriptive data, centers with collective agreements generally paid somewhat higher wages than those without agreements. However, the size of this gap was only large (and significant) in the United States, Canada, and Germany.

TABLE 5.3 Median pay and pay inequality, coordinated European and liberal countries*

	Call centers (GCC)				All workplaces (OECD)	
	Median (uw)	Median (w)	Coefficient of variation (w)	Gini (uw)	Mid-2000s ntl. Gini	Mid-2000s ntl. median
Austria	$15,181	$16,075	0.59	0.23	0.27	$23,374
Denmark	$41,935	$41,935	0.15	0.09	0.23	$30,200
France	$21,962	$20,910	0.17	0.10	0.28	$20,502
Germany	$26,208	$26,208	0.27	0.18	0.30	$21,443
Netherlands	$15,480	$12,900	0.44	0.18	0.26	$27,107
Spain	$14,640	$12,216	0.29	0.16	0.32	$14,731
Sweden	$30,375	$32,076	0.13	0.08	0.23	$23,252
UK	$27,300	$26,390	0.20	0.13	0.34	$25,336
Canada	$30,000	$26,400	0.31	0.17	0.32	$24,078
US	$29,000	$26,000	0.38	0.24	0.38	$26,990

*The call center measures are reported both unweighted (uw) and weighted by number of agents in each center (w).
Source: Global Call Center Project survey and OECD national surveys.

A further question is whether patterns of inequality between centers with different collective bargaining institutions or in different market segments differed across countries. Multivariate analyses of pay differentials account for factors such as skill level or sector that could explain these differences. Batt and Nohara (2009) found that unionized call centers paid significantly higher wages in the liberal United States and Canada—but also in coordinated Germany and Denmark (although Denmark's union differential was small at 7.8 percent compared to 29.7 percent in Germany). Similar calculations showed a union differential of 16 percent in the Netherlands (Lloyd, Weinkopf, and Batt 2009). Denmark and France had particularly low pay differentials between in-house call centers and subcontractors, at 7.8 percent and 6.6 percent, respectively—compared to 26.2 percent in Germany (Batt and Nohara 2009). Meanwhile, in the UK, Austria, and France, there was no union effect on pay, and the UK showed no difference between in-house and subcontractor centers.

This comparison again shows that findings from the United States and Germany may be broadly representative of trends in "liberal" and "coordinated" countries, but that national differences also are evident within those two groups. The United States and Canada had a high degree of pay inequality overall, as well as high pay differentiation between union and nonunion or in-house and subcontracted workplaces. However, patterns of inequality in the UK more closely resemble those in Europe, with low pay dispersion and no significant differences based on union or subcontracting status. Within Europe, Germany is unusual for the degree and effects of institutional erosion. However, it is not unique: Austria and the Netherlands also had quite unequal wage structures despite their more encompassing collective bargaining institutions. This may be due to the common use of nonstandard employment forms in these countries, as well as highly segmented labor markets and traditions of sectoral wage inequality.

Denmark and France stand out here as well, but this time for their similarities: they are the two national cases that consistently demonstrated low internal inequality. In both countries, encompassing institutions provide a high minimum wage floor and more effectively reduce differentials between sectors. However, in the case of France, low differentials were coupled with low wages overall. French unions are relatively weak and rely on the government to set minimum standards, with wages clustering around these legal minimum levels. In addition, low inequality was accompanied by high monitoring and low discretion. Again, Denmark was the "best case" viewed in terms of worker outcomes: strong union presence at workplace level, a tradition of social partnership, and (relatively) solidaristic wage structures secured through encompassing agreements appear to have resulted in both low inequality and greater use of high-involvement management practices.

Telecommunications Call Centers in France

France is particularly interesting to compare with the United States and Germany, as the survey data show both low take-up of high-involvement employment practices and low inequality across workplaces. To examine why this is the case, I discuss findings from a study of telecommunications call centers in France, based on research conducted with colleagues on the Global Call Center Project, Hiroatsu Nohara and Robert Tchobanian (Doellgast, Nohara, and Tchobanian 2009). This presents a convenient parallel to the telecommunications case studies discussed in earlier chapters.

France and Germany have similar traditions of strong social and political regulation of work. However, the industrial relations systems in the two countries present significant contrasts. First, in France, codetermination rights and institutions are considerably weaker than those in Germany. This is due to more constricted formal participation rights, as well as low membership density, divisions among the major unions, and a generally conflictual tradition of bargaining. *Comités d'entreprise* (workplace committees, often compared with German-style works councils) are elected by the workforce in companies with at least fifty employees and include both the head of the company and employee representatives. Establishments with more than ten employees are covered by a separate system of *délégués du personnel* (workforce delegates), who represent employees when they have individual or collective grievances. However, neither body has formal codetermination rights, and union agreements have priority in all areas concerning pay and employment practices (Amadieu 1995).

At the same time, France has in place stronger formal mechanisms to extend collective agreements to poorly organized sectors and workplaces compared to Germany. The French government commonly declares agreements generally binding on all establishments within a particular industry, provided they are negotiated by unions deemed "representative." Although the German Ministry of Labor can also formally declare sectoral agreements generally binding, this power is rarely used as it requires the agreement of three representatives each from the two major peak organizations: the Confederation of German Employers (BDA) and the Confederation of German Trade Unions (DGB).

Collective Bargaining and Employment Systems

These institutions have shaped the strategies that France Télécom and its major competitors adopted as they adjusted to changes in the markets, leading to quite different outcomes from those in Germany or the United States. France Télécom only established comités d'entreprise in 2005, when the French state sold its majority stake and became a minority shareholder. The corporate group had in place similar representative bodies that worked closely with the unions, but negotiations tended to focus on topics traditionally important to civil servants such as promotions, mobility, and individual grievances. Managers had begun to discuss decisions concerning organizational changes, technology adoption, or work design with the comités, but worker representatives did not have veto rights over these decisions. In addition, multiple (and competing) unions were present in France Télécom, which created additional barriers to building strong countervailing power at the workplace level. Members affiliated with these different unions often took distinct or even opposing positions, particularly with regard to potentially disruptive restructuring measures.

Because of this fragmented and weak structure of local bargaining, managers were able to implement new employment practices unilaterally as they reorganized call center work. Similar to management strategies in the United States case studies, France Télécom managers mainly used local structures to communicate planned changes to worker representatives. Meanwhile, unions focused on regulating employment in the areas where they traditionally enjoyed some degree of power, through central agreements on pay, job classifications, and promotions. Union presence was lower outside of France Télécom, leaving management at these firms with broad discretion over work redesign—though these decisions were often influenced by the job security clauses, job classifications, and pay rates set by sectoral and company agreements.

Management used this discretion to adopt employment practices that relied heavily on work intensification, monitoring, and scripting. Similar to the CWA in the United States, the unions at France Télécom played some role in setting out the rules within which practices were implemented but did not participate in the design of those practices. For example, annualization of hours was negotiated between the comités or delegués and management. These agreements restricted managers' ability to change schedules at short notice, with some flexibility in the rules during high-volume seasons. However, they gave individual agents little choice over their schedules. The comités were consulted on rules concerning the use of electronic monitoring, but they were unable to negotiate agreements that developed alternatives to increased monitoring intensity or the use of scripts to standardize customer interactions.

At the same time, France Télécom had assigned a broader range of tasks to individual agents, increasing skill and job complexity. Here, work design more closely resembled that at Deutsche Telekom, as managers could draw on the resource provided by its highly skilled and stable professional workforce developed through strong internal labor markets (Reynaud and Reynaud 1996). France Télécom also continued to employ a large number of civil servants, or *fonctionnaires,* with iron-clad job security, making it difficult to use the threat of dismissals to discipline employees. Supervisors cross-trained call center agents in products and skills to improve internal flexibility, allowing management to route different call types across call center locations and between teams at one location. Increased task complexity required investment in training and skills but also led to work intensification and increased agent stress (Théry 2006; SUD and CGC 2008).

Collective Bargaining and Organizational Restructuring

Collective bargaining institutions at France Télécom and at the sectoral level also developed quite differently from those in Germany or the United States. Collective bargaining at France Télécom continued to be influenced by the legacy of state ownership. The majority of employees at France Télécom were civil servants, whose working conditions were determined by centralized civil service negotiations.[4] As France Télécom established subsidiaries in the early 2000s, such as Orange (mobile) and Wannadoo (internet), civil servants had the option to transfer to the new companies with rights of return. However, most of their workforce was hired externally and thus covered under private sector agreements. Civil servants were also gradually moved to other jobs in the public sector following several waves of downsizing. Each new subsidiary negotiated separate agreements covering subjects such as variable pay and scheduling, but they were also bound to follow the minimum terms in France Télécom's central collective agreement.

Like Germany, France did not have sectoral collective bargaining institutions in the telecommunications industry when markets were liberalized in 1998. However, France Télécom and its major competitor Cegetel established an employers' association, UNETEL, and signed an agreement in December 1998 with five major unions. Then in 1999 the French State extended the UNETEL agreement to all firms in the "new" telecommunications sector, which was broadly defined to include telecommunications and internet providers, cable operators, television and radio broadcasting units, and call centers owned by firms in these industries. In April 2000, a new global collective agreement defined job classifications, social benefits, length and types of work schedules, and minimum salaries. Call center subcontractors were also covered by a sectoral agreement, which was negotiated in 2001 as an amendment to the service providers agreement. The state extended this to all firms in 2002. In addition, France has a high minimum wage that is indexed to inflation, which effectively restricted the lower end of base pay rates in these agreements.

The presence of encompassing collective agreements across France Télécom and at the sector level contributed to different patterns of restructuring and wage differentiation from those in the United States and Germany. In contrast to the trend of decentralization in these countries, France Télécom centralized and standardized pay for call center jobs. Managers initially adopted separate employment models for fixed-line and subsidiary (wireless and internet) call centers, although base pay was the same across the corporate group. However, in the mid-2000s they consolidated and networked these centers while adopting a more standardized set of compensation and performance management practices and job definitions. The corporate group made use of subcontractors for peak call times and certain low-value activities, but did not pursue the wholesale selling off of call centers to third-party firms observed at Deutsche Telekom.

At the same time, French employers had fewer incentives to seek additional cost savings, as call center workers historically were paid much less in France compared to Germany or the United States. The starting salary at T-Com, the fixed-line division of Deutsche Telekom, was €34,620 (for a thirty-four-hour week) in 2006, compared to €19,826 (thirty-five-hour week) for equivalent jobs at France Télécom; while the subcontractor Walter Telemedien was paying around €16,000 (forty-hour week) compared to a €15,375 (thirty-five-hour week) minimum in France's subcontractor agreement. Pay levels at the U.S. company AT&T were more similar to Germany, with an average salary of between $50,618 and $58,457 (roughly €38,000–€44,000) for equivalent service and sales jobs. Concession bargaining at Deutsche Telekom in 2008 reduced pay for call center work to €23,490 for a thirty-eight-hour week, which brought wages closer to those at France Télécom.

In addition, subcontracting was becoming a more popular practice in France despite the lower labor cost differential. In 2007, the mobile company SFR sold three of its centers to two subcontractors and shifted nineteen hundred employees to the new owners. As in Germany, the new owners were obligated to maintain existing collective agreements for a period of one to two years, after which time the employees were shifted to the subcontractors' (lower paid) sectoral agreement.

Explaining Differences

This brief case study provides a useful point of comparison to recent developments in the United States and Germany. Encompassing bargaining was established in the "new" telecommunications sector in France due to government policies and union strategies. The French state placed strong pressure on all parties to enter into negotiations through the policy of extending collective agreements. The presence of a high national minimum wage in France set a high level of base pay that these agreements could not undercut.

In addition, unions in France adopted strategies early on that focused on developing encompassing bargaining institutions. Ver.di's close relationship with the former monopolist, and its role in promoting legislation favorable to Deutsche Telekom, made it difficult for the union to develop bargaining relationships in other telecommunications firms. In contrast, France Télécom's workforce was represented by more radical leftist unions, such as CGT and SUD, and more reformist unions closer to the centre, such as the CFDT. The major unions were both less clearly associated with France Télécom's interests and more willing to expand the scope of their bargaining and organizing activities to new employee groups, including those at call center subcontractors.

Encompassing institutions reduced the potential payoff from outsourcing and subsidiary creation, and encouraged growing centralization in wage setting. As a result, there was less inequality in pay and working conditions across French call centers compared to those in Germany and the United States. At the same time, institutional supports for worker participation remained weak. France Télécom was subjected to a great deal of negative press in 2009 and 2010 due to a wave of employee suicides, which unions publicly blamed on work intensification, forced relocations or job changes, and a culture of bullying associated with restructuring. Under pressure from the government, the company responded by freezing employee transfers and putting in place counseling for staff, while the deputy CEO resigned. In 2010, a series of new accords were negotiated with the unions aimed at improving management support for work life balance and reducing employee stress. While this represented a historic shift toward increased labor-management cooperation, union representatives were largely skeptical that the accords would result in real change in working conditions in a climate of increasing performance pressure.

The suicides at France Télécom are a particularly tragic example of the negative outcomes associated with top-down work reorganization and organizational restructuring. Lack of participation rights and weak bargaining power at the workplace level meant that decisions concerning work design and staff transfers were made unilaterally by managers, without meaningful employee or union involvement in decision making. Unions were able to publicly critique management decisions but were not able to participate substantively in developing alternatives. In this area, the German case studies presented in this book illustrated better outcomes. At the same time, the limits on monitoring and safeguards to worker discretion that German works councils were able to negotiate for in-house call center staff rested on a fragile base of power. The absence of industrywide institutions and the growing gap in pay and working conditions between companies were clearly undermining this power and forcing concessions, despite works councils' strong formal bargaining rights.

Discussion

International survey and case study data show patterns of between- and within-country differences that are broadly consistent with U.S. and German case study findings. German centers were more likely to adopt high-involvement employment practices than those in the United States, and within each country subcontractors and centers without collective bargaining were more likely to use a low-road, low-discretion model. These patterns were to some extent mirrored in other liberal and coordinated countries, with a few notable exceptions. Overall, findings support the argument that call centers are more likely to offer workers high-quality jobs in those countries and workplaces with collective bargaining institutions that support worker participation in management decision making. France was a useful counterexample, where comparatively weak participation rights allowed managers to adopt practices relying on intensified monitoring and low discretion.

The United States and Germany looked more similar in having high levels of pay inequality—again, with the largest gaps between establishments with different bargaining arrangements and between in-house centers and subcontractors. Here, there was more variation within each group of liberal and coordinated countries. Germany had a larger pay gap between workplaces and segments compared the other European countries, which can be explained by growing opportunities to exit collective arrangements and its (unusual) lack of mechanisms to extend collective agreements or minimum standards. A case study of the French telecommunications industry illustrated the role of state intervention in encouraging sectoral bargaining and closing off these kinds of exit routes. Encompassing bargaining thus made a difference for patterns of inequality and organizational restructuring but was not enough to overcome union weakness at the workplace level. Though not examined in detail here, Denmark appears to represent a "best case," where institutions both encouraged workplace democracy through strong participation rights and structures and were encompassing due to a mixture of strong union bargaining power, state support for minimum terms, and voluntary compliance to sectoral agreements by employers. This supported a range of "high-road" outcomes for Denmark's call center workers: high-involvement employment systems, high pay, and low inequality.

6

Conclusions

Call centers are often described as the service sector equivalent of Taylorist factories, known for pervasive monitoring and work intensification. This book has shown that poor job quality is not universal in these workplaces. At a time when U.S. telecommunications firms were rationalizing and deskilling their frontline service and sales jobs, similar German firms were investing in skills and expanding worker discretion. These high-involvement employment models were not adopted by employers who sought to gain competitive advantage in high-end, high-quality market segments. Instead, worker representatives used their participation rights and bargaining power to negotiate constraints on unilateral management, which in the short-term safeguarded employee discretion and skills while helping firms to adapt to new competitive pressures.

At the same time, the institutions that supported these alternative models were increasingly fragile. Strong codetermination structures in German telecommunications call centers were the legacy of an industry that long enjoyed encompassing collective agreements and high union membership.

Legislation in the late 1990s led to increased competition in both the U.S. and German telecommunications markets, contributing to bargaining decentralization, the growing market presence of nonunion firms, and the expansion of the subcontracting industry. These developments gave employers new incentives and opportunities to bypass strong collective agreements. Major firms responded with similar organizational strategies, using restructuring measures such as outsourcing and the establishment of subsidiaries to move call center jobs outside of existing bargaining units. The end result of this process was to weaken bargaining coordination and increase the pressure on managers to reduce labor costs. This undermined worker participation structures in German workplaces and contributed to growing wage inequality and wage concessions in both countries.

Survey data showed similar outcomes at the national level in the United States and Germany. German call centers were more frequent adopters of high-involvement practices, but certain of these practices were most common where both unions and works councils were present—in particular, limits on performance monitoring and discipline. At the same time, both countries had a high degree of pay inequality between call centers, with subcontractors generally representing a poorly organized and low-wage segment of the market.

International survey data and case studies provided further evidence of the relationship between national institutions, collective bargaining structures, and management strategies. Across liberal and European coordinated countries, subcontractors tended to have weaker collective bargaining institutions, to pay lower wages, and to use more control-oriented employment practices compared to in-house centers. However, outcomes varied at the workplace and national levels. Call centers in coordinated countries that had works councils and unions were most likely to limit monitoring and discipline, while those countries with more encompassing bargaining institutions had the most equal pay structures.

A case study of the French telecommunications industry was used to examine how a different configuration of institutions influenced employment systems for call center jobs. France is known for having stronger traditions of state intervention in collective bargaining and pay setting compared to Germany, with a high national minimum wage and mechanisms to extend collective agreements to all employers in a sector. Bargaining at the industry and corporate group-level ensured that wage setting remained centralized and pay levels relatively egalitarian; but weak participation rights allowed management to unilaterally intensify monitoring and constrict employee discretion. Denmark represented a contrasting case, where traditions of workplace democracy and encompassing bargaining appeared to support the "high-road" outcomes of high pay, low inequality, and strong use of high-involvement practices.

Based on these findings, I have argued that national differences in industrial relations institutions can explain variation in the use of high-involvement employment systems and patterns of inequality in easily rationalized service workplaces. "Good jobs" are best fostered across networked workplaces where participation rights support strong forms of workplace democracy and encompassing institutions prevent escape from these democratic arrangements. Coordinated industrial relations institutions serve as important constraints that prevent management from pursuing narrow goals of cost reduction where there are strong external pressures and incentives to do so.

Implications for Comparative Theory and Research

This book has sought to explain both cross-national variation in employment systems and changing patterns of inequality within countries. The comparative capitalism literature has focused on mapping out the relationships between complementary bundles of national institutions and employers' competitive strategies. Theories of institutional change similarly derive from observations of national or institutional trends in actor preferences and outcomes. The current study has brought the focus of analysis down to the microlevel, examining the politics of restructuring inside similar firms and workplaces. This gives a unique lens on how restructuring strategies are contributing to institutional change in different national political economies, as well as the effects of these changes on workers.

One contribution of the research presented here is to demonstrate the central, and distinctive, role of industrial relations institutions in encouraging employers to adopt high-involvement employment systems in more peripheral service workplaces. Managers have more obvious incentives for investing in worker skills and discretion where they have designated a group of employees as core resources or where they compete in high value-added market segments. Much of the comparative literature argues that coordinated bargaining and participation rights in countries like Germany support employers as they seek to invest in these resources or pursue competitive advantage in these segments.

Employers face much stronger incentives to rationalize work and to reduce investments in human capital in the call center workplaces studied here. In these settings, countervailing power exercised by local worker representatives can help to challenge the easy pursuit of cost-cutting and to implement alternatives. Past theorists have argued that encompassing collective agreements encouraged labor-management cooperation in social European countries, as they provided unions with institutional security while removing more conflictual zero-sum bargaining out of the firm and workplace (Fox 1974; Katz and Sabel 1985). Solidaristic bargaining typical of these countries also promoted redistribution of risk away from more poorly organized employee groups and sectors, with the broader effect of standardizing or "decommodifing" labor (Polanyi 1944).

Recent trends in Germany demonstrate that this coordinated social model is increasingly fragile in the face of eroding union power and bargaining coverage. Some observers of these trends argue that participation structures continue to promote trust and cooperation in core German workplaces (Herrigel 2008; Höpner 2007). This study has shown that absent strong and encompassing collective agreements, organizational restructuring can be used to substantially shrink the size of this core. Under these conditions, codetermination often becomes more narrowly a resource for firms to gain worker cooperation, rather than a means for developing negotiated alternatives that provide "mutual gains." This was illustrated vividly in the case studies of call center subcontractors and the telecommunications firms who outsourced work to these subcontractors. Expanding opportunities for employers to exit formal bargaining arrangements were weakening the countervailing power and institutional security that supported high trust labor relations in the past. Maintaining and strengthening workplace democracy in coordinated countries thus requires not only employer commitment to retaining competitive advantage in high value-added market segments, but also institutions that constrict exit options, ensuring that managers are obligated to cooperate with both peripheral and core groups of worker representatives.

A second contribution of this book is to demonstrate the value of study-ing the politics of restructuring at the level of the "networked firm." Con-temporary research on "convergence and divergence" in employment systems (Katz and Darbishire 2000) or new patterns of "segmentalism" in coordinated economies (Thelen 2009) describe national trends of growing differentiation in pay and working conditions, but draw their empirical evidence from major unionized employers and core workplaces. Here, I have shown that the organizational strategies of major firms can be closely related to changes in employment systems for their internal work-force, as well as for the distribution of pay and working conditions across their subcontractors and subsidiaries.

Describing and explaining contemporary changes in management strate-gies increasingly requires research at the level of these boundary-spanning relationships. Several recent single-country studies have adopted this approach, including the research of Marchington et al. (2005) on inter-organizational forms in the UK, Greer's (2008a) study of the effects of verti-cal disintegration on industrial relations in the German auto industry, and Sako's (2006) analysis of changing corporate structures and union strate-gies in the Japanese auto industry. Lane's (2008; Lane and Probert 2009) work on global production networks in the pharmaceutical and clothing industries and the research of Huws et al. (2009) on value chain restructur-ing in Europe go further in comparing the international organization of networked firms headquartered in different countries.

This book contributes to this growing body of research. It is distinct in using cross-national comparison to analyze both the dynamics of or-ganizational restructuring and internal negotiations over work reorga-nization. Findings show that these two dimensions of restructuring are closely related, as employers face changing incentives to cooperate with worker representatives and changing opportunities to escape or avoid these arrangements. Formal participation rights characteristic of the Ger-man Model thus prove to be a necessary but not a sufficient condition for encouraging high-road management strategies. For codetermination in-stitutions to continue to make a difference to the strategic choices of firms, they need to be supported by new structures that regulate pay and work-ing conditions at the interorganizational level. "Democracy at work" can no longer be taken for granted in the vertically disintegrated German firm, and has become an even more distant goal for U.S. unions faced with weak participation rights and increasingly fragmented bargaining structures.

Implications for Unions and Policymakers

The findings from this book provide lessons for policy debates on effective responses to growing inequality in income distribution and access to good jobs. These debates often focus on how best to invest in worker skills and opportunity. If market forces inevitably lead to the erosion of job quality on the bottom, policymakers should help companies create more good jobs at the top. The journalist Thomas Friedman (2007) makes this case succinctly in his book *The World is Flat:* advanced industrial economies can only sustain their competitive edge through supporting the innovations that will create new waves of knowledge-intensive jobs. Management strategy scholars advise firms to outsource noncore activities, allowing them to develop a unique and sustainable competitive advantage in higher-value-added segments that capitalize on their "core competencies" (Prahalad and Hamel 1990; Hammer and Champy 1994). Leading policy advisors and management consultants counsel national governments to liberalize trade rules and clear the way for these firms to offshore their noncore activities, as this frees enterprising managers to create new jobs in more capital- and knowledge-intensive areas (see, e.g., Berger 2005: 4).

Meanwhile, institutions that raise standards for workers stuck on the wrong side of the skills divide are often viewed as obstructing efficiency and stymieing job creation. Economists blame high unemployment rates in Europe on rigid labor market rules, high wages, and strong unions (Siebert 1997; Neumark and Wascher 2008). Fearing negative effects on job growth, the U.S. government has allowed its meager minimum wage to fall by more than 30 percent of its value in the 1970s. Today, labor unions represent a shrinking proportion of the American workforce. Where they are still present, they are popularly perceived as special interest groups that raise wages to inefficient and unsustainable levels and make it difficult for firms to adjust flexibly to changes in markets and technologies.

These arguments suggest that labor market institutions work best when they minimize constraints on employers while supporting the innovations that help firms to compete in value-added markets. However, this market-oriented approach to policymaking has not uniformly raised living standards in the United States, where it has been most consistently and enthusiastically embraced. Wages for less-skilled workers have stagnated or fallen since the 1970s as returns to education have grown. New information and communication technologies have not only increased skill demands, but also given companies new options for rationalizing a range of service and manufacturing jobs. Supply-side investments in human capital and innovation do not on their own address problems of low pay and poor working conditions at the bottom of the labor market.

The findings in this book demonstrate that growing inequality in access to good jobs is not the necessary result of changes in markets and skills, but instead can be shaped by political choices. Labor unions in many successful economies have traditionally played a central role in wage setting and management decision making, helping to promote cooperative approaches to restructuring while redistributing gains from productivity improvements. Case studies showed that they can successfully play this role in "new economy" service workplaces—even in settings typically viewed as peripheral to employers' core competency. However, this requires bargaining power, which is secured in large measure through labor law and public policy.

The argument I put forward here suggests that policies aiming to redress the increasingly uneven balance of power in postindustrial economies should target two fronts: improving unions' role in democratic decision making at the workplace level and building encompassing institutions at the industry (and increasingly cross-industry) level. These two dimensions of social regulation are key to achieving what Budd (2004) calls "employment with a human face," or "a productive and efficient employment relationship that also fulfills standards of human rights," balancing equity, efficiency and voice.

In the abstract, it is easy to agree that equity and voice are worthwhile objectives, particularly if they complement employer interests in increasing efficiency. However, concretely employers have a range of interests. Firms pursue contradictory objectives—for example, seeking both consent and control (Hyman 1987) or cost reduction and quality improvement (Korczynski 2002). Democratic institutions at the workplace level can serve as a resource for managers in developing a strong basis for consent, by encouraging collective voice (Freeman and Medoff 1984) or drawing on employees' commitment to shared standards of professionalism (Matuschek, Arnold, and Voss 2007; Holtgrewe 2006). The extent to which performance benefits are matched with true gains for workers, however, depends on their ability to exercise countervailing power in these negotiations. This often conflicts with management interests in retaining control over decision making or in allocating profits to investors.

The past experience with collective regulation in social Europe has shown that strong industrial relations and labor market institutions are necessary to bring about a more equitable balance of power in the economy. Participation rights are legislated, while government decisions to extend collective agreements or enforce bargaining and organizing rights determine the ease with which employers can bypass collective institutions. The goal of strengthening these institutions should be placed at the center of a broader public agenda aimed at improving job quality and reducing labor market inequality.

In the United States, unionized firms have a strong tradition of negotiating labor-management partnership agreements. Case studies in the 1990s of innovative partnerships at auto manufacturers such as Saturn and NUMMI (Kochan and Osterman 1994), as well as recent studies of airline carriers Southwest and Continental (Bamber, Gittell, and Kochan 2009) or the healthcare and insurance provide Kaiser Permanente (Kochan et al. 2009) have shown that these agreements can lead to mutual gains. However, they rely heavily on management goodwill, due to weak formal participation rights and low union density. As a result, they are often abandoned or substantially weakened when management comes under pressure to cut costs (Osterman 1999).

Unions and their supporters have repeatedly called for reforms to U.S. labor law that would strengthen organizing and participation rights. Past efforts such as the 1993 Dunlop Commission made the academic and policy case for encouraging worker participation in management but lacked broader public support and resulted in no concrete reforms. The recent window of opportunity presented by the proposed Employee Free Choice Act—passed by the House of Representatives but blocked in the Senate—appears to have closed. Surveys of U.S. workers show large demand for workplace voice, but more uncertainty concerning whether unions are the most effective means to this end (Freeman and Rogers 1999; Freeman, Boxall, and Haynes 2007).

Moving toward institutional reform in the United States will thus require making a stronger case to the public and to policymakers that an expanded worker role in management decision-making can have broad social and economic benefits, and that labor unions are best placed to secure these benefits. Here, the new organizing efforts of unions to link up with community-based organizations, advocate living wages, and remake themselves as social movement actors show promise (Osterman 2002; Milkman, Bloom, and Narro 2010; Tattersall 2010). However, these campaigns will have limited long-term effectiveness if they do not also focus on establishing democratic structures for worker participation—and campaigning for legal support for these structures.

Other Anglo-Saxon countries provide qualified models for possible legal reforms. The UK Labour government elected in the 1990s invested in a "Partnership Fund" and "Union Learning Fund" to encourage labor management cooperation (Guest and Peccei 2001; Wallis, Stuart, and Greenwood 2005). Past Australian Labor governments passed legislation encouraging the establishment of joint consultative committees (Holland et al. 2009), while the Labor government elected in 2007 adopted a wide-ranging set of legal changes that, among other things, reestablished minimum pay awards by industry (Cooper 2009). These examples show that labor law reform can be a useful starting point for supporting workplace democracy, even in "liberal market economies" where collective bargaining has been declining.

In Germany, as in social Europe more generally, workplace democracy is embedded in stronger political and legal traditions (Frege 2005). However, unions face the challenge of reestablishing encompassing institutions, at a time when bargaining density and coverage are declining. There are recent efforts in this direction. Ver.di is putting more resources into organizing members and strengthening the role of works councils in low-wage service workplaces (Turner 2009; Greer 2008b). IG Metall has launched campaigns to improve pay and working conditions for auto workers employed by temporary agencies and suppliers (Greer 2008a). These campaigns are promising but have not yet reversed trends of union decline.

Other European countries again provide models. In France, a high national minimum wage and system of encompassing agreements has helped to establish minimum standards despite generally weak union power within firms (Caroli and Gautie 2008). Austrian and Dutch unions have organized successful campaigns to improve collective and legal protections for different categories of contingent or nonstandard workers (Shire, Schönauer et al. 2009; Salverda, Klaveren, and Meer 2008). These examples show that unions in countries with traditions of strong social regulation can use established institutions in creative ways, mobilizing state support for minimum standards and extending bargaining within new service workplaces.

At the same time, across Europe, unions face the challenge of finding new ways to organize public and political support, at a time when their traditional roles are changing. This case cannot be made solely on the basis of their contribution to improved productivity and national competitiveness. Instead, it should be presented as a central piece of policy measures aimed at reversing trends of growing inequality and declining job quality at the bottom of the labor market.

Increased capital and labor mobility mean that national regulation can provide only a partial solution to downward pressure on pay and working conditions. Employers today are able to move jobs and production across national borders. Supply chains are increasingly international. These trends have had a large impact on the international division of labor in service activities like call centers. Here, the efforts of international labor organizations such as Union Network International (UNI) to build global institutions show some promise. France Télécom has negotiated a framework agreement with UNI, which includes a commitment to respecting labor and organizing rights in its foreign subsidiaries. The CWA and ver. di are working together on a campaign to organize Deutsche Telekom's mobile subsidiary, T-Mobile, in the United States. This builds on past efforts by ver.di representatives to use their leverage at corporate headquarters in Germany to encourage the company to take a more neutral stance toward unions seeking to organize T-Mobile locations in other countries. These campaigns are relatively new, and have had limited success to date. However, they demonstrate that unions are beginning to change their strategic focus and are seeking to build encompassing bargaining across multinational firms and their production networks.

The case studies and survey findings in this book demonstrate that the degradation of work in secondary jobs is not inevitable in globalized, service-based economies. Strong participation rights and traditions of workplace democracy can encourage alternative, high-involvement approaches to organizing work and motivating workers. These employ-ment models provide benefits for firms, such as improved worker com-mitment and cooperation. Most striking, however, is the positive effects these institutions can have on job quality, in service workplaces commonly viewed as offering little worker discretion, poor working conditions, and often low pay. As such, they should serve as a model for governments worldwide concerned with improving access to "good jobs."

Labor unions continue to play an important role in helping to set up a framework of rules and incentives that can push employers toward the high road while extending democratic decision-making structures to new industries—benefiting not only core groups of workers but also those tra-ditionally seen as peripheral in easily rationalized or lower skilled settings. These efforts face an uphill battle, but are essential for pursuing broader goals of economic justice and dignity in the workplace.

Appendixes

	Site visits	Manager (HQs)	Manager (CCs)	Team leader	Agent	Union reps	Works council reps	Total
US interviews								
US Telecom	3	9	7	5	7	6	n/a	34
US Mobile	1	0	3	4	9	7	n/a	23
Client Help USA	3	1	17	3	0	n/a	n/a	21
US Vendotel	1	2	3	2	1	n/a	n/a	8
Other telcos	2	5	6	5	9	18	n/a	43
Other subcontractors	3	0	4	3	0	n/a	n/a	7
Other call centers	5	0	7	1	0	0	n/a	8
Total	**18**	**17**	**47**	**23**	**26**	**31**		**144**
German interviews								
Deutsche Telekom	4	3	8	10	16	7	6	50
German Mobile	2	2	7	4	2	7	5	27
Client Services Germany	2	2	3	4	3	3	6	21
German Vendotel	2	n/a	3	4	1	n/a	n/a	8
Other telcos	3	0	7	4	3	3	6	23
Other subcontractors	4	1	3	0	0	3	10	17
Total	**17**	**8**	**31**	**26**	**25**	**23**	**33**	**146**

* Additional follow-up interviews were carried out in the United States and Germany between 2007 and 2010.

APPENDIX B: Organizational characteristics and employment practices by country, in-house and outsourced centers

	In-house		Outsourced	
	US	DE	US	DE
Organizational characteristics				
Age of center (years)	17.6	8.3	14.3	7.7
% outbound centers	12.3	8.3	28.1	41.2
Average number of contact employees	163	79	295	108
Staffing and skill				
Education level: % University degree	23.1	11.2	9.5	10.1
Education level: % Apprenticeship (Germany)	n/a	77.9	n/a	73.6
Weeks initial and on the job training	40.2	35.7	24.7	32.3
% employees with <1 year tenure	22.7	18.8	37	32.4
% part time	16.1	44.8	42.4	42.7
Scheduling				
>50% workforce with flex scheduling	33.3	61.2	33.9	51.5
% high discretion over breaks	36.8	75.5	25	74
Work design				
Average call duration (seconds)	379	203	350	247
>50% workforce in self-managed teams	17.1	36.7	11.1	28.6
>50% workforce in quality circles	32.8	30.6	17.7	34.4
>50% workforce with flex job descriptions	13	29.2	14.3	39.2
% high work discretion	40.3	66	23.4	58
% high customer discretion	81	82	59.4	57
% high script use	76.4	46	40.6	37.8
Coaching and monitoring				
Average % work continuously monitored	45.3	63.1	66.2	61.7
% frequent commun. of performance stats	53.7	30.6	68.8	49.5
% frequent supervisor monitoring	45.9	6	65.1	23.2
% high use of performance info for discipline	74.1	20.4	87.5	33.3
Compensation				
Annual pay (USD)	31,326	34,311	26,505	27,241
% pay based on individual commission	14.1	7.2	13.4	17.8
Outcomes				
% absent	5.5	12.1	7.6	9.4
% quit	11.9	2.1	19.5	6.7
% dismissed	7.7	2.1	13.9	7.3
Observations	**400**	**50**	**64**	**100**

Source: Global Call Center Project survey

APPENDIX C: Organizational characteristics and employment practices by collective bargaining arrangements, United States and Germany

	US		Germany		
	Union	Non-union	Union + works council	Works council only	No union or works council
Organizational characteristics					
Age of center (years)	19.9	16.9	10	8.2	6.8
% outbound centers	9.5	14.8	3.1	8.8	54.1
Average number of contact employees	318.6	167.6	76.0	232.6	53.3
Staffing and skill					
Education level: % University degree	11.9	22.3	9	8.5	11.6
Education level: % Apprenticeship (Germany)	n/a	n/a	84	79.1	71.2
Weeks initial and on the job training	58.8	36	40.4	33.7	30
% employees with <1 year tenure	10.7	26.1	15.4	13.7	38.1
% part time	18.2	19.7	35.8	48.7	41.3
Scheduling					
>50% workforce with flex scheduling	26.2	34	79.4	54.5	42.9
% high discretion over breaks	26.2	36	67.6	77.1	76.3
Work design					
Average call duration (seconds)	520.3	361.7	219.9	169.7	276.4
>50% workforce in self-managed teams	4.8	17.5	31.3	18.2	36.4
>50% workforce in quality circles	21.4	31.9	28.1	33.3	35.1
>50% workforce with flex job descriptions	4.8	13.7	39.4	28.1	38.7
% high work discretion	23.8	39.3	67.6	54.3	61
% high customer discretion	76.2	78.1	64.7	77.1	61
% high script use	69	71.8	35.3	52.9	39.5
Coaching and monitoring					
Average % work continuously monitored	61.5	46.8	68.9	63.7	59.5
% frequent commun. of performance stats	58.5	55.4	29	50	45.5
% frequent supervisor monitoring	38.1	49.6	6.1	5.7	27.4
% high use of performance info for discipline	69	76.5	23.5	27.3	33.3
Compensation					
Annual pay (USD)	36,094	30,088	35,342	30,927	26,155
% pay based on individual commission	9.0	14.5	8.3	8.7	20.2
Outcomes					
% absent	7.0	5.6	9.0	11.3	10.4
% quit	4.5	13.8	1.8	3.6	7.0
% dismissed	4.5	8.9	2.1	2.6	8.2
Observations	**42**	**420**	**34**	**35**	**77**

Source: Global Call Center Project survey

NOTES

1. Introduction

1. For the large literature on work organization in call centers, see, e.g. Baldry, Bain, and Taylor 1998; Callaghan and Thompson 2001; Deery, Iverson, and Walsh 2002; Kinnie, Hutchinson, and Purcell 2000; Taylor et al. 2002; Frenkel et al. 1999; Gorjup, Valverde, and Ryan 2009; Holtgrewe, Kerst, and Shire 2002; Holtgrewe 2006; Matuschek, Arnold, and Voss 2007; Kleemann and Matuschek 2003; Moss, Salzman, and Tilly 2008.

2. Changes in Markets and Collective Bargaining

1. Much of the history of restructuring in telecommunications is drawn from the following sources: (1) US: (Turner 1991; Bahr 1998; duRivage 2000; Darbishire 2005; Vogel 1996; Boroff and Keefe 1994; Katz, Batt, and Keefe 2003; Keefe and Batt 1997; Keefe 2005); (2) Germany: (Darbishire 1997, 2005; Katz and Darbishire 2000; Sako and Jackson 2006; Sarkar 2000; Turner 1991; Vogel 1996; Althaus 2000; Blutner, Brose, and Holtgrewe 2002; Mickler 2002). I also draw on interviews with managers, union representatives, policymakers, and works councilors; annual reports from major telecommunications firms; and union publications. General information found in multiple sources is not cited.

2. In 2009, 57 percent of total share capital was owned by institutional investors, 11 percent by retail investors, and 32 percent by the federal government. The Blackstone Group owned 4.4 percent of shares (DT Annual Report 2009).

3. In Germany, only 0.5 percent of residents in 2006 subscribed to cable broadband services and 16.4 percent to DSL; while in the US, 10.3 percent subscribe to cable broadband and

only 8.5 percent to DSL (OECD 2007). However, the cable market was beginning to experience a boom, with the market more than doubling to 1.5 million broadband customers in 2008 (Bundesnetzagentur 2009).

4. The CWA negotiated expedited elections at AT&T, BellSouth, GTE Southwest, and Lucent; and card check recognition at Ameritech Cellular, BellAtlantic, and SBC.

5. Personnel councils are covered by the Personnel Representation Law (*Personalvertretungsrecht*), while works councils are covered by the private sector Works Constitution Act (*Betriebsverfassungsgesetz*).

6. The other four unions were: Deutschen Angestelleten-Gewerkschaft (DAG), Gewerkschaft Handel, Banken und Versicherungen (HBV), Industriegewerkschaft Medien (IG Medien) and Gewerkschaft Oeffentliche Dienste, Transport und Verkehr (ötv). Ver.di was organized into 13 *Fachbereiche,* or departments, and telecommunications was placed in FB9: Telekommunikation, Informationstechnologie, Datenverarbeitung.

7. The major telecommunications companies with collective agreements in 2009 included the DT group (131,300), Vodafone/Arcor (13,000), and O2 (5,100) which adds up to around 150,000 employees covered by an agreement—out of an estimated 187,000 employees in the industry (Bundesnetzagentur 2009).

4. Losing Power in the Networked Firm

1. These numbers are taken from an internal consultant report provided by a DT works councilor. I do not discuss T-Systems here because call centers represented a smaller proportion of employment and involved qualitatively different work for large business customers.

2. In 1998 Arcor and the railworkers' union (Gewerkschaft der Eisenbahner Deutschlands, GdED) signed a package of nine collective agreements. GdED later changed its name to "Transnet."

5. Broadening the Comparison

1. The U.S. survey was administered in mid-2003 to a stratified random sample of 472 call centers, as part of a larger telephone survey of telecommunications establishments conducted by the Survey Research Institute at Cornell University's Industrial and Labor Relations School. The survey was supported by grants from the Alfred P. Sloan Foundation and Russell Sage Foundation, and conducted by a research team consisting of professors Rosemary Batt and Harry Katz at Cornell University, and Jeffrey Keefe at Rutgers University. Around 40 percent of the sample was drawn from the Dun and Bradstreet listing of establishments in the telecommunications industry, which were stratified by size (10–99 employees; 100-plus employees); by SIC code (cellular, fixedline, and cable); and by state location. Telecommunications call centers are thus overrepresented. The remaining cases came from a nationally random sample of call center managers drawn from subscriber lists of the industry publication *Call Center Magazine.* At the time, these lists included some seventy thousand names, representing a very large and diverse database covering every industry and region of the country. There was a 62 percent response rate, and the telephone interview averaged forty minutes.

An identical survey was administered in Germany in 2004 to a random sample of 154 call centers by the Sozialwissenschaftliches Umfragezentrum (Social Science Survey Center) of the University of Duisburg/Essen. The German survey was supported by a grant from the Hans Boeckler Stiftung and conducted under the direction of Professor Karen Shire and P.D. Dr. Ursula Holtgrewe at the University of Duisburg/Essen. The sample was drawn from a database of twenty-seven hundred call centers that the German team compiled from lists provided by regional development agencies in eight German *Bundesländer* (states) and ver.di's SOCA project (Soziale Gestaltung der Arbeit in Call Centern—social work design in call centers), as well as internet-based membership and marketing lists of call center organizations. This sampling method probably led to underrepresentation of in-house call centers, reflected in the large percentage of call center subcontractors in the sample (56 percent). There was a 51 percent response rate, and the telephone interview averaged forty-five minutes.

2. This is a brief summary of a study that is reported in more detail in Doellgast (2008a)

3. National medians are taken from OECD figures from 2004; and are not based on purchasing power parity.

4. Ninety-seven percent of employees at France Télécom were civil servants in 1995; falling to 70 percent in 2008. In contrast, 50 percent of Deutsche Telekom's workforce were civil servants in 1995 and 28 percent in 2008.

BIBLIOGRAPHY

Albert, Michel. 1993. *Capitalism vs. Capitalism: How America's Obsession with Individual Achievement and Short-Term Profit Has Led It to the Brink of Collapse.* New York: Basic Books.

Althaus, Sarah. 2000. Deutsche Telekom Income Falls 45%. *Financial Times,* January 21, 26.

Amable, Bruno. 2003. *The Diversity of Modern Capitalism.* Oxford: Oxford University Press.

Amadieu, Jean-Francois. 1995. Industrial Relations: Is France a Special Case? *British Journal of Industrial Relations* 33 (3): 345–51.

Appelbaum, Eileen, and Rosemary Batt. 1994. *The New American Workplace: Transforming Work Systems in the United States.* Ithaca, NY: ILR Press.

Bahr, Morton. 1998. *From the Telegraph to the Internet.* Washington, DC: National Press Books.

Baldry, C., P. Bain, and P. Taylor. 1998. Bright Satanic Offices: Intensification, Control, and Team Taylorism. In *Workplaces of the Future,* edited by P. Thompson and C. Warhurst. London: Macmillan Business.

Bamber, Greg, Jody Hoffer Gittell, and Thomas Kochan. 2009. *Up in the Air: How Airlines Can Improve Performance by Engaging Their Employees.* Ithaca, NY: ILR Press.

Batt, Rosemary. 2000. Strategic Segmentation in Front-line Services: Matching Customers, Employees, and Human Resource Systems. *International Journal of Human Resource Management* 11 (3): 540–61.

——. 2001. Explaining Wage Inequality in Telecommunications Services: Customer Segmentation, Human Resource Practices, and Union Decline. *Industrial and Labor Relations Review* 54 (2A): 425–49.

Batt, Rosemary, and Owen Darbishire. 1997. Institutional Determinants of Deregulation and Restructuring in Telecommunications: Britain, Germany, and the United States Compared. *International Contributions to Labour Studies* 7: 59–79.

Batt, Rosemary, David Holman, and Ursula Holtgrewe. 2009. The Globalization of Service Work: Comparative International Perspectives on Call Centers. *Industrial and Labor Relations Review* 62 (4): 453–88.

Batt, Rosemary, and Hiroatsu Nohara. 2009. How Institutions and Business Strategies Affect Wages: A Cross-National Study of Call Centres. *Industrial and Labor Relations Review* 62 (4): 533–52.

Batt, Rosemary, Hiroatsu Nohara, and Hyunji Kwon. 2010. Employer Strategies and Wages in New Service Activities: A Comparison of Coordinated and Liberal Market Economies. *British Journal of Industrial Relations* 48 (2): 400–435.

Beraud, Mathieu, Thierry Colin, and Benoit Grasser. 2008. Job Quality and Career Opportunities for Call Center Workers: Contrasting Patterns in France. In *Low-Wage Work in France,* edited by E. Caroli and J. Gautie. New York: Russell Sage Foundation.

Berger, Suzanne. 2005. *How We Compete: What Companies around the World Are Doing to Make It in Today's Global Economy.* New York: Doubleday.

Berger, Suzanne, and Ronald Dore, eds. 1996. *National Diversity and Global Capitalism.* Ithaca, NY: Cornell University Press.

Berggren, Christian. 1992. *Alternatives to Lean Production: Work Organization in the Swedish Auto Industry.* Ithaca, NY: ILR Press.

Best, Michael H. 1990. *The New Competition: Institutions of Industrial Restructuring.* Cambridge, MA: Harvard University Press.

Blutner, Doris, Hanns-Georg Brose, and Ursula Holtgrewe. 2002. *Telekom: Wie Machen Die Das?* Konstanz: UVK Verlagsgesellschaft mbH.

Boersch, Alexander. 2007. *Global Pressure, National System: How German Corporate Governance Is Changing.* Ithaca, NY: Cornell University Press.

Boroff, Karen, and Jeffrey Keefe. 1994. Telecommunications Labor-Management Relations: One Decade after the AT&T Divestiture. In *Contemporary Collective Bargaining in the Private Sector,* edited by P. Voos. Madison: Industrial Relations Research Association.

Bosch, Gerhard, and Steffen Lehndorff, eds. 2005. *Working in the Service Sector: A Tale from Different Worlds.* New York: Routledge.

Bosch, Gerhard, and Claudia Weinkopf, eds. 2008. *Low Wage Work in Germany.* New York: Russell Sage Foundation.

Bowman, Edward H., and Harbir Singh. 1993. Corporate Restructuring: Reconfiguring the Firm. *Strategic Management Journal* 14: 5–14.

Boyle, Kevin, and Sue Pisha. 1995. Building the Future through Quality Unions in the Telecommunications Industry—Communications Workers of America and US West. In *Union, Management and Quality Opportunities for Innovation and Excellence,* edited by E. Cohen-Rosenthal. Boston, MA: Irwin.

Brandt, Torsten, Thorsten Schulten, Gabriele Sterkel, and Jörg Wiedemuth, eds. 2008. *Europa im Ausverkauf: Liberalisierung und Privatisierung öffentlicher Dienst leistungen und ihre Folgen für die Tarifpolitik.* Hamburg, Germany: VSA-Verlag.

Braverman, Harry. 1974. *Labor and Monopoly Capital: The Degradation of Work in the Twentieth Century.* New York: Monthly Review Press.

Budd, John. 2004. *Employment with a Human Face: Balancing Efficiency, Equity, and Voice.* Ithaca, NY: ILR Press.

Bundesnetzagentur.2009.Jahresbericht2008.http://www.bundesnetzagentur.de/Shared Docs/Downloads/DE/BNetzA/Presse/Berichte/2008/Jahresbericht08Id15901pdf. pdf?__blob=publicationFile

Cairncross, Frances. 1997. *The Death of Distance: How the Communications Revolution Will Change Our Lives.* Boston: Harvard Business School Press.

Callaghan, George, and Paul Thompson. 2001. Edwards Revisited: Technical Control and Call Centres. *Economic and Industrial Democracy* 22: 13–37.

Caroli, Eve, and Jerome Gautie, eds. 2008. *Low-Wage Work in France.* New York: Russell Sage Foundation.

Cooper, Rae. 2009. Forward with Fairness? Industrial Relations under Labor in 2008. *Journal of Industrial Relations* 51 (3): 285–96.

Crouch, Colin. 2005. *Capitalist Diversity and Change: Recombinant Governance and Institutional Entrepreneurs.* Oxford: Oxford University Press.

Crouch, Colin, and Helmut Voelzkow, eds. 2009. *Innovation in Local Economies: Germany in Comparative Context.* Oxford: Oxford University Press.

Darbishire, Owen. 1997. Germany. In *Telecommunications: Restructuring Work and Employment Relations Worldwide,* edited by H. C. Katz. Ithaca, NY: ILR Press.

———. 2005. Radical Restructuring: The Transformation of Industrial Relations in the Telecommunications Industry. Ph.D. diss., Cornell University, Ithaca, NY.

Deeg, Richard, and Gregory Jackson. 2007. Towards a More Dynamic Theory of Capitalist Variety. *Socio-economic Review* 5 (1): 149–79.

Deery, Stephen J., Roderick D. Iverson, and Janet P. Walsh. 2002. Work Relationships in Telephone Call Centers: Understanding Emotional Exhaustion and Employee Withdrawal. *Journal of Management Studies* 39 (4): 471–97.

Djelic, Marie-Laure, and Sigrid Quack. 2003. *Globalization and Institutions: Redefining the Rules of the Economic Game.* Cheltenham, UK: Edward Elgar.

Doellgast, Virginia. 2006. Negotiating Flexibility: The Politics of Call Center Restructuring in the U.S. and Germany. Ph.D. diss., Cornell University, Ithaca, NY.

———. 2008a. Collective Bargaining and High Involvement Management in Comparative Perspective: Evidence from US and German Call Centers. *Industrial Relations* 47 (2): 284–319.

———. 2008b. National Industrial Relations and Local Bargaining Power in the US and German Telecommunications Industries. *European Journal of Industrial Relations* 14 (3): 265–87.

———. 2009. Still a Coordinated Model? Market Liberalization and the Transformation of Employment Relations in the German Telecommunications Industry. *Industrial and Labor Relations Review* 63 (1): 3–23.

Doellgast, Virginia, Rosemary Batt, and Ole Sorensen. 2009. Introduction: Institutional Change and Labour Market Segmentation in European Call Centres. *European Journal of Industrial Relations* 15 (4): 349–71.

Doellgast, Virginia, Ursula Holtgrewe, and Stephen Deery. 2009. The Effects of National Institutions and Collective Bargaining Arrangements on Job Quality in Frontline Service Workplaces. *Industrial and Labor Relations Review* 64 (4): 489–509.

Doellgast, Virginia, Hiroatsu Nohara, and Robert Tchobanian. 2009. Institutional Change and the Restructuring of Service Work in the French and German Telecommunications Industries. *European Journal of Industrial Relations* 15 (4): 373–94.

Dore, Ronald. 1973. *British Factory, Japanese Factory: The Origins of National Diversity in Industrial Relations.* Berkeley, CA: University of California Press.

——. 1986. *Flexible Rigidities: Industrial Policy and Structural Adjustment in the Japanese Economy, 1970–80.* Stanford, CA: Stanford University Press.

DPG. 2001. Geschaeftsbericht des Hauptvorstandes, des Gewerkschaftsrates sowie der Kontroll- und Beschwerdekommission der Deutschen Postgewerkschaft vom 1.7.1997 bis 31.12.2000.

Dribbusch, Heiner. 2004. *Working Time Cuts Agreed in Exchange for Job Guarantees at Deutsche Telekom.* EIRO. http://www.eiro.eurofound.eu.int/2004/05/feature/de0405 205f.html 2004, accessed August 26, 2005.

Dunlop, John. 1958. *Industrial Relations Systems.* New York: Holt.

duRivage, Virginia. 2000. CWA's Organizing Strategies: Transforming Contract Work into Union Jobs. In *Nonstandard Work: The Nature and Challenges of Changing Employment Arrangements,* edited by F. Carre, M. A. Ferber, L. Golden and S. Herzenberg. Madison, WI: Industrial Relations Research Association.

Economist, The. 2002. Ringing the Changes. *Economist.com/ Global Agenda,* July 18, 2002, 1.

——. 2008. Bad Connection: A Class Action of Sorts for Germany's Disillusioned Shareholders. *The Economist,* April 10, 2008.

Edwards, Tony, Chris Rees, and Xavier Coller. 1999. Structure, Politics, and the Diffusion of Employment Practices in Multinationals. *European Journal of Industrial Relations* 5 (3): 286–306.

Elger, Tony, and Chris Smith, eds. 1994. *Global Japanization: The Transformation of the Labour Process.* New York: Routledge.

FCC. 2005a. Local Telephone Competition: Status as of December 31, 2004. Washington, DC: Federal Communications Commission, Industry Analysis and Technology Division, Wireline Competition Bureau.

——. 2005b. Trends in Telephone Service. Washington, DC: Federal Communications Commission.

——. 2008. Trends in Telephone Service. Washington, DC: Federal Communications Commission.

Form, William. 1979. Comparative Industrial Sociology and the Convergence Hypothesis. *American Review of Sociology* 5 (1): 1–25.

Fox, Alan. 1974. *Beyond Contract.* London: Faber.

Freeman, Richard B., Peter Boxall, and Peter Haynes, eds. 2007. *What Workers Say: Employee Voice in the Anglo-American Workplace.* Ithaca, NY: ILR Press.

Freeman, Richard B., and James L. Medoff. 1984. *What Do Unions Do?* New York: Basic Books.

Freeman, Richard B., and Joel Rogers. 1999. *What Workers Want*. Ithaca, NY: ILR Press.

Frege, Carola. 2005. The Discourse of Industrial Democracy: Germany and the US Revisited. *Economic and Industrial Democracy* 26 (1): 153–77.

Frenkel, Steve, Marek Korczynski, Karen Shire, and May Tam, eds. 1999. *On the Front-line: Organization of Work in the Information Economy*. Ithaca, NY: Cornell University Press.

Friedman, Thomas L. 2007. *The World Is Flat: A Brief History of the Twenty-First Century*. New York: Farrar, Straus and Giroux

Funk, Lothar. 2004. *Questionnaire for EIRO Comparative Study on Industrial Relations in the Public Sector, Focusing on the Public Utilities—Case of Germany*. European Industrial Relations Observatory (EIRO) 2004. Available from http://www.eiro. eurofound.ie/2005/02/word/de0411105s.doc, accessed October 23, 2005.

Gautié, Jérôme, and John Schmitt, eds. 2009. *Low Wage Work in the Wealthy World*. New York: Russell Sage Foundation.

Gittleman, Maury, Michael Horrigan, and Mary Joyce. 1998. "Flexible" Workplace Practices: Evidence from a Nationally Representative Survey. *Industrial and Labor Relations Review* 52 (1) (October): 99–115.

Godard, John. 2009. Institutional Environments, Work and Human Resource Practices, and Unions: Canada versus England. *Industrial and Labor Relations Review* 62 (2): 173–99.

Gorjup, María Tatiana, Mireia Valverde, and Gerard Ryan. 2009. In Search of Job Quality in Call Centers. *Personnel Review* 38 (3): 253–69.

Gospel, Howard, and Andrew Pendleton, eds. 2005. *Corporate Governance and Labour Management: An International Comparison*. New York: Oxford University Press.

Greer, Ian. 2008a. Organized Industrial Relations in the Information Economy: The German Automotive Sector as a Test Case. *New Technology, Work, and Employment* 23 (3): 181–96.

——. 2008b. Social Movement Unionism and Social Partnership in Germany. *Industrial Relations* 47 (4): 602–24.

Greer, Ian, and Marco Hauptmeier. 2008. Political Entrepreneurs and Co-Managers: Labour Transnationalism at Four Multinational Auto Companies. *British Journal of Industrial Relations* 46 (1): 76–97.

Guest, David, and Riccardo Peccei. 2001. Partnership at Work: Mutuality and the Balance of Advantage. *British Journal of Industrial Relations* 39 (2): 207–36.

Hall, Peter A., and David Soskice, eds. 2001. *Varieties of Capitalism: The Institutional Foundations of Comparative Advantage*. Oxford: Oxford University Press.

Hammer, Michael, and James Champy. 1994. *Reengineering the Corporation: A Manifesto for Business Revolution*. London: Nicholas Brealy.

Hancke, Bob, Martin Rhodes, and Mark Thatcher, eds. 2008. *Beyond Varieties of Capitalism: Conflict, Contradictions, and Complementarities in the European Economy*. Oxford: Oxford University Press.

Herrigel, Gary. 2008. Roles and Rules: Ambiguity, Experimentation and New Forms of Stakeholderism in Germany. *Industrielle Beziehungen* 15 (2): 111–32.

Herrigel, Gary, and Volker Wittke. 2004. Varieties of Vertical Disintegration: The Global Trend toward Heterogeneous Supply Relations and the Reproduction of Difference in U.S. and German Manufacturing. In *Changing Capitalisms?* edited by G. Morgan, E. Moen, and R. Whitley. Oxford: Oxford University Press.

Hirsch, Barry T., and David A. Macpherson. 2010. *Union Membership and Coverage Database 2009*. Available from http://www.unionstats.com.

Holland, Peter, Amanda Pyman, Brian K. Cooper, and Julian Teicher. 2009. The Development of Alternative Voice Mechanisms in Australia: The Case of Joint Consultation. *Economic and Industrial Democracy* 30 (1): 67–92.

Holman, David, Stephen Frenkel, Ole Sorensen, and Stephen Wood. 2009. Work Design Variation and Outcomes in Call Centers: Strategic Choice and Institutional Explanations. *Industrial and Labor Relations Review* 62 (4): 510–32.

Holst, Hajo. 2008. The Political Economy of Trade Union Strategies in Austria and Germany: The Case of Call Centres. *European Journal of Industrial Relations* 14 (1): 25–45.

Holtgrewe, Ursula. 2006. *Flexible Menschen in flexiblen Organisationen: Bedingungen und Moeglichkeiten kreativen und innovativen Handelns*. Berlin: Edition Sigma.

Holtgrewe, Ursula, and Virginia Doellgast. Forthcoming. A Service Union's Innovation Dilemma: Limitations on Creative Action in German Industrial Relations. *Work, Employment and Society*.

Holtgrewe, Ursula, Christian Kerst, and Karen Shire, eds. 2002. *Re-Organising Service Work: Call Centres in Germany and Britain*. Aldershot: Ashgate.

Höpner, Martin. 2007. Coordination and Organization: The Two Dimensions of Nonliberal Capitalism. *MPIfG Discussion Paper 07 / 12*, http://www.mpifg.de/pu/mpifg_dp/dp07-12.pdf.

Höpner, Martin, and Gregory Jackson. 2003. Entsteht ein Markt für Unternehmenskontrolle? Der Fall Mannesmann. In *Alle Macht dem Markt? Fallstudien zur Abwicklung der Deutschland AG*, edited by W. Streeck and M. Höpner. Frankfurt: Campus Verlag.

Huws, Ursula, Simone Dahlmann, Jörg Flecker, Ursula Holtgrewe, Annika Schönauer, Monique Ramioul, and Karen Geurts. 2009. *Value Chain Restructuring in Europe in a Global Economy*. Leuven: HIVA.

Hyman, Richard. 1987. Strategy or Structure. *Work, Employment, and Society* 1 (1): 25–56.

Jackson, Gregory. 2003. Corporate Governance in Germany and Japan: Liberalization Pressures and Responses during the 1990s. In *The End of Diversity? Prospects for German and Japanese Capitalism*, edited by K. Yamamura and W. Streeck. Ithaca, NY: Cornell University Press.

Jacoby, Sanford. 1985. *Employing Bureaucracy*. New York, NY: Columbia University Press.

———. 2005. *The Embedded Corporation: Corporate Governance and Employment Relations in Japan and the United States*. Princeton: Princeton University Press.

Jaikumar, R. 1986. Postindustrial Manufacturing. *Harvard Business Review*, November–December: 69–76.

Kanter, Rosabeth Moss. 1978. *Men and Women of the Corporation.* New York: Basic Books.

Katz, Harry C., Rosemary Batt, and Jeffrey H. Keefe. 2003. The Revitalization of the CWA: Integrating Collective Bargaining, Political Action, and Organizing. *Industrial and Labor Relations Review* 56 (4): 573–89.

Katz, Harry, and Owen Darbishire. 2000. *Converging Divergences.* Ithaca, NY: ILR Press.

Katz, Harry C., and Charles Sabel. 1985. Industrial Relations and Industrial Adjustment in the Car Industry. *Industrial Relations* 24 (3): 295–315.

Katzenstein, Peter. 1985. *Small States in World Markets: Industrial Policy in Europe.* Ithaca, NY: Cornell University Press.

Keefe, Jeffrey. 2005. Racing to the Bottom: How Antiquated Public Policy Is Destroying the Best Jobs in Telecommunications. Washington, D.C.: Economic Policy Institute.

——. 2009. Is Digital Technology Reshaping Employment Systems in U.S. Telecommunications Network Services? *Industrial and Labor Relations Review* 63 (1): 42–59.

Keefe, Jeffrey, and Rosemary Batt. 1997. United States. In *Telecommunications: Restructuring and Employment Relations Worldwide,* edited by H. C. Katz. Ithaca, NY: ILR Press.

Kern, Horst, and Michael Schumann. 1984. *Das Ende der Arbeitsteilung? Rationalisierung in der industriellen Produktion.* Muenchen: Beck.

Kerr, Clark, John Dunlop, Frederick Harbison, and Charles Meyers. 1964. *Industrialism and Industrial Man.* Cambridge, MA: Harvard University Press.

Keune, Maarten, Janine Leschke, and Andrew Watt, eds. 2008. *Privatisation and Liberalisation of Public Services in Europe: An Analysis of Economic and Labour Market Impacts.* Brussels: European Trade Union Institute.

Kinnie, Nick, Sue Hutchinson, and John Purcell. 2000. "Fun and Surveillance": The Paradox of High Commitment Management in Call Centers. *International Journal of Human Resource Management* 11 (5): 967–85.

Kitschelt, Herbert, and Wolfgang Streeck, eds. 2004. *Germany: Beyond the Stable State.* Portland, OR: Frank Cass.

Klaveren, Maarten van, and Wim Sprenger. 2008. Call Center Employment: Diverging Jobs and Wages. In *Low-Wage Work in the Netherlands,* edited by W. Salverda, M. v. Klaveren and M. v. d. Meer. New York: Russell Sage Foundation.

Kleemann, Frank, and Ingo Matuschek, eds. 2003. *Immer Anschluss unter dieser Nummer.* Berlin: Edition Sigma.

Kochan, Thomas A., Adrienne E. Eaton, Robert B. McKersie, and Paul S. Adler. 2009. *Healing Together: The Labour-Management Partnership at Kaiser Permanente.* Ithaca, NY: ILR Press.

Kochan, T. A., H. C. Katz, and R. McKersie. 1986. *The Transformation of American Industrial Relations.* New York: Basic Books.

Kochan, Thomas, and Paul Osterman. 1994. *The Mutual Gains Enterprise.* Boston, MA: Harvard Business School Press.

Korczynski, Marek. 2002. *Human Resource Management in Service Work.* London: Palgrave.

Lane, Christel. 2008. National Capitalisms and Global Production Networks: An Analysis of Their Interaction in Two Global Industries. *Socioeconomic Review* 6 (2): 227–60.

Lane, Christel, and Jocelyn Probert. 2009. *National Capitalisms, Global Production Networks: Fashioning the Global Value Chain in the UK, USA, and Germany.* Oxford: Oxford University Press.

Lehndorff, Steffen, Gerhard Bosch, Thomas Haipeter, and Erich Latniak. 2009. From the 'Sick Man' to the 'Overhauled Engine' of Europe? Upheaval in the German Model. In *European Employment Models in Flux: A Comparison of Institutional Change in Nine European Countries,* edited by G. Bosch, S. Lehndorff and J. Rubery. Basingstoke: Palgrave Macmillan.

Lepak, David P., and Scott A. Snell. 1999. The Human Resource Architecture: Toward a Theory of Human Capital Allocation and Development. *Academy of Management Review* 24 (1): 31–48.

Lloyd, Caroline, Claudia Weinkopf, and Rosemary Batt. 2009. Restructuring Customer Service: Labor Market Institutions and Call Center Workers in Europe and the United States. In *Low Wage Work in a Wealthy World,* edited by J. Gautié and J. Schmitt. New York: Russell Sage Foundation.

Locke, Richard, Thomas Kochan, and Michael Piore, eds. 1995. *Employment Relations in a Changing World Economy.* Cambridge: MIT Press.

Marchington, Mick, Damian Grimshaw, Jill Rubery, and Hugh Willmott, eds. 2005. *Fragmenting Work: Blurring Organizational Boundaries and Disordering Hierarchies.* New York: Oxford University Press.

Marginson, Paul, Keith Sisson, and James Arrowsmith. 2003. Between Decentralization and Europeanization: Sectoral Bargaining in Four Countries and Two Sectors. *European Journal of Industrial Relations* 9 (2): 163–87.

Markovits, Andrei S. 1986. *The Politics of the West German Trade Unions.* Cambridge: Cambridge University Press.

Marsden, David. 1999. *A Theory of Employment Systems: Micro-foundations of Societal Diversity.* Oxford: Oxford University Press.

Marx, Karl, and Frederick Engels. 1986. *The German Ideology, Part One.* New York: International Publishers.

Matuschek, Ingo, Katrin Arnold, and G. Guenter Voss. 2007. *Subjektivierte Taylorisierung: Organisation und Praxis medienvermittelter Dienstleistungsarbeit.* Munich, Germany: Reiner Hampp Verlag.

Maurice, Marc, Francois Sellier, and Jean-Jacques Silvestre. 1986. *The Social Foundations of Industrial Power.* Cambridge, MA: MIT Press.

McKinley, William, and Andreas Georg Scherer. 2000. Some Unanticipated Consequences of Organizational Restructuring. *Academy of Management Review* 25 (4): 735–52.

Mickler, Otfried. 2002. Arbeitsverhältnisse in der Telekommunikation: Trends und Widersprüche in der Organisation von Wissensarbeit. In *Transformation der Arbeit,* edited by D. Claussen, O. Negt and M. Werz. Frankfurt: Verlag Neue Kritik.

Milkman, Ruth, Joshua Bloom, and Victor Narro, eds. 2010. *Working for Justice: The L.A. Model of Organizing and Advocacy.* Ithaca, NY: ILR Press.

Morgan, Glenn, Richard Whitley, and Eli Moen. 2005. *Changing Capitalisms? Institutional Change and Systems of Economic Organization.* Oxford: Oxford University Press.

Moss, Philip, Harold Salzman, and Chris Tilly. 2008. Under Construction: The Continuing Evolution of Job Structures in Call Centers. *Industrial Relations* 47 (2): 173–208.

Neumark, David, and William L. Wascher. 2008. *Minimum Wages.* Cambridge, MA: MIT Press.

OECD. 2004. Regulatory Reform in Telecommunications. In *OECD Reviews of Regulatory Reform—Regulatory Reform in Germany.*

———. 2007. OECD Broadband Statistics to December 2006. *OECD Directorate for Science, Technology and Industry.* At http://www.oecd.org/document/7/0,3343,en_2649_34225_38446855_1_1_1_1,00.html.

Ohmae, Kenichi. 1994. *The Borderless World: Power and Strategy in the Interlinked Economy.* London: Harper Collins.

Osterman, Paul. 1984. *Internal Labor Markets.* Cambridge, MA: MIT Press.

———. 1999. *Securing Prosperity.* Princeton: Princeton University Press.

———. 2000. Work Reorganization in an Era of Restructuring: Trends in the Diffusion and Effects on Employee Welfare. *Industrial and Labor Relations Review* 53 (2): 179–96.

———. 2002. *Gathering Power: The Future of Progressive Politics in America.* Boston: Beacon Press.

Piore, Michael J., and Charles F. Sabel. 1984. *The Second Industrial Divide: Possibilities for Prosperity.* New York: Basic Books.

Polanyi, Karl. 1944. *The Great Transformation: The Political and Economic Origins of Our Time.* Boston: Beacon Press.

Porter, Michael E. 1990. *The Competitive Advantage of Nations.* New York, NY: Free Press.

Prahalad, C. K., and G. Hamel. 1990. The Core Competence of the Corporation. *Harvard Business Review* 68 (3): 79–91.

Rechenbach, Jeff, and Larry Cohen. 2002. Union Global Alliances at Multinational Corporations: A Case Study of the Ameritech Alliance. In *Unions in a Globalized Environment,* edited by B. Nissen. Armonk, NY: M. E. Sharpe.

Reynaud, Emmanuele, and Jean-Daniel Reynaud. 1996. La régulation des marchés internes du travail. *Revue Française de Sociologie* 37: 337–68.

Royle, Tony. 2004. Employment Practices of Multinationals in the Spanish and German Quick-Food Sectors: Low-Road Convergence? *European Journal of Industrial Relations* 10 (1): 51–71.

Sako, Mari. 2006. *Shifting Boundaries of the Firm: Japanese Company—Japanese Labour.* Oxford: Oxford University Press.

Sako, Mari, and Gregory Jackson. 2006. Strategy Meets Institutions: The Transformation of Management-Labor Relations at Deutsche Telekom and NTT. *Industrial and Labor Relations Review* 59 (3): 347–66.

Salverda, Wiemer, Maarten van Klaveren, and Marc van de Meer, eds. 2008. *Low-Wage Work in the Netherlands.* New York: Russell Sage Foundation.

Sarkar, Ranjana S. 2000. *Akteure, Interessen und Technologien in der Telekommunikation: USA und Deutschland im Vergleich.* Frankfurt: Campus Verlag.

Schmidt, Vicki. 2002. *The Futures of European Capitalism.* Oxford: Oxford University Press.

Schmitter, Phillipe, and Gerhard Lehmbruch, eds. 1979. *Trends towards Corporatist Intermediation.* Beverly Hills, CA: Sage.

Schröder, Lothar. 2007. Der Tarifkonflikt bei der Deutschen Telekom AG. *WSI Mitteilungen* 9: 515–18.

Shire, Karen, Hannelore Mottweiler, Annika Schönauer, and Mireia Valverde. 2009. Temporary Work in Coordinated Market Economies: Evidence from Front-line service Workplaces. *Industrial and Labor Relations Review* 62 (4): 602–17.

Shire, Karen, Annika Schönauer, Mireia Valverde, and Hannelore Mottweiler. 2009. Collective Bargaining and Temporary Contracts in Call Centre Employment in Austria, Germany and Spain. *European Journal of Industrial Relations* 15 (4): 437–56.

Siebert, Horst. 1997. Labor Market Rigidities: At the Root of Unemployment in Europe. *Journal of Economic Perspectives* 11 (3): 37–54.

Sørensen, Ole. 2008. Pay and Job Quality in Danish Call Centers. In *Low-Wage Work in Denmark,* edited by N. Westergaard-Nielsen. New York: Russell Sage Foundation.

Sørensen, Ole H., and Claudia Weinkopf. 2009. Pay and Working Conditions in Finance and Utility Call Centres in Denmark and Germany. *European Journal of Industrial Relations* 15 (4): 395–416.

Stewart, Paul, Ken Murphy, Andy Danford, Tony Richardson, Mike Richardson, and Vicki Wass. 2009. *We Sell Our Time No More: Workers' Struggles Against Lean Production in the British Car Industry.* London: Pluto Press.

Streeck, Wolfgang. 1984. *Industrial Relations in West Germany: A Case Study of the Car Industry.* London: Heinemann.

———. 1991. On the Institutional Conditions of Diversified Quality Production. In *Beyond Keynesianism: The Socio-Economics of Production and Full Employment,* edited by E. Matzner and W. Streeck. Aldershot: Edward Elgar.

———. 1996. Lean Production in the German Automobile Industry: A Test Case for Convergence Theory. In *National Diversity and Global Capitalism,* edited by S. Berger and R. Dore. Ithaca, NY: Cornell University Press.

———. 2009. *Re-Forming Capitalism: Institutional Change in the German Political Economy.* Oxford: Oxford University Press.

Streeck, Wolfgang, and Kathleen Thelen, eds. 2005. *Beyond Continuity: Institutional Change in Advanced Political Economies.* Oxford: Oxford University Press.

SUD and CGC. 2008. *Observetoire du Stress et des Mobilités Forcées—France Télécom.* Available at http://www.observatoiredustressft.org.

Tattersall, Amanda. 2010. *Power in Coalition: Strategies for Strong Unions and Social Change.* Ithaca, NY: ILR Press.

Taylor, Phil, Gareth Mulvey, Jeff Hyman, and Peter Bain. 2002. Work Organization, Control and the Experience of Work in Call Centres. *Work, Employment, and Society* 16 (1): 133–50.

Thelen, Kathleen. 1991. *Union of Parts: Labor Politics in Postwar Germany.* Ithaca, NY: Cornell University Press.

———. 2001. Varieties of Labor Politics in the Developed Democracies. In *Varieties of Capitalism,* edited by P. Hall and D. Soskice. New York: Cambridge University Press.

———. 2009. Institutional Change in Advanced Political Economies. *British Journal of Industrial Relations* 47 (3): 471–98.

Théry, Laurence, ed. 2006. *Le travail intenable: Résister collectivement à l'intensification du travail.* Paris: La Découverte.

Turner, Lowell. 1991. *Democracy at Work: Changing World Markets and the Future of Labor Unions.* Ithaca, NY: Cornell University Press.

———. 2009. Institutions and Activism: Crisis and Opportunity for a German Labor Movement in Decline. *Industrial and Labor Relations Review* 62 (3): 294–312.

Van Jaarsveld, Danielle, Andries De Grip, and Inge Sieben. 2009. Industrial Relations and Labour Market Segmentation in Dutch Call Centres. *European Journal of Industrial Relations* 15 (4): 417–35.

Van Jaarsveld, Danielle, Hyunji Kwon, and Anne Frost. 2009. The Effects of Institutional and Organizational Characteristics on Numerical Flexibility: Evidence from US and Canadian Call Centers. *Industrial and Labor Relations Review* 62 (4): 573–601.

Vogel, Steven K. 1996. *Freer Markets, More Rules: Regulatory Reform in Advanced Industrial Countries.* Ithaca, NY: Cornell University Press.

Wallis, Emma, Mark Stuart, and Ian Greenwood. 2005. "Learners of the Workplace Unite!" An Empirical Examination of the Trade Union Learning Representative Initiative. *Work, Employment, and Society* 19 (2): 283–304.

Weinkopf, Claudia. 2009. Job Quality in Call Centres in Germany. *International Labour Review* 148 (4): 395–411.

Wever, Kirsten S. 1995. *Negotiating Competitiveness: Employment Relations and Organizational Innovation in Germany and the United States.* Boston: Harvard Business School Press.

Whitley, Richard. 1999. *Divergent Capitalisms: The Social Structuring and Change of Business Systems.* Oxford: Oxford University Press.

Whyte, William H. 1956. *The Organization Man.* New York: Simon and Schuster.

Womack, James P., Daniel D. Jones, and Daniel Roos. 1990. *The Machine that Changed the World: The Story of Lean Production.* New York: Macmillan.

Yamamura, Kozo, and Wolfgang Streeck, eds. 2003. *The End of Diversity? Prospects for German and Japanese Capitalism.* Ithaca, NY: Cornell University Press.

Zysman, John. 1983. *Governments, Markets, and Growth: Financial Systems and the Politics of Industrial Change.* Ithaca: Cornell University Press.

INDEX

"In *Disintegrating Democracy at Work*, Virginia Doellgast compares the changes in the organization of frontline call center jobs in the United States and Germany. Doellgast conducted nearly three hundred interviews with key informants in both countries and compared the qualitative findings with the quantitative results of an international survey. This is an innovative book; there are not many internationally comparative studies on wages and work organization with such a broad empirical base and such a profound knowledge of institutions and the organization of an industry."
—Gerhard Bosch
Universität Duisburg Essen

"This unique and original book makes a major contribution to comparative industrial relations. It is a solid empirical analysis based in the growing service sector and examines a globally growing occupation, the call center customer service representative. Virginia Doellgast argues that both participation rights and union bargaining power are important supports for the adoption of high involvement employment systems."
—Jeffrey H. Keefe
Rutgers, The State University of New Jersey

THE shift from manufacturing- to service-based economies has often been accompanied by the expansion of low-wage and insecure employment. Many consider the effects of this shift inevitable. In *Disintegrating Democracy at Work,* Virginia Doellgast contends that high pay and good working conditions are possible even for marginal service jobs. This outcome, however, depends on strong unions and encompassing collective bargaining institutions, which are necessary to give workers a voice in the decisions that affect the design of their jobs and the distribution of productivity gains. Doellgast's conclusions are based on a comparative study of the changes that occurred in the organization of call center jobs in the United States and Germany following the liberalization of telecommunications markets. Based on survey data and interviews with workers, managers, and union representatives, she found that German managers more often took the "high road" than those in the United States, investing in skills and giving employees more control over their work.

ISBN 978-0-8014-7799-7

ILR/Cornell Paperbacks

Cornell University Press
www.cornellpress.cornell.edu

ISBN 978-0-8014-7799-7
90000
9 780801 477997